GOD

Don't
Like

UGLY

GOD

Don't
Like
UGLY

African American
Women Handing on
Spiritual Values

Teresa L. Fry Brown

Abingdon Press
NASHVILLE

GOD DON'T LIKE UGLY:
AFRICAN AMERICAN WOMEN HANDING ON SPIRITUAL VALUES

Copyright © 2000 by Abingdon Press

This book is printed on recycled, acid-free, elemental-chlorine–free paper.

Library of Congress Cataloging-in-Publication Data

Brown, Teresa L. Fry, 1951-
    God don't like ugly : African American women handing on spiritual values / Teresa L. Fry Brown.
    p. cm.
    Includes bibliographical references and index.
    ISBN 0-687-08799-6 (alk. paper)
    1. Afro-American women—Religious life. 2. Parenting—Religious aspects—Christianity. I. Title.

BR563.N4 B68 2000
277.3'0089'96073—dc21
                                                                                    00-056599

All scripture quotations, unless otherwise indicated, are taken from the HOLY BIBLE, NEW INTERNATIONAL VERSION®. Copyright © 1973, 1978, 1984 by International Bible Society. Used by permission of Zondervan Publishing House. All rights reserved.

Scripture quotations marked (NRSV) are from the *New Revised Standard Version of the Bible,* copyright 1989, Division of Christian Education of the National Council of the Churches of Christ in the United States of America. Used by permission. All rights reserved.

Scripture quotations marked (KJV) are from the King James Version of the Bible.

Excerpts from BABY OF THE FAMILY, copyright © 1989 by Tina McElroy Ansa, reprinted by permission of Harcourt, Inc.

Excerpt from "Legacies" from MY HOUSE by Nikki Giovanni. Copyright © 1972 by Nikki Giovanni. Reprinted by permission of HarperCollins Publishers, Inc.

Excerpt from "Our Grandmothers" from I SHALL NOT BE MOVED by Maya Angelou. Copyright © 1990 by Maya Angelou. Reprinted by permission of Random House, Inc.

Excerpt from "Still I Rise" from AND STILL I RISE by Maya Angelou. Copyright © 1978 by Maya Angelou. Reprinted by permission of Random House, Inc.

Excerpt from I KNOW WHY THE CAGED BIRD SINGS by Maya Angelou. Copyright © 1969 and renewed 1977 by Maya Angelou. Reprinted by permission of Random House, Inc.

Excerpt from "mrs. martha jean black" from SPIN A SOFT BLACK SONG by Nikki Giovanni. Copyright © 1971, 1985 by Nikki Giovanni. Reprinted by permission of Hill and Wang, a division of Farrar, Straus and Giroux, LLC.

Excerpt from "I'm So Grateful" by Gloria Griffin. Copyright © 1993 by Leric Music Inc. (administered by Copyright Management International). All rights reserved. International Copyright secured. Used by permission.

Excerpt from "He's Worthy" by Sandra Crouch. Copyright © 1983 by Bud John Songs, Inc./Sanabella Music. All rights reserved. Used by permission.

Excerpt from "If It Had Not Been for the Lord" by Margaret Pleasant Douroux. Copyright © 1980 Margaret Pleasant Douroux. All rights reserved. Used by permission.

Excerpt from "What Is This?" by Joan Golden and Willie Morganfield. Copyright © 1961 by Sue Records, Inc. Used by permission.

Excerpt from "Trees" by Margaret Pleasant Douroux. Copyright © 1981 by Margaret Pleasant Douroux. All rights reserved. Used by permission.

Excerpt from "Call Letters Mrs. V. B." from AND STILL I RISE by Maya Angelou. Copyright © 1978 by Maya Angelou. Reprinted by permission of Random House, Inc.

"Women" from REVOLUTIONARY PETUNIAS & OTHER POEMS, copyright © 1970 and renewed 1998 by Alice Walker, reprinted by permission of Harcourt, Inc.

01 02 03 04 05 06 07 08 09—10 9 8 7 6 5 4 3

MANUFACTURED IN THE UNITED STATES OF AMERICA

ACKNOWLEDGMENTS

The writer of Ecclesiastes states that every event has a season or time to occur. This work was conceived almost twelve years ago and only by God's grace has it finally been birthed.

To Tessie Bernice Parks, my grandmother, thank you for being my inspiration for passing on values to all persons.

To my mother, Naomi Parks Fry, incapacitated by illness yet spiritually vibrant, thank you for teaching me about the wonders of God.

To all grandmothers, mothers, othermothers, my sistahs in the spirit, my nieces and nephews, my "adopted" children and former students around the world, and all the nurturing brothas I have known, thank you.

To two special men in my life, Lyman Parks and William Fry, Sr., who taught me that love comes in many different forms, and that courage is often overlooked. God bless.

To my sister, Richelle Fry, thank you for typing the early manuscripts and believing in me.

My deep appreciation to Dr. Jean Miller Schmidt, who nurtured my intellectual side, and Rev. Jesse L. Boyd, who gave me room to develop my spiritual side.

Last, but never least, to Veronica Nadyne Tinsley, who has sacrificed much so I could be a preacher, teacher, scholar, and "special mom," and to my husband, Frank David Brown, who is my blessing from on high. Thank you both for allowing me to be me.

"I am because we are." PASS IT ON!

CONTENTS

PREFACE

Backbone, courage, durability, energy, fortitude, nerve, stability, tenacity, and vitality are just a few of the descriptive attributes of my ancestors. The mentality, strength, intensity, faithfulness, and forbearance of those who survived and thrived in spite of forced immigration, a deadly Middle Passage, government-sanctioned enslavement, sharecropping, a Great Migration, Jim Crow, and institutional slavery are often overlooked by progeny who only know twenty-first century materialism, tentative entitlement, and superficial equality.

Over fifty years ago, African American poet Margaret Walker stated, "My grandmothers were strong."[1] She reminisced about the smells of soap and vegetables, the sound of singing voices, and the sight of new life birthed at the hands of her grandmothers. She reflected on the lives of those black women who worked, cared, reminisced, and shared life's wisdom with those who took the time to observe and listen.[2] She experienced and questioned the same resolve that many African American women face today. How were our ancestors so capable of resisting systemic evil while we seem to collapse, or at least bend, under the contemporary weights of oppression, neglect, and overbearing responsibility? Walker questioned her own resolve when observing grandmothers' patterned behavior. Likewise, my ninety-year-old maternal grandmother, Tessie Bernice Ray Parks (Mama Tessie), has been my strongest influence on how to live a full, productive life as a black woman in America. Her example of how to live above social or political circumstance ranged from lovingly creating large dinners out of meager resources, cleaning someone else's house, greeting the world while sitting on her own front porch, praising God from the choir stand every Sunday at the Baptist church, to shopping at stores where we couldn't try things on for the first fourteen years of my life.

Mama Tessie always seemed to have a word of instruction or Mother Wit[3] to keep me going, quell my indignation at social injustice, or give some semblance of order to life.

One such saying that has stuck with me throughout life is "God don't like ugly," meaning God is not pleased with negative or unattractive behavior. God is present in everything we do or say, so we have an obligation always to behave in a manner that is pleasing to God. This translates into a corrective of "Act like you got parents," or "Remember where you came from and don't do anything to make us ashamed," and the biblically inspired mandate of "You reap what you sow." The essence of these sayings is that one has been taught the difference between right and wrong and is already equipped to act in a certain fashion when away from home. Although many women and men have challenged, prodded, manipulated, cajoled, demanded, pushed, and taught me how to survive,[4] it is the voice and protective presence of my grandmother that resounds above and overshadows all others.

As I contemplate distressing reports on crises in the black family, church, and community I am frustrated by political cries for quick fixes, blaming the victim, and disregard for positive methods already being used to transmit moral wisdom, particularly by African American mothers, grandmothers, and othermothers. Granted, there are black mothers and grandmothers who have not provided positive, loving nurture or guidance for children and grandchildren. Many adopt an attitude of hopelessness and pass it on to their children. Yet the majority of black mothers and grandmothers seek social change by beginning with changing family dynamics. There are black women who care not only for children, but also for grandchildren and anyone else's child who visits. Correcting behavior or telling someone else's child how to behave is risky, but is a daily occurrence in black churches and communities. What about those women whose voices have been silenced just because they are African American and female? The Mother Wit of our foreparents is ridiculed at times as old-fashioned until time and life experience prove otherwise.

What becomes of the voices of black women in songs, sermons, novels, poems, autobiography, political speeches, and recited family histories? One of my elders' earliest instructions to me was to invest in books because the entire world could be mine if I learned to read. My mother made us children spend two full hours every Saturday morning at the library or at least reading. My grandmother and aunts would read great works of black literature. My sister-friends sit, eat, discuss, argue, laugh, and cry as we find ourselves, our lives, our modes and methods for healing our wounds, or affirmations for our beings in contemporary African American women's literature.[5] In each of these instances black women assisted in framing means for living life that they shared with others.

I learned the secrets of a productive, liberative, Christian life through precept and example, direct chastisement and instruction, indirect modeling, telling stories, humming songs, discussing the last sermon, and sharing family history. Through the urgings of the grandmothers and othermothers of my life I determined that there was no choice but to make my own space in the world while respecting the place of others. I could not accept the social or spiritual paralysis that others chose for me; for a God of possibilities had created me and I must live in spite of the circumstance, not only spiritually free but also physically and socially free.

Some of my life instruction was neither positive nor romantic. Growing up in an age of corporal punishment, I was spanked at times with a switch I was sent to get from a tree. I was chastised verbally and had privileges rescinded, but I was rarely verbally abused or demeaned. Some of the othermothers I have met along the way skated just on the edge of legality, in terms of compliance with legal statutes, but I discovered the boundaries of acceptable behavior. They were loving individuals despite social castigation and choice of lifestyle. I learned many hard lessons, ran into many walls, but there always seemed to be a grandmother or othermother there for me when my own mother was not available.

All suggested means of transformation were not successful, but I was taught to build from the defeats as well as the victories. When all the doors in my life seemed closed, all the paths blocked, I envisioned the faces of my grandmothers sweating over someone else's kitchen floor so I could eat, or heard them humming about a God who made everything all right, and that was enough for me to continue. In the midst of all, there was talk of a God who loved everyone and "could do anything but fail."

During my teen years this made no sense, and I began to question the status quo. I would confront my grandmothers and othermothers about how a God of love could allow evil to flourish, permit blacks to be lynched, keep me out of the recreational activities my white classmates enjoyed, or prevent my parents from working jobs that paid little more than subsistence wages. Some of the grandmothers, mothers, and othermothers were teachers, entrepreneurs, nurses, and homemakers, but the majority worked for less than minimum wage. I was even embarrassed that my grandmothers worked as domestics and were called by their first names by white children. The response kept coming back, "You got to love them like God loves us" or "We're doing this so you never have to do it." They went into the world with their heads "bloodied but unbowed" and kept on thanking God for preserving their lives. Like Walker, I ponder why many of my contemporaries (and at times, myself) do not have or cannot find the inner strength—physically, morally, ethically, spiritually—to live "in spite of" circumstance like "our grandmothers."[6] Realizing that I had been given a small part of a possible solution to some of the difficulties African American families face in contemporary society, I began a process of unearthing some of the core beliefs of black families, churches, and communities that have been communicated across generations. Even at this stage in my life I am continually surrounded by grandmothers and othermothers who mentor me and love me into a deeper understanding of black women's moral wisdom and character development. The nature of this wisdom and how it is transmitted is the subject of this book.

Buttressed by the wisdom and guidance of my elders, I approach the study of transmission of spiritual values by grandmothers and othermothers from a variety of viewpoints: as an ordained itinerant elder and preacher in the African Methodist Episcopal Church I have been assigned the task of spiritual barometer and transmitter of beliefs for my community of faith. As a Progressive Baptist musician's daughter and deacon's granddaughter, former youth director, Sunday school teacher and superintendent, choir director and worship leader, I have come to know the history, trials and tribulations, and inner workings of the black church. As the founder of several women's support groups such as Sisters Working Encouraging Empowering Together (SWEET) in Denver and Sistah Circle in Atlanta, and as faculty advisor/sponsor for sororities and black student groups at Central Missouri State University in Warrensburg, Missouri, and Candler School of Theology in Atlanta, Georgia, and as Consultant for Personal and Organizational Development for the African Methodist Episcopal Church Women in Ministry, I have attempted to help women and men of all ages build bridges and support one another. This was accomplished through open discussion, seminars, ethnographies (oral interviews of older women and men), and most important through reading groups focusing on the literature of African American women, and the voicing of our own concerns and solutions to life's problems.

As seminary professor and ordained minister I have been afforded the opportunity to analyze what it means to develop a personal and cultural hermeneutic that accounts for who and what I am, and not what others think I am or should be. I have also been able to pursue a fifteen-year personal investigation of what values are present in black families, churches, and communities based on informal surveys, small group discussions, church conferences, community action groups, and dialogue with black men and women regarding where and from whom they learned how to live with their "head held up, looking them in the eye." As Naomi's daughter; Tessie's granddaughter; Veronica's mother; Miriam, Richelle, and LaWanda's blood sister; Rikesha and Tyree's aunt; Carrie, Marcia, Sandy, and Rosetta's fictive sister; Margaret, Ruth, and Sally's sister-in-law; and "othermother" to people across the United States, I am compelled to examine what I say, what I do, why I make particular choices, with whom I talk, and where I learned about empowerment and spirituality, because I have the power to influence lives by passing on positive or negative prescriptions just like the grandmothers who came before me.

DUE
9/26/07

Reported To : MALCOLM BRANTZ
COLORADO CHRISTIAN UNIVERSITY
LIBRARY
180 S GARRISON STREET
LAKEWOOD CO 80226

Delivery Type	Format	Quantity
Electronic Mail	Citation	
Electronic Mail	Full Text	
Total Documents Electronic Mail		10
On Line	Abstract	1,009
On Line	Citation	85
On Line	Full Text	1,94
On Line	Image	672
Total Documents On Line		3,70
Total searches by word @ no charges		1,94
Total searches by source @ no charge		822
Remaining Pre-paid Documents	(Abstract)	UNLIMITE
Remaining Pre-paid Documents	(Citation)	UNLIMITE
Remaining Pre-paid Documents	(Full Text)	UNLIMITE
Remaining Pre-paid Documents	(Image)	UNLIMITE

As a social/political activist I have had extensive opportunities to observe the development of relationships and results of contact between older, mature Christian women and younger people as they sought to maintain community and family against all odds. I have seen the benefit and outcomes of youth learning wisdom and knowledge at the feet of elders in intergenerational mentoring groups. Who is better able to speak a word of truth on what it means to survive than the same one who has done so, someone who is bruised and battered yet living?

The strength gained when a "grandmother or othermother" gently lays on hands, or holds a younger person through tears, or soothes fears with words of faith cannot be replaced with psychological or sociological analysis of the situation. This sense of connectedness and transmission of faith based on lived experience is one of the most powerful tools I have observed. The intersection of black family, church, and community in my life has been built on elders articulating premises such as "God is everywhere you go." Therefore, God-talk permeates conversations in all three areas. There is no separation of life into the secular and the sacred. Regardless of the willingness of the younger people to listen, elders have imbued this holistic tradition. It is the doing of theology— "Practicing what you preach," "Living so God can use you," or "Do what God called you to do and don't waste time explaining it"—coupled with the articulation of one's beliefs—"The Lord will make a way somehow," "Prayer changes things," or "God don't have no stepchildren"—that undergirds the spirituality of a family, church, or community under siege.[7]

The foundation of my research is formed by a black community saying (Mother Wit), "You can't lead where you won't go and can't teach what you don't know." Whatever I am able to transmit to my daughter, sisters, friends, students, or community comes from my lived experience and the proof of those community sayings that have instilled a sense of empowerment in my life. African American by birth and Christian by choice, I have struggled with the incomprehensible notions that God loves some people more than others; that as a black female I have few or no rights in a world dominated by white Americans; that black men are of more value than black women and are therefore automatically the authoritative spokesmen blacks need or want; and that as one ages he or she is to be discounted as senile and unable to contribute to the betterment of society. Through my mother, grandmothers, othermothers, father, grandfathers, and otherfathers I have learned that these presuppositions are untrue and that I must challenge them whenever the opportunity presents itself. This book is that opportunity.

INTRODUCTION

This book is about the intergenerational transmission of African American spiritual values by grandmothers and othermothers in African American families, churches, and communities. It is the mothers, grandmothers, teachers, or neighbors who provided early guidance in faith development or taught one how to act in relationships.

This is not an attempt to exclude black men who have taught values to black children and who work within the black church and community to ensure preservation of what is good, and change from what is negative. Rather there has been an unwritten assumption in our society that black men, following a patriarchal model, are the leaders of the black family, church, and community with an often intentional denial of the importance or presence of black women as viable teachers, leaders, or nurturers of their children. Yet, I know that I can speak about black women, their spirituality, and methods of value transmission based on my social location, cultural hermenuetic, and worldview as a black woman. Black women and men strive in a sometimes diluted partnership—social structures based on artificial power dynamics which may skew reality—to edify, regenerate, and rediscover spiritual values in the black family, church, and community. The voice of African American women has been muted or ignored in the area of spirituality. As one advantaged to articulate a part of the story, I choose to do so without prejudice or insult to African American men.

This study will use history, sociology, ethics, and spirituality, focusing on African American history, African American ethics, black theology, and womanist theology and ethics as primary disciplines. Ethical presuppositions stem from a womanist hermeneutic of liberation for all people. I firmly ascribe to the saying that "None are free until all are free." Even when I do not fully grasp the belief system, lifestyle, sense of humor, lack of passion, justice stance, or political position of another person I am obligated to "hear him or her into speaking" and work to walk with him or her in that person's particularity. This type of freedom means that I do not own the table, where we sit by invitation only, selectively deciding who is worthy to be human. It means that together we seek a place to sit and talk through our humanity, without hierarchical seating charts. My grandmother continues to teach me that no one is better than another person: each is just differently blessed. In God's personnel department everyone has specialized skills, an obligation to use these talents for the good of all, and a legacy or record of all positive or negative acts. Persons who use this life as a means to abuse, misuse, or confuse others are a disappointment to God. Those who use the time establishing relationships with all of God's children are ultimately rewarded. My grandmother says that to be treated well, to be validated as a child of God, one must treat others well. Empowered through a quest for love and justice, black women are committed to the survival and wholeness of all women, men, and children. Historically denied legal and personal freedoms, black women still work for the equal distribution of God's love. Love of oneself and others in spite of who or what they are is critical to womanist ethics. There is no room for hatred, discrimination, ethnocentrism, or any other power-based injustice in a womanist paradigm. Although they did not wear the name of womanist, I believe that numerous real and imagined black women, including my grandmother, have exemplified womanist thought.[1]

The book is written purposely in two distinct voices: academic and culturally specific vernacular. African and African American proverbs, community sayings, African American religious jargon, and Mother Wit are juxtaposed with academic language. It is written for an academic audience as a contribution to womanist ethics and African American spirituality. It is written for scholars interested in black women's literature as a source of discovering and defining black women's spirituality, and as a means of passing on spiritual instruction to children and adults. It is also written for African American women in particular, and all persons in general, who search for a voice to articulate how they raise their children. The work details how African American women contribute to the black church even when limited by black male hegemony, and how they continue to labor behind the scenes to maintain and advance the course of the black community. It is compiled to reach both academics and nonacademics who seek information and understanding about power-filled and power-depleted black family, church, and community.

African American women's literature (poetry, songs, novels, short stories, autobiography) written since the 1960s is analyzed for information regarding how black women transmit values. The date was chosen to limit the scope of the literature studied and because of the sociopolitical transitions which took place beginning in the late 1950s and into the 1960s. The beginning of the modern Civil Rights movement in 1954 with the Montgomery Bus Boycott, Student Nonviolent Coordinating Committee, and Freedom Rides; Camelot and the Presidency of John F. Kennedy; the assassinations of John Kennedy, Martin Luther King, and Robert Kennedy; the war in Vietnam, Haight-Ashbury, and flower children; sit-ins, wade-ins, antiwar protests; voting and civil rights bills; and the threat of nuclear war were but a few of the dramatic social events of the time that influenced the very core of American life—the family.

Chapter 1, "Reaffirming Cultural Roots: Yah Bettah Hold Ontah Whatcha Got," explores the development, adaptation, use, and transmission of mores or core beliefs in the black family, church, and community through a brief overview of the realities, changes, myths, charges, challenges, and expectations of black Americans. The effects of social, political, and spiritual change are also discussed.

"Wisdom Bearers: The Mother Wit of Sistuh Girlfriends" is the title of chapter 2. African American theology and ethics lay the groundwork for a discussion of womanist ethics and theology. The roles and responsibilities of African American women, ascribed and assumed, as the carriers of tradition and shared knowledge for survival are examined. African American women's moral agency, affirmation of self, and the onus of conveying these affirmations despite racism, sexism, and classism are considered.

Chapter 3, "Listening to Experience: Why Are You Actin' Like You Don't Hear Me?" delineates the rationale for using African American women's literature as a source for demonstrating the transmission of black women's moral wisdom intergenerationally. There is a brief review of the history of black women's literature highlighting selected literary forerunners. Black women's literary criticism, themes, characters, and didactics are addressed. Additionally, I explore why there is often an aversion to accepting black women's literature as a legitimate source of information about black family, black church, and black community. Society often characterizes the "voice" of black people as decidedly male. Black women, however, have developed strategies to articulate their point of view, even in silence.

Chapter 4, "Acting Lessons: God Don't Like Ugly," chapter 5, "Spiritual Connections: We Are All Aunt Haggie's Children," and chapter 6, "Faith-Filled Perseverance: Trouble Don't Last Always" constitute my analysis of selected African American women's literature using an interpretive framework on values transmission across generations. The moral/ethical interpretive framework consists of religious sources, ethical presuppositions, and transformative effects. Presence of religious themes, African American traditions, use of Bible, authority, and justification beliefs are basic elements of African American spirituality.[2] The interpretive framework has five parts: Pedagogy,

Social Location, Relationships, Moral/Ethical Considerations, and Transformative Possibilities. These three chapters represent moral/ethical presuppositions I developed from an in-depth study of African American values—such as reverence for God and elders, respect for self and others, responsibility for one's own actions, restraint from impulsive or destructive behaviors, reciprocity (mutuality) through racial bonding or solidarity, perseverance (hope), and compassion (forgiveness)—as discussed in the first three chapters. These presuppositions are investigated separately but may occur simultaneously within the black family, black church, and black community.

The interpretive framework evolved from my reading African American women's literature, examining scholarly supportive information, and personal observations of African American women's intentional, inductive teaching of values to children and younger persons. The framework is placed over each literary work as a way of discerning the presence or absence of African American women's moral wisdom and the means by which the spiritual values are passed on to others.

In each chapter, gospel music, poetry, short stories, novels, and autobiographies are examined for social location, ontological stance, cultural hermeneutics, presence of Mother Wit, faith language, moral agency, and pedagogy. The consequences of oppression and survival, intergenerational relationships or connectedness, spirituality of the grandmother or othermother in the literature, and the particularity or universality of the core belief taught, passed on, or modeled (i.e., care, compassion, perseverance, forgiveness) are also examined. The framework also evaluates possibilities for transformation or rejection of the moral wisdom drawn from the teachings of the grandmother or othermother.

Chapter 7, "Community Responsibilities: It Takes an Entire Village to Raise a Child," is the constructive womanist paradigm for ways in which contemporary families, churches, and communities can transmit spiritual values and be responsible for their own social change. Opportunities for liberation, social change, and transformation are presented as possibilities rather than panaceas. Examples are the Full Circle Intergenerational Program in Denver, Colorado (developed by Anita West Ware), and a Rites of Passage Program for Young Women at the Bridge Street A.W.M.E. Church in Brooklyn, New York (developed by Rev. Kimberly Detherage). I present two church-based paradigms that I have developed for transmission of values across generations: mentoring for youth, and additional ways to use African American women's literature as a resource for value transmission intergenerationally by African American women. These paradigms may be adapted by any racial, ethnic, age, faith, or gender focus group using their own cultural resources.

1

REAFFIRMING CULTURAL ROOTS

You
Bettah
Hold
Ontah
Whatcha
Got

T his chapter focuses on historical and social elements of African American spirituality and religion, the black family, and the black extended family (community) as the fundamental elements for development of African American theology and ethics, which are intergenerationally transmitted. De facto secularism, materialism, moral confusion, and chaotic public policies threaten all persons in America today. Television talk shows, call-in radio programs, political campaign speeches, public policies, crime statistics, Sunday morning sermons, and Monday morning coffee machine conversations allude to the destructive nature of black Americans and the threat to the safety of America. Yet the typical fear of young black men based on demeanor and dress, and disdain for outspoken and outcast black women evidenced in those communications, is grounded in centuries of stereotypes now perpetuated by mass media.

Marian Wright Edelman, president of the Children's Defense Fund, states that the cultural myths regarding the black family are fundamental to societal views of black responsibility for the disintegration of the moral core of America.

> In their concern over the effects of slavery, urbanization, and unemployment on black families, a number of scholars have identified female-headed households or matriarchy as the characteristic and pathological element making and keeping black families "inferior" to white families. Until the 1960s many analysts assumed that there was something wrong with the black family, which was described at best as nonfunctional and disorganized.[1]

Unfortunately, thirty years later the same critique echoes in political debate, sociological reports, and even some sermons. The historical target for all that is wrong with "black America" is those uppity, angry, illiterate, or loose black women. Little time is spent on the reality of social, political, economic, and educational power disparities, and continual denial of societal complicity in the retention of centuries-old stereotypes. I find it amazing that even though government statistics declare that the majority of persons on welfare are not black families, the media/political agenda still holds up the black family as government dependent.

In 1986, Lerone Bennett, African American social historian, described ten prevalent myths about the black family perpetuated by sociologists and historians. Each myth may be found in one form or another in media reports, contemporary novels, movies, or small group discussions today. According to Bennett, the myths are:

1. Raw and uncontrolled sex is at the root of the black family problem.
2. The root cause of the problem is loose morals.

3. Blacks lack a family tradition and came to America without a sense of morality and a background of stable sexual relationships.
4. The bonds of the black family were destroyed in slavery.
5. The black family collapsed after Emancipation.
6. The black family collapsed after the Great Migration to the North.
7. The black family is a product of white paternalism and government welfare.
8. The black family has always been a matriarchy characterized by strong and domineering women and weak and absent men.
9. Black men cannot sustain stable relationships.
10. The history of the black family is a history of fussin' and fightin' by hard-hearted men and heartless women.[2]

The anthropologic observers who formed these myths of the African American community are generally European Americans. The myths are often reinforced by misinformation garnered from small sociological samples, such as the current tendency of news reporters to seek out the most dysfunctional person in a crowd (drug addict, gang member, or illiterate person) to give an account of what is going on in the black community.

If one follows the logic of these myths, blacks are unethical and immoral people dominated by black women. Although there are certainly persons within African American communities who seem unable to function socially, are economically deprived, or are violent, the tendency to paint all persons with the same brush is unwarranted. These myths entrench stereotypes about black men, women, and families that lead to characterizations that have taken centuries to begin to transform. There is no mention of any complicity by anyone else, including those responsible for the black presence in America. Pushing the onus of moral degradation off on one segment of society exonerates others from any responsibility for the problems or solutions.[3]

Edelman concurs with Bennett's assessment of the perpetuation of these myths by stating that there are millions of black families who are not welfare recipients, who have children who are not dropouts, who stay out of prisons, who are not prone to violence, and who do not get pregnant as a badge of maturity or social acceptance.[4] Bennett and Edelman recognize that there are problems within the black family, but they caution that making sweeping generalizations about the total demise of the black family is premature and detrimental.

An example of the root cause of the negative characterization of the black family has been laid at the feet of black women. All too often the black mother is charged with being instrumental in the rise in crime and other social maladies in the black family and community. Single mothers have been considered particularly at fault because of their "low morals" and "unchurched families." As the divorced mother of a five-year-old, I remember being told my child was "at risk." She was tested by her school district and to the surprise of the psychologist was an "above average, bright, sociable child." She was then recommended to attend a special program at a private school to ensure that she would progress through school and not become a statistic. After I filed my income tax statement and financial profile, she was offered a full scholarship at an exclusive school for six years. I found it interesting that no one asked about my academic background, current or future plans for my child's education, or my support systems. The system chose to focus on the label "divorce, black, female, child." At the time, I was completing a second master's degree program, had been admitted into a doctoral program, had worked as a university professor and a college and public school speech/language pathologist, had entered ministry, and had strong familial, church, and community support systems for raising my daughter. The societal myths and cultural realities again collided. Veronica received an education that cost more than my tuition, and the system was happy to have "saved" another "at risk" black child.

The nature of the black church, black extended family, and values embraced by the majority of black women have been ignored in search of a scapegoat. Although black women have been raising families in America for over 380 years, media reports often infer that this group possesses few or no parenting skills.[5] Their attitudes and values of commitment to employment, egalitarianism, and raising children to adulthood have been overlooked in recent studies as if these areas are new for black women. The fact that African American women may be single by choice, divorced, or widowed is forgotten. Most single mothers are viewed as deviant, although the majority may be in relationships where the father is absent due to work, military service, incarceration, or by choice. Studies regarding the negative side of the African American community do not account for the number of persons who are neither criminals nor unchurched. In addition, there are relatively few studies of single female-headed households that produce conscientious citizens and devout Christians. One must again consider that there are black women who lack education, finances, or even the will—for example, mothers addicted to crack cocaine—to be responsible parents, but they represent a small percentage of all black mothers.[6]

The black church, black family, and black mothers are interconnected as a fertile source of ethics and morals in the African American context. Each is essential in the development of the black child as a responsible individual. There is a plethora of problems in some black communities such as addictions, violence, divorce, and generational conflicts. These mirror the general dysfunction of the larger society in terms of family systems, political debates, moralizing over the rights of women, health care for those living with AIDS, legalization of drugs, terrorism, domestic abuse, care of the elderly, or welfare reform.

In the face of oppressive situations—racism, classism, sexism, denominationalism, and ageism—African Americans have maintained solidarity defined by skin color, values, geography, and their shared history. The church, family, and those who are designated as the "teachers" have assigned community roles. Core beliefs are established and perpetuated covertly and overtly. Preachers tell of the healing power of the "God of the oppressed." Families pass on stories about what happens when one rushes into something without weighing the consequences. Mothers tell their children to "Do the best you can" or "Don't be led by anybody dumber than you." Children observe all the good and bad, acceptable and unacceptable, positive and negative, life-affirming and life-taking events in their community and decide what to do to survive, thrive, or become participants in community or in self-destruction.[7]

The brunt of responsibility for the incidence of crime, teen pregnancy, divorce, unemployment, and illiteracy in the African American community has been placed on the black church and family. The contention of this chapter is that in a majority of instances the black church, the black family, and the black extended family have been able to provide and nurture the spiritual seedbed for development of mores and values. The purpose of teaching relevant values and beliefs is to ensure that the majority of black children lead full and productive lives with a strong sense of personhood. A brief historical review of the black church, family, and community will shed light on this proposition.

When All God's Children Get Together

> A religion is a unified system of beliefs and practices relative to sacred things, that is to say, things set apart and forbidden—beliefs and practices which unite into one single moral community called a Church, all those who adhere to them.[8]

This definition of religion by Emile Durkheim is based on solidarity. He says that the object of religion is to regulate relations of persons through prayers, sacrifices, beliefs, and rites. Moral rules, based on beliefs and rites, are acted out in community. Persons classify things around them as either sacred or profane. Words, expressions, and formulas may be sacred. Persons consecrated or positioned high on the social structure may be or use the sacred. Others are in the realm of the mundane or profane. A certain number of sacred objects sustain relations in a unified system of beliefs. Religious beliefs are common to a specific group or community. The sacred things that are translated into common practices connect one to another. Solidarity evolves from a shared sense of the sacred.

Born in slavery, the black church is a gathering of the disinherited who possess their own sense of the sacred, revere their own icons, and establish their own sense of solidarity. The black church has been the source of comfort and hope for a people with minimal or nonexistent social recognition. Slavery deprived blacks of their African "tribal religions," which were considered pagan by whites and cited as a source of black rebellion against chattel slavery. The idea of a transcendent God made slavery more tolerable for blacks by offering a solace beyond the immediate situation. The black church began as a protest movement against the racism and discrimination of the white church. It provides identity with the black community and takes on its own identity as a "civil religion."[9] There is no separation of the sacred and secular in many black faith communities. Those faith communities focusing on individual change, often described as "prosperity gospel oriented" and some termed "charismatic" or "neo-Pentecostal ministries," may be exceptions to the rule. For the majority of black faith communities (particularly traditional denominations), however, God is in everything because God created all that is and ever will be. Politics, social action, and faith development are integral, unapologetic aspects of the black church. The pulpit is the place of explanations of the salvation story, forthright voting and human rights discussions, and proclamation regarding the need for individual conversion.

African religious elements such as polytheism, polygamy, ancestor worship, spirits, and the phenomena of nature were evident in early worship services in the invisible churches of enslaved Africans. God is Creator, Judge, Redeemer, and Supreme Being. The dominant motifs of African religions are affirmation and enjoyment of life.[10] African slaves carried inside them the African religions and belief systems passed down through generations. So-called "slave religion" elements such as the ring shout, "everywhereness" of God, and God in all creation—rocks, streams, earth, and wind—were passed on to me in the institutional black church of my grandparents and elders. The difference in the religion of the slaves and that of the black church is the European denominational influence and the freedom of worship. Personal salvation is a prerequisite for receiving God's help in the liberation of self and others. Conversion is transcendent, spiritual, and solitary at times. It is both communal and personal.[11]

During slavery African religious practices such as dance, drumming, and free expression of emotions were ridiculed as pagan rites and outlawed by white Christian missionaries and slave owners.[12] The slave owners came to understand the power of the African religious rites. Members of specific tribes united around ritual. Solidarity was reinforced through common religious practices. The laws became yet another method of breaking the will and common personhood of the enslaved.

Why the transition from African or slave religion to the institutionalized black church? Unable to rationalize the White Christian concept that a person could be a slave or slave owner and be a Christian, the slaves adapted basic Christian tenets such as love and neighborliness, and rejected others such as the often quoted Ephesians 6:5, "Slaves, obey your earthly masters with respect and fear, and with sincerity of heart, just as you would obey Christ." The irreconcilability of what white Christians practiced and what they preached was instrumental in black Christianity reinterpreting scripture in ways that made it applicable to their own daily existence. The idea that God loved creation and was "no respecter of persons," alongside the facts that blacks were owned, traded, raped, and lynched by whites, set up cognitive dissonance. Blacks sought affirmation for their personhood and empowerment to fight for the liberation of all persons.[13] A new tradition was needed to validate and affirm the black ideology of racial solidarity. Social deprivation was too great and the next step to independence and self-help seemed to be an institution that was owned and operated by blacks. This led to the establishment of the traditional independent black denominations: "Bluestone" African Baptist Church (1758), Free African Society (1787), which became the African Methodist Episcopal Church (1816), African Methodist Episcopal Zion Church (1796, 1820), and the Colored Methodist Episcopal Church (1870), which became the Christian Methodist Episcopal Church in 1954.[14]

Historically, some black churches, such as the African Methodist Episcopal Church, used Afrocentric scripture interpretations, stories, icons, and symbols in place of Eurocentric hermeneutic and images. Bishop Henry McNeil Turner, the twelfth Bishop of the A.M.E. Church (1888–1915), was an early proponent of black consciousness. Early in his ministry in Charleston, South Carolina, he spoke of the inequities of life for blacks in America, advocated for the return of blacks to Africa, and insisted that God was black.

> We have as much right biblically and otherwise to believe that God is a Negro, as you buckra or white people have to believe that God is a fine looking, symmetrical and ornamented white man. . . . Every race of people since time began who have attempted to describe their God by words, or by paintings, or by carvings, or by any other form or figure, have conveyed the idea that the God who made them and shaped their destinies was symbolized in themselves, and why should not the Negro believe that he resembles God as much as other people?[15]

Often the Jesus represented as white-skinned, blue-eyed, blond-haired Jesus of European American Christians is replaced with an image of Jesus with black skin, brown eyes, and tightly curled black hair for African American Christians.

This is particularly evident in Afrocentric or black independent churches. Portraying a loving God who looks like the black believer reinforces blacks' faith stance by enabling them to pray to someone who they envision looks, thinks, and therefore feels what they feel, including oppression based on color of skin. For some blacks it was incomprehensible that they were made in the image of a white figure, not least because this white image had been used to indicate that blacks were a damned people for they were so unlike the white Christian image of God. Many African Americans began to believe that God was multifaceted and could be any color God chose to be in order to be one with a variety of children.[16] As the thirst grew for freedom of religious expression and practice and for cultural affinity and community allegiance, the independent black church was established.[17]

The black church is that Christian aggregation whose origin, establishment, administration, function, life, order, symbols, and structure are exclusively in the hands of African American people. Emmanuel McCall, quoting Howard Thurman, refers to the black church as the background for black existence and ecclesiology ("It keeps the black race from community suicide"). It is the place where oppression is converted to poetry; exploitation to creativity; humiliation to hunger for justice; and haunting fears to hymns of praise. It is the womb of education and the cradle of freedom.[18] McCall postulates that the black church provides a vehicle for creative hope. It is where blacks come together and experience integrity and wholeness. Social unity and cultural freedom are there.[19]

During slavery and up to the present, the central location for tutoring the black community has been the black church. In the early black churches the black preacher was one of the only literate members of the community. Black teachers who learned to read in Sunday school returned the favor by teaching black children skills for jobs and classical education.

Since the time of Nat Turner, Denmark Vesey, and Harriet Tubman, freedom movements have grown out of the black church. On a more mundane level the church is the community meeting house, recreation center, and at times home for new members. Benjamin E. Mays and Joseph Nicholson, African American educators and theologians writing in the 1930s, identify the black church as a source of racial and ethnic validation for African American people. It provides an opportunity to be a person of value and dignity.[20] It affords status, pride, and self-respect to every janitor, domestic, salesperson, cashier, doctor, teacher, lawyer, and unemployed person who attends church. It replaces institutionally segregated housing, clubs, schools, churches, and professions. The black church encourages black participation in education, business, politics, economic development, and cultural stability. The fundamental values of freedom, justice, equality, mutuality, life, and love are reinforced.[21] There is a traditional community saying that the black church "counts you in when everyone else counts you out."

It has been my experience that the black church has also proved to be an oppressive place for some persons. The role of women in the many black churches has traditionally been to sing in choirs, teach children, serve the pastor, give financial support, and keep the building clean. The pulpit is most often the exclusive male domain. In other cases of oppression or exclusion, the black church may "lock out" those who have disabilities, those with different sexual proclivities, those who sell themselves for money or drugs, the underclass, boisterous young people, and anyone who does not agree with the politics or power of the senior pastor. At its worst, the black church repeats the exclusivity of the white churches prior to the independent black church movement of the late 1700s. At its best, the black church is the healing and nurturing place of black communities.

According to sociologists Jualyne Dodson and Cheryl Gilkes, the black church is built around a common ethos of struggle for and with the entire community. The black church strives to function holistically.[22] There is something within the church that is a driving force that enables the people to resist oppression, and hope for a better tomorrow. The group, an extension of the individual, encourages regeneration, resistance, and redemption from societal depression, confusion, and restriction. The church is a place of spiritual liberation; it is there that one may freely express one's innermost feelings in prayer and praise. This shared culture of resistance to racism turns stereotypes into accolades. The church functions to mobilize the community to seek justice and demand social change. The church holds up a banner of universalism seeking comfort and advocacy for all persons. Members are called to seek the elimination of suffering for themselves and their children.

According to biblical scholar Cain Hope Felder, the Bible is a source of personal piety in the black church.[23] It is the cornerstone of the pursuit of justice and full political rights. It allows the individual to know God, an incarnate Savior, and the workings of the Holy Spirit. In the church, the use of the Bible is central and diverse. It is used in the community narratives, art, sermons, education, testimonies, and music. It brings an awareness of the oppressed conditions of the people and the liberating aspects of God. In some African American denominations the Bible is literally interpreted and inerrant. Some use exegesis and hermeneutic exposition to relay information on Christian responsibilities for individuals and community. Regardless of interpretative styles, there is a fundamental community understanding that the Bible details extended families as the bedrock of the church. The Bible guides our lives in relationship to God and one another. This reinforces the organization of the black church and community.

Wallace C. Smith claims that the black church and the black family are inextricably linked through role definition and function.[24] God, the Creator, is the universal parent (*mother to the motherless* and *father to the fatherless*). The pastor and spouse or older members of the congregation are often called *father* or *mother*. Jesus, God's Son, is called the *elder brother*. The belief that we are God's children is reflected in calling members of the congregation *brothers* and *sisters*. The connection of the black church and the black family is essential to the survival of the black community. Each has prescribed responsibilities to the church and to one another. Many black families turn to the black church in times of crisis as well as for inspiration and nurture. This is evident in the number of food and clothing banks or distribution centers set up in black communities through even storefront churches.

Smith lists four central intersecting elements of the black religious system, of family, and of community. First, each person must be involved in education—mentoring the young, caring for the elderly, feeding the hungry, or working with the homeless in the concept of a suffering community. If one suffers, all suffer. Second, the church is an inclusive community. This model is adapted from African heritage. There is a reverence for age and for women. No one is left out of the power structure. Patriarchs and matriarchs are revered. Surrogate mothers, fathers, aunts, uncles, cousins, sisters, brothers, and grandparents are provided for church and community members. The children belong to the entire church and are generally reared accordingly. There are no orphans, which leads to the third point. The black church is an *adoptionist* community. Through evangelism new members are acquired. Each new "family member" has full participation (depending on the polity of the church in terms of access to ordained ministry) in the life and customs of the church. Members share joys, pains, loves, and struggles of their "family" members. Fourth and finally, at its finest the black church is a hopeful community. Practical eschatology is a central focus. There is a better life to come for everyone. This means that whatever happens to black church members, there is hope. This is accomplished through mutuality and love for one another as demonstrated in black family systems. The black church, when it fails to live up to its original mission, may become an exclusive, judgmental institution in regard to those who look different or who think, live, or worship differently than the leadership.[25]

Patricia Hunter suggests that even with a majority female membership masculine language is prevalent in descriptions of God, but the traditional understanding is that God possesses both maleness (father) and femaleness (mother). The gender is internally translated depending on who is listening and their worldview. God looks after "His helpless children" and concurrently empowers them to engage evil and overcome oppression. The use of inclusive language in black churches has been slow in evolving due to the entrenched masculine leadership and cries that the black church is the "only place black men are in unchallenged leadership." Generally, women academicians, seminarians, and ministers have been at the forefront of a summons to transform exclusively male language, icons, and polity to include women.[26] (This will be discussed further in chapter 2.)

The mission of the church is to reach out to all in need, all fellow sufferers, regardless of who they are. With the growth of class stratification among African Americans the primary groups that are unchurched are the underclass and upper class. Segments of each view the church as irrelevant. The underclass feels shut out because of materialism, lack of education, and social barriers. There is also a feeling of institutional betrayal for some. Many upper-class blacks view religion as an emotional substitute for success. Figures from 1989, however, indicate that 85 percent of African Americans who attend church belong to one of the traditional black denominations.[27] The remaining percentage attend mainline traditionally white denominations or new religious movements. Those who remain in black denominations often cite links to their cultural heritage, cultural connectedness, and freedom of worship as their rationale for attendance.

Bless Be the Tie That Binds

A principal characteristic of the West African Dahomey people was family stability.[28] This area was also known as the Gold Coast because of the seemingly endless supply of slaves bound for the Caribbean, South America, and North America. The consanguineal relationships of the West Africans were the source of community. Conjugal relationships were secondary and contingent on the blood relationships of the compounds. A family council completed all matters of inheritance, law, and decision making. The eldest male of the compound settled all internal disputes. Husbands and wives had distinct roles in decision making and familial relations. The entire compound was responsible for the socialization of children. Divorce and remarriage were acceptable if determined by the family council as necessary. Husbands had little control over the property of wives, who were often powerful and influential.

The African Diaspora family value system incorporated reverence, reconciliation, respect, responsibility, restraint, and reciprocity. Among the Ashanti, fathers were responsible for the obedience and moral deference of the children. The mothers were the chief counsels of the sons. Daughters learned social skills and character from women in their community.[29]

Slave owners and traders disregarded these social structures. Familial solidarity was purposely destroyed in the name of economic advancement, resulting in alienation and death for many Africans. Torn from their homelands and thrown into the cargo holds of slave ships, the Africans began to form new communities and alliances based on survival and ethnicity. Because it was not uncommon for Africans to be multilingual, some speaking as many as five languages, and because of their common bondage, communicative barriers broke down. These diverse cultures—Ibo, Dahomey, Mandinka, and Mende tribes—became intertwined and the cord yielded a strong, enduring people. Pacts were made to protect one another unto death. New "families" were formed using an oral tradition to keep their shared heritage alive. Self-sacrifice was evident in pledges to take punishment for the weaker members and give food to children.[30] The unsettling of the African family unit began during slavery. Children were often sold to other plantations shortly after weaning. African women were made into breeders and the men were made into workhorses. Everyone attached to a particular plantation became a member of one large family. Differentiation evolved primarily from the slave masters raping African women and producing children of mixed blood and varied skin color. Specialized skills and "Caucasian" features were rewarded by assignment of blacks to assorted jobs and single "family" homes. Those who worked in the master's house were young women thirteen or older who cared for the master's children. Older women cooked, sewed, or cleaned. Older men worked as butlers and handymen. Young, darker men worked the fields with older, darker women. Lighter-skinned blacks are often referred to as beautiful because of the closeness to Caucasian features. Darker-skinned blacks are today still held in disdain in some communities because of their African features. This "color-struckness" is also prevalent in some contemporary families, churches, and communities.

Patricia Hill Collins, a black feminist, reports changes in the black family due to slavery.[31] Before slavery African women combined work and family without conflict. Children often accompanied their mothers to the fields or marketplaces. During slavery women were powerless labor units still combining children and work. Communal childcare resulted in a few older women being accountable for all the children. Reproduction was controlled for capitalism instead of the assurance of lineage. Childbearing became a way for enslaved women to anchor themselves in a particular location. Because life expectancy for black women was 33.6 years, and because between 1850 and 1860 two out of three black children survived to age ten, women gave birth to many children. Birth prizes, such as new clothing or special privileges, were often given to the enslaved woman who produced the most children. And yet, conversely, black infanticide was a means of ensuring children would not have to endure the pain of slavery.[32]

Between Emancipation (1863–65) and the Great Migration (1890–1940) blacks began to work as wage laborers. Communal childcare was maintained as women entered the labor force as paid domestics or field workers. With an increasing number of black men working, particularly in the North, women began to stay at home to strengthen the political and economic position of the family. Working in the home also lessened the sexual harassment and rape black women encountered. The shift from sleeping over to day work as domestics, and entering manufacturing fields, gave black women more time for their children. The practice of behaving or taking actions in consideration of what was good for the family, community, or race sustained the family in the new environment. Black women also began to create black communities focused around churches, child care, and neighborhood activities. These self-contained, segregated communities helped strengthen family structures.[33]

African American men and women filled factory and armament positions during World War II, which resulted in a strengthening of the Northern black economic base. However, after the war, with the return of white workers, blacks were forced out of positions. Numbers of blacks were laid off or demoted. The unemployment rate hit the black community with a vengeance. Members of entire neighborhoods lived in poverty. Economic stratification began to separate the black community. Seventy to 75 percent of blacks were working class. Family economic insecurity again led to fathers migrating across the country to find jobs. Mothers returned to the workforce as domestics or blue-collar workers. This period saw the advent of welfare programs such as Aid to Families with Dependent Children.[34] An increasing number of single, separated, and divorced families was evident. There was a shift from everyone working for the good of the community to individuals striving to become part of the "American Dream." Changes in the overall structure of the black community accelerated after 1960. Recreation moved to black community centers often outside the neighborhood. The number of adolescent single mothers was increasing. Especially among the poor, communal child care was replaced by grandmothers caring for their own grandchildren.[35] This was the same model employed during slavery when older women on plantations cared for children while mothers worked.

One of the most controversial reports on the black family in the twentieth century was the 1965 Moynihan Report.[36] Based on federal census information from 1940 to 1963, Senator Daniel Patrick Moynihan released "The Negro Family: The Case for National Action." He concluded that "the heart of the deterioration of Negroe society is the decline of the family." Apparently based on his reading of statistics, he said that the black middle class was strong and successful while the lower class was disadvantaged and disorganized.

> There is probably no single fact of Negro American life so little understood by whites. The white family has achieved a high degree

of stability and is maintaining that stability. By contrast, the family structure of lower class Negroes is highly unstable, and in many urban centers is approaching complete breakdown. (Moynihan Report, 5)

Ironically, there was no such report on the white middle class and white youth at that time, who were also rejecting family values. The grave difference is that economically and politically, whites could afford to leave the family, divorce, or have someone else raise their children. They had a privileged power base that would not question shifts in their family structure.[37] At that time there were no widely circulated assessments of white families by black psychologists or politicians. Few gave attention to contradictory "living" evidence of black family life.

In his evaluation of the black family, Moynihan cited role reversal of black males and females. He defined black women as "castrating matriarchs." These so-called matriarchs were said to be better educated and worked more often than black males. In Moynihan's estimation, black females were responsible for the breakdown of the black family due to their dominance over black males. The result of this "power" of black women was children who grew up without fathers, with no familial work ethic, low intelligence quotients, and poor school performance. Conversely, Moynihan said that white youth were products of stable homes, egalitarian mothers, and working fathers. Even whites from divorced families were said to be surrounded with working male role models, supposedly nonexistent in black families.

White children without fathers at least perceive all about them the pattern of men working. Negro children without fathers flounder— and fail. Broken homes mean low intelligence quotients and school performance. (Moynihan Report, 35)

Moynihan's report was completed by external observers with little or no concept of the internal mores, history, or extended connections of the black family. Census information is rarely inclusive of all persons. There is no accounting for persons who give false information through fear of government intervention, or for exceptions to the statistics. Blacks are taught to "keep your business to yourself," which translates into not telling anyone, particularly outsiders, anything about yourself. Moynihan did not consider the appropriation of white values by blacks in his assessment. He also ignored the number of black men in the military during the period of the census, those incarcerated, those looking for jobs or working in other states, black male homosexuals, those married to women of a different racial-ethnic background, those active in protest movements that would take them away from their families, or those living in common-law situations.[38]

Bettina Aptheker suggested that the Moynihan Report was strategically timed to coincide with the apex of the Civil Rights movement.[39] The purpose was to turn the black community back on itself and absolve the white community of any responsibility or complicity in racism and discrimination. It fueled a battle of the sexes and further entrenched the black patriarchy that sought to parallel the white patriarchy. A result of the modern Civil Rights movement was the opening of opportunities for blacks to enter the workforce in new and more profitable positions. One of the critiques of this phenomenon was that black women, judged by the white power structure as less threatening and better educated than black men, were taking jobs away from black men. Often black women were targeted by white society as "castrating matriarchs" and by black society as "betrayers of the race."

bell hooks denies the existence of a black matriarchy in the United States.[40] She defines "matriarch" as one who has equal power with men. The matriarch has control over her own body and is economically secure. Few women hold this privilege, particularly black women. In spite of these difficulties black women continued to work with black males, usually in a subordinate role, for the edification of all persons. Black women continued to seek jobs to assist in supporting the extended black family. The Moynihan Report left its mark on perceptions of the strength and formulation of the black family. In the past forty-five years black activists, psychologists, historians, and social scientists have written numerous rebuttals of Moynihan and affirmations about the black family.

Marian Wright Edelman contends that in the past twenty years researchers have begun to look also at the strengths of the black family.[41] There has been an effort to distinguish between the myths and realities of the black family, and to investigate the effect of social, economic, and discrimination factors on black family structure. She cites three theoretical approaches to the study of black families—cultural deficiency, cultural variance, and social class—widely used by social scientists, yet problematic. The cultural deficiency view uses the white middle class as the norm. Black families are seen as different and distinct from white families. This results in a belief that black families are unstable and suffer from economic trouble, discrimination, promiscuity, and patriarchy. The cultural variance view is based on socialization. Black and white cultures are different but equal. Black families are judged on the African mores and behavioral norms that distinguish them as a culture. A subsection of this theory is cultural equivalency used primarily by historians. Blacks have had two-parent intact families that are similar, but not identical, to white families. Finally, the social class view holds that given equal opportunities black families will parallel white families. If blacks are not poor, experience no racism or discrimination, and have equal access to goods and services they will resemble white families. It is important to remember that black and white social scientists have used these views in assessing black families. One must ask what is it about the black, poor, single-parent head-of-household family that succeeds without emulating or behaving like white families? What are the accepted criteria for being a good family? How do blacks challenge, rebut, or at least reassess the Moynihan Report or all the Moynihan clones?

Sociologist Andrew Billingsley countermands negative stereotypes of African American families. He defines the African American families as "an *intimate association* of persons of African descent who are *related to one another* by a variety of means, including blood, marriage, formal adoption, informal adoption, or by appropriation; sustained by a history of common residence in America; and deeply embedded in a network of social structures both internal and external to itself."[42]

The strongest element of the African American family is blood ties and lineage. The African American extended family developed through informal adoption, appropriation, and fictive kin.[43] Hallmarks of black community are shared geography, shared sets of values, identification with heritage, and institutions or organizations such as schools, churches, and businesses that have grown out of African American heritage. During slavery 45 to 50 percent of free blacks lived in families with other free blacks, slaves, white partners, or Native Americans.

At every period since slavery until 1980 the majority of African American families were married couples. By 1990 57 percent of African American families were single-parent families. Billingsley points to shifts from a Southern agricultural lifestyle (90 percent of all blacks in 1890) to a Northern industrial lifestyle (90 percent of all blacks in 1980), social and racial discrimination, and economic marginality as factors for "marring" the African American extended family. He says that families cannot be strong unless the community is strong. The changes in community are external factors that are often precipitated by changes within individuals, such as a lack of self-esteem.

Joseph Scott and James Steward, African American sociologists, name three reasons for the shift in black family structure and values since slavery: *institutional decimation* is the numerical shortage of black males. The killing of black males necessitated female-headed households. Scott and Steward cite slavery, lynching, the Vietnam War, crime, police brutality, accident, disease, hypertension, drugs, alcohol, and prisons as sources and means of the decrease in viable black men. The second reason is *institutional deprivation*. Blacks are shut out of areas of gainful employment, facing a 50 to 85 percent unemployment rate in older urban areas. Blacks are often underemployed. They have skills that exceed the job specifications but are not hired in positions that match those skills.

Many blacks of all socioeconomic groups "hustle" to survive. Between 1960 and 1970 enterprises included gambling, selling "hot" items, and running numbers. More money could be made by *hustlin'* than by being a domestic or a porter. As income increased so did family tensions because *hustlin'* was contradictory to Christian teachings about honesty. The tension of providing for the family by any means necessary and the living out of Christian values was a difficult choice for many families. Children grew up knowing that there was extra money but many did not know where it came from or what happened to their fathers when caught *hustlin'*.[44] The reality was that working two and three jobs was a tradition for the majority of black families. Many times children accompanied their parents to work or worked themselves in order to earn extra money for the family. Children learned to make "extra" money by observing their parents. The ends justified the means for many families existing in poverty. Moynihan challenged that black youths did not possess an occupational tradition. Perhaps he was looking for traditionally defined nine to five work or white-collar work, not the black tradition of working two to three jobs or *hustlin'* to make ends meet.

The third reason listed by Scott and Steward is *institutional subsidization*. During this period the number of unemployed black males swelled as the number of black women seeking welfare spiraled. Black males moved out of the home in order for their families to qualify for assistance. As the female looked to the white male-dominated system to supply family needs, the black male became an appendage in many homes. The welfare system and its by-products inadvertently and, in some views, purposely destroyed black family life in working-class families. Yet this welfare system "Catch 22" is often ignored by researchers: if the father remained with the family they would starve, and if he left, he was called a deserter or felt emasculated. In this way, the United States government supported the beginnings of fragmentation of the black family, according to Scott and Steward.

In this impasse, kinship bonds in black families became crucial, according to social workers Joanne and Elmer Martin.[45] Most African societies were based on kinship through nuclear, extended, clan, tribe, and community groups. African families were based in helping others and caregiving. The well-being of the community through mutuality was paramount. *Fictive kin* were persons cared for though not necessarily blood relatives. Selfish people were ostracized.

During slavery the helping tradition continued with men and women working side by side, but it began to decline in the 1930s during the Great Migration. Blacks were looking for a better life while shifting from rural to urban life. In order to fit in, newly citified blacks were told not to "act country" and not to trust city people. Friends and family members already living in the North responded by reorienting emigrants and forming neighborhoods and churches with "folks from down home." With expanded urbanization, secularism, and competition blacks assimilated dominant urban values of individualism. Big city survival was based on "me first." Economics, occupation, church affiliation, and education stratified old neighborhoods as blacks pursued the "American Dream." This trend continued through the 1960s. Integration of schools added to the shift in values from group, family, or community to professionalization of caregiving, meritocracy, and class issues over race.[46] The values the emigrants possessed on arriving in the urban areas gave way to those of persons in power in the big city. Those who sought to retain former ways were called old-fashioned or backward. Regardless of the outside pressures, they had affirming families, churches, and communities that allowed and taught them to "act" as God intended them to act.

You Always Have Your Family

Bridging the gap of who to be at home and who to be in the world proved difficult for blacks in general and black youth in particular. Few black youth in the 1960s and 1970s could afford to go "seeking the meaning of life" like many of their white counterparts. Life was all too real for black youth. They worked as well as went to school. They faced discrimination and tried to find their place in society through endurance and at times, protest. Even when in jail many received the message that their families would always be there for them. Their "extended families" were responsible for providing love and assurance to help them face the adversities of life.

The *black extended family* is a multigenerational, interdependent kinship system. It is welded together by a sense of obligation to relatives. It is centered in a *family-based* household and is guided by a *dominant family figure*. The black extended family reaches across geographical boundaries and can be both a moral and financial support system. It is not unusual that it provides emotional, social, material, and economic support for several generations of relatives. It is the place where leadership, security, sense of true family, group direction, and personal identity evolve and are reinforced.[47]

The *family base* is generally the home of the *dominant family member,* often the grandparent(s). It is the place of large family activities such as reunions and holidays, and times of family celebrations, sorrow, and crisis. In two or three generations the subextended family (nuclear unit) may become extended units in and of themselves.

When I was growing up my grandparents' homes in Sedalia, Missouri, were "Grand Central Station" for holidays and summer vacations. The city was divided by a railroad track and blacks crossed over to the other side to go to work, to go to a segregated movie theater, and to shop for—but not try on—

clothing. The black high school and black swimming pool/park were located within one block of my maternal and paternal grandparents' respective blocks. My mother's five brothers and sisters, their families, and an assortment of aunts, uncles, and church members would sleep on the floor, in chairs, on the porch, or wherever they could find a spot, and look forward to a family dinner. Even while in college and working my first job, the house at 401 West Morgan Street was a place of physical and spiritual renewal. Regardless of activities on Saturday night we were each expected in church on Sunday morning. My grandparents were martial law in their home.

One block away my paternal grandparents provided a different yet equally viable form of nurture. It was in their home that I learned to dance, cook, and play "grown-up card games" like Bid Whist. They taught us how to respect ourselves, live in a world transitioning slowly from segregated to integrated, and value the strength of all family configurations. I remember my paternal stepgrandmother advising me to "Learn all you can, do not settle for being someone's domestic, I want you to be somebody. If I ever think that you have to work cleaning up after someone else, I will get out of my grave and whip you myself." Whenever I feel like giving up, Grandma Cloria's words echo in my head. Both grandparental homes were like mansions to me as I matured. I still long for those times when love came in the form of food, hugs, spankings, talks, laughter, and tears from persons whom society valued little, but who worked to make sure those who followed became more than they could ever imagine.

The *dominant family member* in most African American families provides leadership either through assumption or appointment. He or she is usually the oldest living member of the family, similar to the pattern found in African families. Often it is the grandparent, aunt, or uncle who keeps the family alive and is the totem for its survival. Although it is clear that family members must be able to stand up for themselves, be self-sufficient, work, and go to school, family members turn to this person in times of need—such as when they need temporary shelter, economic support, or interim child care. The dominant family member spends energy keeping the family together, exemplifying familial closeness, love, and concern. He or she helps socialize children, passes down family history, conveys African American heritage, teaches skills and techniques of survival, helps regulate the moral behavior of the family members, upholds the family spiritual life, and keeps individual and collective family secrets. Part of the power ascribed to the dominant family member comes through awareness of the burdens and concerns of the family. Coercion and manipulation are rare attributes. The position of the dominant family member is similar to that of a charismatic leader in a larger social context. He or she has unquestioned authority and is the source of wisdom and law.[48]

In a similar vein, an older sibling may be the one designated to raise the children while the parents work two jobs or one is absent from the home. He or she becomes the *dominant family member by substitution*. The member has responsibility but limited power. An older, retired member of the neighborhood who becomes the monitor for all the children, seeing everything and reporting back to parents when they return from work, may also supplement the socialization.

My grandmother, Mama Tessie, age ninety, is the source of our family nurture and news. She has lived in the same house for over sixty years. She knows about each child, grandchild, and great-grandchild and can be counted on to supply the sick and shut-in report as well as news on who has been promoted, married, birthed, or just maintaining. She always has time to listen, pray, laugh, advise, and visit. She is the dominant family member for her own six children, over thirty grandchildren, and a number of great-grandchildren as well as persons in the community and the church where she still teaches Sunday school.

Extended families are formed through procreation, marriage, adoption, and absorption. (Absorption is taking care of the homeless and those unable to fend for themselves due to age, sickness, or unemployment.) The family is flexible yet stable enough to withstand the change in the immediate structure. The *home base* is opened to all family members, and at times friends, no matter where they live. The rationale is that, "Mary would do the same for us." Informal adoption primarily involves children whose natural parents are unable to care for one or all of their children. A family member (or members) is willing to adopt the children temporarily or permanently. Persons who are not blood relatives also adopt children of close friends. The continuation of the extended family is particularly relevant in working and middle-class families. Typically the adopted child is the only child in the family, the last or only child in a subextended family, a child born out of wedlock who returns home with the mother, or the child of a single father. Other possible situations that result in a child being adopted are: the mother is pregnant again and needs assistance, parental inability to discipline the child, a parent who wants to avoid a child being raised around "bad kids," the illness or death of the mother, an abused or unwanted child, or a parental request for freedom from child-rearing responsibility. Grandma, Mamma, Mama, Nana, or Granny often takes the child to avoid formal adoption and the loss of the child to the welfare social service system. The child is raised with religious beliefs, strict (corporal) discipline, respect for parental authority, and relevance of experience or Mother Wit (common sense).[49]

African American family structure is fluid and at times indefinable. It has rarely conformed to the 1950s husband, wife, and two children *Leave It to Beaver* model. Members of the extended family may be of any age, racial group, or faith system. A guiding principle is that no one should be alone. In the 1990s several studies produced definitive information about the varieties of black family structure. Archie Smith explored the changing structures of African American families, such as adolescent (families within families), non-procreating, and cohabiting structures, in addition to the traditional nuclear, extended, and augmented structures.[50] He also infers that black people are in danger of a loss of collective solidarity and common struggle in an exploitative society if they become fully integrated in mainstream materialism. It is the quest for materialism that has lessened the extended family structure of the black community, he suggests.

This progression from solidarity to individualism is marked by a loss of collective memory. In the past, the majority of black people had *anamnesis,* a recollection of the buried past and participation in a common memory and hope. The conscious identification with one another and the quest for freedom resulted in *anamnestic solidarity.* This relationality of black people signifies the indwelling presence of others in our concrete reality and of our presence in others. We learn to respond to the intentions and actions of others and self. The dominant family member was traditionally the community therapist. The spiritual healer, glad tidings bearer, interpreter of the unknown, comforter in sorrow, expresser of community resentment of a stolen and oppressed people, in Smith's thought, is endangered. The increasing diversity and decreased unity in the black community is due to assimilation and an inward orientation rather than community salvation. The African American community must reclaim its solidarity in order to survive fully.

African Americans have a rich heritage of values-based extended families. Yet, family structures are as varied as the rainbow of skin colors found in the black community. Just as there are families that are loving, caring, and spiritually grounded there are also those families that are grossly fragmented. Researchers who present sweeping reports on the disintegration of the black family typically charge that the black mother lacks parenting skills and the black father is absent. The full story is much more complex than lack of stable parental relationships. One also must consider the social history of blacks in America, overall treatment of black women, denigration of black men, socially acceptable behaviors, and waning membership in Christian institutions.

Constant shouts regarding a lack of role models in the black community assume that the only people who can teach black children about life are athletes and entertainers. Increasingly credence is given to the role models already present in the community like ministers, teachers, the woman next door, or members of the overlooked extended family. These ordinary mentors should be remembered before global statements of the ineffectiveness of black parenting are cavalierly tossed out.

It is crucial to understand that blacks teach their children "particular" values and ways of living in this society. Black children have a different set of doors to try to get through in order to "fit in." The majority of African Americans recognize the value of their distinct culture and heritage, those practices and teachings that have survived the 380 years since the Jamestown Landing, the vibrant black church, and the wealth of parenting knowledge found in the community. African Americans seek to obliterate and transform those debilitating myths and stereotypes regarding the black family, the black church, and the black community.

Much can be learned by studying what has worked in establishing and nurturing vital black families, as well as what has proved detrimental. It is well to remember that all values found in the black community are not socially accepted as positive in the dominant culture. For example, *hustlin'* may border on illegality. Many values stem from a survivalist instinct, a type of situation ethics not lived or understood beyond the black community. Regardless of the proscribed ideal family structure, the African American family flexes to meet the needs of the members. A family may appear to be five members yet has over thirty as immediate members. The composition of the family may be through natural birth, marriage, and fictive kin. A mantra of the black family is, *there is always room for one more*. Fundamental to the composition of these extended family configurations is what, why, and how they are sustained. The role of the African American woman as dominant family member, mentor, nurturer, and spiritual advisor of black family is the focus of the succeeding chapters.

2

WISDOM BEARERS

The
Mother Wit
of
Sistuh Girlfriends

Why cannot we do something to distinguish ourselves, and contribute some of our hard earnings that would reflect honor upon our memories, and cause our children to arise and call us blessed? Shall it any longer be said of the daughters of Africa, they have no ambition, they have no force? . . . How long shall the fair daughters of Africa be compelled to bury their minds and talents beneath a load of iron pots and kettles?   —Maria W. Stewart, 1832.[1]

Almost two hundred years later, these questions continue to reverberate in the minds of black women. When women are silent they are over-looked, ignored, or thought to be ignorant, with nothing of value to contribute to anyone. When they speak up they are branded as insolent, aggressive, or domineering man-haters. In the excerpted September 1832 speech in Boston, Maria Stewart called on black women to develop their intellectual, spiritual, and occupational abilities in order to work effectively for the liberation of black people, with no apology for being female. This clarion call has been transmitted intergenerationally. It reverberates as a challenge to move from passive resistance to ignorance and bigotry toward active self-sufficiency. It is a central pillar of *womanist* perspectives and has been elaborated by African American women scholars such as Jacquelyn Grant and Katie Cannon.[2] Unnamed millions of black women have urged their sisters and daughters to do something to make the world know they have lived, rather than merely become statistics in actuarial charts. They have suggested that women live a Christ-like life, become president, or own their own business.

The intent of this study of black women's transmission of values is to give voice to such women. Hence, this chapter will analyze the roles and responsibilities of black women in the black family, the black church, and the black community. Foundational to understanding the intergenerational transmission of African American spiritual values by black grandmothers and othermothers is a brief review of African American ethics. Founding scholars (such as Katie Cannon, Jacquelyn Grant, Cheryl Gilkes) of *womanist* thought began with interest in particular studies in black theology and African American ethics. These disciplines, coupled with an African American women's hermeneutic, evolved into womanist perspectives on theology and ethics. I will examine womanist theology to show that the belief systems of African American women are both similar to and different from that of the black community in general and black males in particular. A perusal of the womanist perspective will focus on the social roles ascribed to black women by society, how black women acknowledge and confront multidimensional oppression, and an analysis of some of the spiritual values black women transmit to children, church, and community as gleaned from my research in African American women's literature, faith systems, and scholarly reports.

African American Christian ethics originated in the African culture, were reinforced in the black church, and blended with adaptations from the society. In response to European American subjugation implemented with the advent of slavery, African Americans have developed a corrective to allow them to live the life God has directed them to live even in the face of horrors like chattel systems and institutionalized oppression. This corrective is a common belief among black Christians in the universality of humanity. Moral improvement within the culture stems from adherence to the principles of good citizenship and benevolence to others. It is believed that God favors the incessant striving of people for freedom, equality, and justice. Sin is the failure of this morality. Therefore, worth and dignity of the person can and must be sought within the social system—judicially, politically, economically, and spiritually. Black women strive to sustain these aspects of morality in the black family, the black church, and the black community. Each has been the site of black women's oppression and freedom. This contradiction has been most evident within the black church.

African American women have supported the creeds of the black church since its inception in the "hush arbors" of slavery. Black women have been the teachers, speakers, comforters, and guardians of the Word of God. They have kept the promise of God alive in the minds of their children, and continue the legacy of their grandmothers in caring for the world. Stemming from this, there are subtle references in the black community to the proclivity of black women to "mother the world" or to be the "Savior" of the world by picking up strays. Yet, they are simply doing what they have been taught by their mothers, grandmothers, and pastors: that all creation should be cared for regardless of race, creed, color, physical attributes, economic status, faith stance, or general abilities.[3]

The Bible Tells Me So

Henry Mitchell and Nicholas Cooper-Lewter, both African American theologians, discuss the core beliefs of the black community as developed in the black church that underlie this concern for the individual and the world.[4] God, God's Son, and the Holy Spirit are ever-present in the lives of the people. We are anchored in the storms of life by the cords of our faith. God preserves us in the midst of perpetual and undeserved pain and suffering. Survival in the face of adversity is based on the learned response of hope.

African Americans learn to cope in adversity through adaptation, self-control, and self-determination. They maintain a hope in a better world through faith in Jesus. They develop the capacity to make something out of nothing to feed nine people on food for three. Through prayer and seeking guidance of the Holy Spirit they learn to "hold on until my change is come."

Mitchell and Cooper-Lewter insist that black Christian ethics are shaped by the struggle to survive. These ethics are based in the Old and New Testament writings and African theology. The providence of God speaks to the community idea that "You may be down but you won't be down always." God is in the midst of all of our struggles and provides for all our needs. Only God is able to lift us up out of the muck and mire. All struggle is for the good of society. This does not mean black women seek out hard times or rejoice in struggle. Nor does it mean that God is the only actor in a situation. Rather, it means that they become agents of their own destiny. The reality that all persons face some kind of trials is understood, as is that persons are directed to act as God leads. One is not to sit in the struggle and complain, but to be "about the Father's business," for there is some blessing or reward "on the other side of through." After the struggle subsides (though for a time it may seem interminable) all persons rejoice in approaching or achieving the goal. However, if we knowingly allow an unjust society to prevail, we are coconspirators in our own demise. That there are destructive forces in the world is accepted, as is the necessity of engaging evil. When some external power is seen to be working against my life, I replay God's question to Jeremiah, "If you have raced with foot-runners and they have wearied you, how will you compete with horses? And if in a safe land you fall down, how will you fare in the thickets of the Jordan?" (Jeremiah 12:5 NRSV). These questions joined with childhood instruction push me to keep up the fight even when it seems that the odds are insurmountable.

This biblical challenge combines in African American spirituality the belief in God's omnipotence, omniscience, and omnipresence. In sermons, songs, prayers, and testimonies it is common to hear, "You can't hide from God" or "God never packs a suitcase because He's already everyplace." The omniscience of God ensures God's knowledge of our state of existence. The assurance of God's presence gives meaning and satisfaction to what we must endure. God is the source of all truth, and God's vision reaches the innermost thoughts and deeds of individuals and society. Because God cares, knows, watches, and heals, persons are empowered to live above their circumstances and thrive in communion with God, self, and neighbor.[5]

It's All About Love

Archie Smith blends all the aforementioned values in his model of Christian social ethics or black liberation ethics.[6] He begins by detailing the agency of self. The individual must create a world that is meaningful for the self, for the individual is the conscious center of activity, creativity, unity, and power within a group. Self-transformation is achieved through recall of past experiences, relating memory to the need for current action, making choices, taking risks, making mistakes, thinking, and reconstructing activity. One gains awareness of self by acting for good or evil in a social context. Black self-consciousness, imagination, and morality are reflections of what it means to comprehend the relationship of self to society.

Smith uses the African proverb "One is only human because of others, with others, and for others" to exemplify the relational self. Our lives have a horizontal and a vertical dimension. We are obligated to be in relationship with God (vertical) and with our sisters and brothers (horizontal). We are challenged to love God, neighbor, and self.[7]

Growing up, there were times when there seemed to be twenty people living in the house. As one of seven children, my responsibility was to cook for the family. My parents, as their parents before them, had an open house. No one was ever turned away from our table, whether we were having beans or turkey. My parents did not believe that anyone should be hungry or without a place to stay. There was always an array of blood relatives and "play cousins" in our home. The family lines blurred and often one did not know the actual relationship until a death. At root, my parents lived in the assurance that God would replace whatever was consumed and that we were not to worry about things, but value people. I find that my home is now also an open house. I get great joy out of inviting people over (or just having them unexpectedly drop by) for dinner, spending the night, or just sitting in quiet friendship and valuing God's family in all of its diversity.

In my parental home and now in my own, *agape* love is applied as the norm in each situation of our social context as in Smith's model of Christian situational ethics. The situation determines the rightness or wrongness of our actions. Judgments are made relative to the circumstances. So although we are taught to tell the truth, in some situations it would be wrong to tell the truth if the result is an unloving or bad consequence. For example, when the bill collector came to our house to pick up money or threaten to turn off or remove some item due to nonpayment, my mother would tell me to say she was not at home. She did not have the money and did not want to be embarrassed by lying about when she would have it. Today, the caller identification monitor on our telephones fulfills a similar function. Persons can check to see if the caller is someone whom they want to speak with or someone to be avoided. Situational ethics makes individual freedom a personal response and determination of the rightness or wrongness of the decision.

Black liberation Christian ethics are revolutionary means to convert the systems of racism, classism, sexism, and denominationalism to emancipatory, God-oriented actions. Core beliefs are located in Scripture, a liberating God, and constant struggle for freedom of all persons. Combining situation ethics and liberation ethics, Smith proposes that African Americans teach their children values based on: (1) action or obligation—what morally ought to be done; (2) character and virtue—commendable or reprehensible personal qualities; and (3) goals or ends—what makes human life good or bad. In summary, Smith holds that the black church, black family, and black community exist in a mutually supportive relationship. Each provides categories of values (alternative for or supplementary to the values of the larger society), which are ultimately beneficial to the social and individual life of the person in community.[8]

These principles of justice, centrality of the Bible, and social activism are both the crux of and challenges to the formation and resilience of the African American church, according to Cain Hope Felder.[9] Felder asserts that although the black religious experience is diverse, people generally share in the view that the supernatural is an extension of nature. Black Christians identify with the heroes and heroines of the faith. They view the Bible as an existential reality, mirroring their own experience, for example, the saga of the Egyptian captivity as chattel slavery and the Exodus as the Emancipation. The Bible is a self-corrective to a range of attitudes about justice. Black Christians share a preoccupation with theodicy—how to account for the justice of God in light of the persistence of suffering and inequalities.

Theologian James Evans, Jr., emphasizes black theology's understanding of both the oppressive and liberative use of the Bible.[10] He says that a marginal social location makes blacks sensitive to the misuse of Scripture. It pushes them to a more open reading of the text. What the Bible means in one's life today takes priority over what the Bible meant when it was written. The inner response to the calling or voice of God directs blacks to use a liberation hermeneutic. One's experience, color, or language does not limit an impartial, transcendent God. God is the infinite within a finite world. God is on the side of the oppressed. The modality of agape or self-sacrificing love is possibly due to the understanding of God's immanence and of a God who suffers with humanity. God sustains us when others objectify us. We love because God loves us.

The basis for African American Christian ethics is best understood by an analysis of black biblical hermeneutics. Even though theologians and social activists question how blacks can give such a central role to a book that was once used to oppress them, many blacks continue to point to it as the source of hope for the community. The Word of God is lifted up as the standard for how we are to act and live in community. Yet, enslaved blacks were often killed for trying to learn to read the King James Version of the Bible, and black women must open the Bible even wider than black men in order to find themselves among "all God's chillun" and determine how they are to live as viable members of the community. Despite such adversities, the Bible did remain vitally important, so much so that even unchurched African American children are often able to quote scriptural passages used to teach them how to behave in community and how to love themselves. The book has a remarkable influence.

You Know You Know How to Act

This educative and ego-building role of the Bible is critical. Instilling a child with working principles for life outside the home includes constant reminders about what he or she already knows. The moment of truth usually comes in the presence of an older relative, one's supervisor, in a department or grocery store, at church, or in front of a teacher. Parents are mortified. The other adults silently, or at times verbally, wonder why you did not teach your child how to behave. "You know you know how to act" or "You'd better mind your p's and q's" reverberate as instantaneous forms of discipline. Many African American children, stereotypically categorized by media-driven society as having few or no values, know these sayings—having been reminded of them throughout their lives by parents, grandparents, in black churches, in predominately black schools, and in the black community. My daughter, Veronica, has been raised as a "preacher's kid" or "PK." She has been surrounded by both precept and example teachings about behavioral expectations in all areas of her life— home, church, and schools. I find myself reminding her whenever she leaves home or I am going on a trip, to "Act like you've got parents" even though I know she is capable of monitoring her own behavior. My grandmother ends phone conversations with me with "Be sweet, I love you." In so many ways a child is reminded that "God don't like ugly." My grandmother passed the saying to my mother, my mother passed it on to me, and I am passing it on to my daughter. The validity of the saying transcends time. This is intergenerational transmission of spiritual values and character development. It is how a child learns that her behavior has repercussions for herself and the world. Learning the truth of core values and transmitting them to others strengthens character and agency of each person.

Developing a sense of agency is a normative feature of most black families, black churches, and black communities. Sociologist Adelbert Jenkins states that increasing reports of psychosocial weakness of African American children are inconsistent with the nurturing nature of the majority of black families.[11] One of the methods used to teach black children values is to develop a sense of agency—a sense of themselves as participants in the events around them. When encouraged to develop a sense of self-awareness and a range of "possible selves," their learning about their true capabilities and how their own intentions influence the world around them is enhanced. One of the major functions of the family is to provide a healthy emotional and psychological environment for the growth and development of children. Such an environment sets up a buffer between the child and the assaults of the world. The African American child is taught that he or she is to be an active contributor to the outcomes and situations of the world. Beginning in infancy, many mothers teach their children that life has meaning and that events are unique. Situations may be presented one way but interpreted and acted upon another way, and the child begins to learn about differentiation and adaptation. Thus when a child is told he or she is ugly, the recognition that that is one opinion and not the definitive one eases the insult.

Depending on their family, church, and community teachings many African Americans use such adaptive abilities to respond objectively, accurately, and to go beyond life's vicissitudes. They use dialectical thinking to envision alternatives. If one way is blocked or one door is closed there is always another route one can test. They use native human capacities actively to develop a sense of reality in keeping with their own understanding of their intentions for themselves and their children. It is difficult to be fully effective in society if one fails to be an agent.

The most important function of the black family is to prepare the child for the external threats in society and how to respond to them with a sense of agency. The awakening of a recognition of the child's ability to survive in an active, intentional setting leads to self-esteem, coping effectiveness, adaptive skills, maintenance of self in crisis, and agency. Jenkins proposes that the child be taught "that I am, rather than what I am." There is an African proverb that says, "The important thing is not what we are called but what we answer to." This means that our sense of self defines us, not external critiques or labeling. The child should be taught to make decisions, take the initiative, and shape the course of his or her life. In extended or supportive families the black child is taught self-development and self-determination. Each child is given responsibilities. Children learn to go forward regardless of what others may say.[12] Whereas some suggest that this type of teaching is accomplished only in privileged families, it has been my experience that even in impoverished settings children are taught how to care for themselves. Adaptive skills may not be socially acceptable, but even in the face of negative teaching, such as telling a child he or she will never succeed or be somebody, there are instances of children who rise above the prophecy. The belief that all children from impoverished backgrounds will fail is a stereotype.

Each family adheres to its own code of conduct. This codification of behavior has been learned over generations and is a blend of cultural mores, situational ethics, and faith-based values. Psychologist Wade Nobles cites black family codes in his assessment of black family mores. Each family is distinctively different and mores may differ from family to family.[13] Values are passed on from parent to child through emphasis on strong family ties and orientation. Unconditional love, respect for self and others, and the assumed natural goodness of children are paramount. Children are taught how to anticipate, address, interpret, manage, and successfully respond to concrete situations or conditions. Family is the source of connection, attachment, validation, self-worth, recognition, respect, and legitimacy. Children develop these attributes within the home to be able to transfer them outside the home where the environment is then more alien and destructive. Generally, even those with few resources come to the aid of those who are experiencing difficulty. There is an "elasticity of boundaries" that gives the black child the latitude and opportunity to stretch out and develop his or her own sense of distinctiveness without violating family mores.

In junior high school my daughter wore baggy shirts, long oversized jeans, and athletic shoes (the complete opposite of her mother's designer shoes and suits), yet she maintained family moral wisdom and deportment. Now in her high school senior year her wardrobe has shifted to heels and skirts, often designer. She developed her distinctive personality and behavior that was not disruptive but antithetical to mine. One of the constant refrains heard during the early teen years was, "I can't do that because my Mom will kill me!" In fact, I did not spend a lot of time threatening or punishing her; she simply knew the standards of the house and the expectations for behavior. She understood the consequences, walked the boundaries of the acceptable behavior, yet rarely crossed them. In conversations with younger children and her friends, she now articulates some of the values I thought she was not internalizing. Her interpretations sound different from mine, but the result is the same. Such development of individual styles, personalities, or conditions strengthens the family member's ability to respond to unique, concrete situations outside the home. Transgenerational sharing of knowledge between mother and child leads to family survival. Pragmatic help enables the child to engage in interpersonal situations while buffeting racism and oppression.

We live in a society that views success as demonstrated ability to be better than someone—to excel at all costs. In African Disapora cultures one is expected to rise to excellence yet remain connected with persons in the culture. A child is constantly reminded to do well in school because someone died in order for black children to receive equal education or equal rights. Each person represents the family, church, or community, and one's behavior can benefit or destroy beliefs about African Americans. The role of the adult is to teach the child how to live a life that is a "credit to the race."

African American children can be socialized to be self-sufficient, confident adults.[14] Black children learn to live in two worlds, black and white, with appropriate behaviors for each. Language, play, child-parent interaction, and responsibilities may differ in these two worlds, but the black child must master the rules of each world. The methodologies employed by black parents are difficult at times for those outside the community to understand. Children are taught to avoid ethnocentric judgments, racial stereotypes, or any negative behavior that meets the expectations of the larger society. Working-class parents may use corporal punishment, deny privileges, or apply verbal discipline that is often judged as harsh or inappropriate by others. A child may be told, "I don't care what John's mother lets him do, I am your mother and you know how to act," meaning the child is not expected to act like other children but as the parent determines is appropriate. Likewise, the mother may say, "Do as I say, not as I do." This is a way of telling the child that there are some behaviors acceptable for adults and others for children. It is also a way of stating that adults make mistakes and occasionally disregard what is socially responsible. Children are encouraged to "do the right thing" anyway and attend to what the situation dictates. This is a tremendous responsibility for a child to assume, yet it is a tough love-survival teaching tool. Black mothers demonstrate two types of love, according to sociologist Margie Peters. Subjective-personal love is responsive to a child's needs, performances, interests, and moods. The mother prepares the child for each new situation or she attempts to anticipate new situations and teaches a lesson just in case. This can be as simple as instructing a child to cross the street or as complex as teaching her or him how to respond to a racist or sexist remark. Status-normative love is based on rules and regulations. The mother teaches the child a task and insists on certain "correct" behavior. The type of love exhibited depends on the mother's socioeconomic and educational background. Each is effective in its own way, depending on the particular child.

In order to understand how African American values are transmitted intergenerationally it is important to recognize how black children develop social roles, interact with adults, and learn from their social setting. Wade Boykin and Forrest Tones describe socialization as the preparation of children to take on social roles and responsibilities.[15] In African American communities the process is incidental and habitual. Boykin and Tones list nine distinct dimensions of African American values passed on from parent to child:

Spirituality is conducting one's life as if the essence is vitalistic rather than mechanistic. Transcendent forces govern all of life. This means that one lives as if he or she knows that God is alive and present in life. God responds to human need and humans respond to God's blessings.

Harmony is the emphasis on wholeness and versatility. The mantra before communion is "If you are in love and charity with your neighbor . . ." Harmony speaks to relationality and community building. If one is not in positive relationship with others in the family, church, or community one is obligated to seek reconciliation.

Movement is a rhythmic approach to life. There is an interwoven mosaic of music, movement, and percussiveness or establishing a beat or rhythm of life. My grandmothers used to cook dinner while humming a song. Regardless of problems, there was a song that spoke to their resolution. Black children are surrounded by movement whether at home, in community, or in church. It is an internal sense of activity that is calming, life giving. Often when a black child moves around in school or sings as he or she walks along, those outside the culture say that the child is disruptive or hyperactive. This aspect is often misinterpreted when working with black children who do not understand the rationale for silence or immobility.

Verve is the psychological affinity for variability and intensity of stimulation. This translates into an ability to do or attend to several projects, conversations, or senses at one time. Boredom often results if one's energies are channeled into one event. A commonplace example is a child's desire to have on the television, sing along with the CD player, talk on the telephone, and occasionally yell downstairs to check if dinner is ready—all at the same time.

Affect is the premium placed on emotional sensibilities and expressiveness. The word "love" is said with numerous intentions. Hugging is socially acceptable behavior for men and women without sexual connotations. Fixing a person dinner, running an errand, singing a song, combing one's hair, doing someone's laundry, or loaning someone clothing with no expectation of return is evidence of affect.

Communalism is a sensitivity to the interdependence of people and the notion that group concerns supersede individual striving. The African proverb "I am because we are" is vital to community existence. Family, church, or community activities are bonding opportunities. Communalism is a hallmark of cultural survival.

Expressive individualism is the cultivation of distinctiveness, spontaneity, and a uniqueness of self-expression. Individualism is the opposite of communalism. Black children are taught that one must be strong individually but exist within the community. There is no imperative to be like everyone else. Many children imitate so-called role models for a time but eventually develop their own sense of style, deportment, and identity.

Orality is the emphasis on oral and aural modes of communication, especially the use of the spoken word, to convey deep contextual meanings. The oral rather than the written word is dominant in the black community, and thus the oral tradition is the principal vehicle for value transmission.

Finally, *social time perspective* is the commitment to time as a social phenomenon. Many black people view clocks, calendars, and other inanimate markers as interfering with social interaction. Although there are cultural jokes about "CP time" (being chronically or consistently late), I was once told by a brother from Kenya that "things begin when the people gather." There is often no hurry to begin events or end events. While the community gathers, time is precious and God is in charge of the completion of the tasks.

Sociologist Andrew Billingsley and theologian Dwight Hopkins trace the origins of African American values, such as the nine listed by Boykin and Tones, to African extended family values.[16] Billingsley supports the continuity of family patterns with strong value placed on the love of children. Besides reverence and respect for the elderly and others in the community the child is taught reciprocity or cooperation. The rights of any person are balanced with those of the family or larger community. This value is termed "restraint." Successive generations give the child a sense of belonging through social support and race pride. Traditional African family values of skills development, self-help, reverence for the transcendence of God, self-governance, service to others, and importance of education are taught to contemporary children. Indeed, Billingsley says that child rearing is the most important function of the contemporary African American family. Parents or grandparents teach children how to manage in a world replete with racial discrimination and prejudice. Giving a child a sense of racial pride, solidarity, knowledge of the struggle for equality, and African heritage prepares the child to enter the mainstream of society and shoulder his or her own responsibilities. With a focus on improving self, there is little or no room for personal bigotry or oppression of others.[17]

Hopkins also posits that enslaved blacks retained religious Africanisms. They were not, contrary to some research, theologically ignorant. They believed in the unbounded power of God who is everywhere and does all things. Dynamic, interdependent relationships between the individual and community assumed a connection to a larger community of invisible ancestors who were actively involved in teaching spiritual beliefs and values. Ancestors were the glue to the sacredness of the culture or way of life and connected the people to past religious traditions and practices.[18] The mothers and fathers of the faith lived out the belief that God would protect, direct, and keep persons who believed in divine intercession. Steeped in this belief, a primary cultural imperative is that God provides for those who follow instructions. When others believe that all hope is gone, God provides a means of living above and beyond expectations.

The legacy of African family values yields an African American ethic of survival that contains three components: *taking-not-stealing, duality of survival,* and *a discourse of solidarity.* Masters and the majority of ministers told slaves that "stealing away" to freedom was against God's will. The enslaved redefined stealing as illegal removal of a fellow bondsman or woman's private property. Taking from the master was the reclaiming of what they believed the master wrongfully stole from them, such as food or clothing for their survival. Duality of survival was the conscious false display of self in front of the master and authentic display of the true self with other blacks. One hears the phrase "scratching when nothing itches and laughing when nothing is funny." A negative outcome of this duality is the entrenchment of stereotypes about shuffling, ignorant blacks by those who don't understand the need for this survival technique. My grandmother used to tell me not to act "uppity" in front of whites. This meant never letting whites know what I knew or what I was really thinking. Her experience had been that the effect of knowing too much was punitive reaction by those who believed blacks were inferior. In essence, at times, one is to feign ignorance to avoid conflict. This protective device, a discourse of solidarity, ensures community survival. The enslaved were taught not to turn in or betray a brother or sister, according to Hopkins. Don't tell on each other; don't tell everything you know. This meant that ensuring the freedom of one would mean the eventual or symbolic freedom of all.[19]

Contemporary African American Christian ethics evolved from the enslaved African's culturally specific reading of the Bible and the need to ensure personal, familial, and community survival. Blacks were also influenced by contact with European religion and culture. This biculturality formed the ethical base for the values and beliefs that were passed across generations from mothers, grandmothers, and othermothers to African American children. The ability to "open the Bible wider" and locate God's message for blacks enabled those responsible for instructing children to provide scriptural support for the humanity and liberation of all of God's people. A culturally specific hermeneutic laid over the Bible enabled blacks to envision a God of the oppressed who was able to provide a space for them in a God-created world as the dominant culture spoke of slaves obeying masters, or cursed races. Armed with the knowledge that God loved them, blacks sought ways to live free and teach their children how to live with their heads up instead of bowed under the weight of oppression. This is particularly important for the black woman, most often denied freedom due to her race, class, and gender.

Girlfriend, Speak for Yourself!

> Only the Black Woman can say, "when and where I enter, in the quiet, undisputed dignity of my womanhood, without violence and without suing or special patronage, then and there the whole *Negro race enters with me*."[20]

Through a personal research quest to find empowering black women models I "discovered" the life of Anna Julia Cooper. Cooper, a nineteenth- and twentieth-century African American educator and social activist, wrote about the voices of black women in 1892. She worked tirelessly to articulate the humanity and equality of African Americans. Her life demonstrated how black women can and do bridge spheres of family, church, and community in teaching values.[21] Cooper wrote and proclaimed the necessity of black women speaking and doing for themselves. No one else could speak about the depth of black women's pain, understand their family, church, and community responsibilities, or faithfully assess their abilities without prejudice. The black woman has a different set of concerns than the black man.

Cooper pushed for a wider arena of participation by black women in spite of men who continued to insist black women ride in the back of the community bus. She was the fourth black woman in history to receive a Doctor of Philosophy degree. She was granted the degree from the Sorbonne in Paris on December 29, 1925. Cooper believed that all married women should earn a living and become independent. She advocated nontraditional roles—extended horizons for women who were not "intended for mothers." When the 1897 American Negro Academy—Reverend Francis Grimke, Reverend Alexander Crummell, and W. E. B. DuBois, among others—barred women from the black think tank, black women created their own spaces for intellectual, social, religious, and political empowerment in the Colored Women's Club movement.

Cooper said that whenever women discussed their rights men regressed to sixteenth-century logic. To ensure places for women's development she also taught at Dunbar High School and served as president of Frelinghuysen University in Washington, D.C., from 1929 to 1941. It was a night school for black men and women that she operated out of her home. She was one of many standard-bearers for the rights of black women and, in turn, black people in America.[22] Her beliefs and her life's work clearly articulate the perspectives of womanist scholars. Cooper, an extraordinary black woman, is but one example of black women's activities in empowering blacks for leading fuller, liberated lives.

Social historian Paula Giddings researched the lives of black women from slavery forward and provides insight into the contributions of black women in American social transformation. She writes that when black women define themselves they are able to speak for themselves. As black women make a concerted effort to work with black men, children, and the world to assure equality for all, they are able to influence the destiny of the entire African American community. Black women, while virtually voiceless in society except as teachers and members of the church, have always had a voice in raising children. Ordinary, everyday black women have also worked for transformation and the survival of the black family, church, and community throughout the centuries of black life in America.

In my experience, black women's contributions to the belief systems of African Americans have often been unnoticed, deferred, or obliterated by black men, white men, and white women. It is vital for these groups in general, and black women in particular, to understand the reality of black women's beliefs and how those are transmitted to children and families. To begin to hear more clearly the voice of black women I will turn to womanist ethical and theological perspectives that grew out of both European American Christian ethics and African American ethics and theology. What are core womanist beliefs? What are the primary roles relegated to or assumed by black women as they transmit values to family, church, and community?

We're Empowered Women

Womanist perspectives take into consideration the social and historical treatment and designations of black women as the necessitating source of belief systems that affirm the humanity of black women, and ways in which black women may speak for themselves and their families. From the early 1600s when black women were brought from the West Coast of Africa, they were viewed as property first, women second, and slaves always.[23] Locked into this position, they were afforded no entitlement or even control of their own bodies. Designated prostitutes, African American women were the body toys for white men and were mated with black men to ensure a continual slave stock. They were raped by men and ridiculed by women of privilege who often used the pain of the black women as a means of establishing their own worth in a patriarchal society. Black female slaves worked in the household and fields. They cared for black and white children, giving priority to the master's children. They nursed, cooked, fed, dressed, groomed, and taught white children values, serving as surrogate mothers and wives. Delores Williams states that some black women were coerced into taking the place of white women as sexual objects or as mothers for white children. Other times black women were voluntary surrogates.

In the postbellum period, black women subordinated themselves by fostering white values in their own families and as domestics nurturing white children. bell hooks describes the devaluation of black women after slavery as a conscious, deliberate effort to sabotage the self-worth and respect of black women.[24] Black men began to achieve a few benefits of freedom, such as opening businesses or political interaction with whites, but black women were still labeled "whores" and "sluts."

Yet, due to the Victorian mores of the time even abolitionists avoided the discussion of the rape of black women. Black women began to emulate the behavior of white women, acting and dressing like white women. They were still raped, beaten, and charged with leading white men into spiritual impurity. Whites romanticized the "strong black woman." Black women were characterized as devoted to motherhood, possessing an innate ability to bear burdens, and yet having a high availability as sex objects. The black women were told that their dignity lay not in liberation but in adjusting, coping, and adapting to the white social structure. Myths about the black woman crippled her womanhood and defamed her in the eyes of all but the black family and church.

The gradual development of self-awareness *(conscientization)* began to allow black women to shape their own personal and social history.[25] This enabled black women to release oppressive stereotypes handed down by slave masters and their progeny. With new insights into their personhood black women could begin to accept their true heritage—empowerment and a sense of "somebodiness."

Self-esteem is built by recognizing one's strengths and weaknesses regardless of what someone else says about them. External pressures tell black people that they are less than others, while internal cues tell them they are God's children and are of value. There is a saying in the community that "God don't make no junk." Children and adults are reminded that they came from a rich heritage and possess unlimited possibilities because they are children of God.

Womanist theologian Kelly Brown Douglas defines the term *womanist* as black women's resistance to multidimensional oppression based on their experience of being black and female in the United States without the privileges afforded white women.[26] Womanists fight for the rights of all women while affirming their own womanhood. For that reason, womanist Christology and theology espouse Jesus as incarnate, a cosufferer. Such belief in the centrality of Jesus is essential to the witness, testimonies, and liberating activities of black women striving to survive and be free. It is through a "spirituality of resistance" that black women transcend negativity and dehumanization. This spirituality encompasses a sense of heritage and connectedness to God that allows black women to "make do and do better" in the face of sexism, racism, classism, ageism, and heterosexism.

Womanist consciousness, according to Elsa Barkley Brown, embraces cultural, sexual, national, economic, and political considerations. Hence, womanists have worldviews that recognize the intersection and interdependence of self-others, male-female, race-sex, community-family, and black-female. Each woman is responsible for care of self and of others. No one is excluded, which enables persons to live their lives unhampered by manipulations of the larger society.[27]

Ethicist Katie G. Cannon, considered to be one of the originators of womanist thought, remembers that she was taught faith and ethics as a child.[28] Her community stressed God's universal parenthood. The social, intellectual, and cultural ethos was the humanity of all persons. Ethics were taken into account in all circumstances, paradoxes, and dilemmas of life. In formulating her womanist perspective she utilized her life experience and academic research.

According to Cannon, the faith and liberation ethics of African Americans defy oppressive rules and standards of the controlling society. Within the insular black community there is a fundamental belief in the interconnectedness of creation and community. A person's life is nurtured, transformed, and sustained by the concern and power of a loving, just, and merciful God who is also present in the life of the entire community. In the pursuit to live "Christ-like" the African American relies on the passage in Luke 4:18 (NRSV):

> The Spirit of the Lord is upon me, because he has anointed me to bring good news to the poor. He has sent me to proclaim release to the captives, and recovery of sight to the blind, to let the oppressed go free.

Each believer is to minister holistically to the entire community. Equality of humanity means attending to the needs of others regardless of who they are. Each person is called to resist oppression and oppose authorities and laws that are contrary to God's will.[29] African American images of God and mandates for moral behavior are derived from a cultural biblical hermeneutic. In many families, churches, and communities the Bible is the principle teaching tool, survival kit, and self-help book.

Jacquelyn Grant, African American systematic theologian, reviews the Christology and use of the Bible by black women. She states that while using the Bible as a major source of her religious validation and God consciousness, the black woman reinterprets her environment to effect a healthier atmosphere for her children.[30] Through direct revelation and witnessing, African American women follow their own agenda rather than that of the dominant social group. Black women face tridimensional oppression by patriarchy (sexism), by white supremacy (racism), and by privileged class (classism). In spite of this, they view Jesus as the incarnate, redeeming, liberating cosufferer empowering them in the midst of the situation. The interplay of Scripture and experience provides an internal critique of the Bible. Black women appropriate what is useful for their communities and discard what is harmful. They may articulate black Christology in the songs, sermons, testimonies, and teachings in the church and at home. Black women utilize the stories of the Bible and situations they face, and develop a system of values and judgments based on the "highest good." They seek the path of what is best for all concerned with the least negative yield.

Theresa Hoover concurs with Grant in a brief analysis of black women's roles in black churches.[31] Black women are traditionally termed "the backbone of the church." Hoover refers to black women as "the glue of the church." Black women also have distinctive roles within the black church, comprising 65 to 95 percent of the total attendance. She asserts that in smaller churches women are more vocal and literally run the church. They are responsible for teaching, outreach, gathering the children, and instructing them in their social and spiritual heritage. Women also supply the economic base to keep the churches open. Additionally, women bridge the church and community. Through foresight, ingenuity, and "stick-to-it-iveness" they keep things going in spite of onerous treatment by male leadership and membership. In urban churches females have limited decision-making power and lower profiles. The male pastor customarily mirrors the dominant culture and social structure to keep women out of positions of leadership.

Although African American women have been entering ministry since the 1800s—Jarena Lee, Amanda Berry Smith, Julia Foote, Zilpha Elaw—few have become established pastors, particularly in larger black denominations. Notable exceptions are Elder Lucy Smith, who in the 1930s founded the All Nations Pentecostal Church in Chicago, and Dr. Oliva B. Stokes, who was ordained in 1952 in the National Baptist Church, the largest independent black denomination.[32] Male preachers and ministers have kept "guard" over the entrance of women into ordained ministry. The black males, and some black females, cite biblical "mandates" against women preachers. They are accustomed to the male entitlement reinforced by the "man of God" image that parallels their male image of God. They also believe women will dilute the only power they have—leadership of the black church. The travesty of this is that the black church was created as a center of liberation. Yet due to assimilation of white patriarchal structures, many churches have become battlegrounds for sexual equality in the black community. The process is painfully slow, but women continue to enter all levels of ministry in the black church. Those women who pioneered in ordained ministry at times transmit both the pain and joys of how to enter and maintain one's status in ministry. They mentor younger women, and at times men, through the obstacles and open doors of the process of ordination. In like manner older women in the church mentor younger women and children in the faith. Although the male pastor may be the perceived power source in the church structure, often the actual source is the older women who have learned to articulate their power subtly.[33]

Cheryl Townsend Gilkes writes of the many roles black women fulfill in the community, family, and church. Respected, powerful, older African American women are often called "Mother," signifying their role and length of service in the church or community. Their "children" are often religious, political, and social leaders who seek advice and support from the "mothers." In the secular sphere, "community mothers" hold positions such as the heads of women's organizations and civil rights interest groups, managing large community and human service agencies and programs. In the sacred sphere, "church mothers" are pastors, evangelists, pastor's wives, and leaders of organized women's religious groups, missionaries, and deaconesses. They have been the founders, administrators, teachers, and financial support for the black church and community. These role models, power brokers, and venerable elders provide continuity and unity during transition, and serve as a counterforce to fragmentation in the community. Such church and community mothers serve as guardians of African American tradition and guides for social change.[34]

African women were mothers, priests, and queen mothers who served as keepers of the traditions and rituals, yet a central feature of African American women's existence has been invisibility, isolation, tokenism, or exclusion from societal privilege. African American women have tried to move African Americans toward social equality through their religious traditions. Through an oral tradition churched and unchurched black women tell of the purpose, meaning, and importance of sociocultural events, and serve as the connective tissue of the community and culture. They hand down religious and community beliefs as educators ("Each one, teach one"), leaders ("You can't lead where you won't go or teach what you don't know"), and businesswomen ("God bless the child that's got his own"). They are deemed "prophetic troublers" in the community, reminding children and adults of their heritage and possibilities.[35]

The grandmothers and othermothers who pass on spiritual values have been given several names and at times virulent definitions throughout history. Patricia Hill Collins, a black feminist, however, also assesses the "mother" in the black family and community.[36] Controlling images of African American women—mammy, matriarch, welfare mother, and Jezebel—have been defined and used by the dominant society to objectify black women and justify race, gender, and class oppression. The mammy is viewed as a "good mother," an obedient, asexual being. She accepts subordination, often showing preference for white children and their values over her own children and black community values. The black matriarch is a "failed mammy." She is a bad mother who spends too much time away from home. Her children are failures because of her inability to raise or supervise them. She is not womanly and emasculates her lovers and husbands. She teaches negative values intergenerationally. The welfare mother is an updated version of the enslaved breeder woman image. This bad mother is unable to control her fertility. She has no work ethic. She is a danger to her children because she has no values. This "woman alone" is not aggressive enough and must have someone take care of her. Finally, a Jezebel is a woman who is sexually aggressive and is incapable of nurturing children. This image originated in slavery with the myth of sexually promiscuous African women who were used as sexual objects for their masters.

Collins examines these images along with those defined and used by the black community. African American women share in a common sisterhood of informal, private, and shared recognition by virtue of their pigmentation and social status. As bonds of sisterhood develop they may affirm one another's humanity, specialness, and right to exist either verbally or in coded mannerism that only black women understand. This is like the unwritten language used by persons in a particular faith system, occupation, or country. It is a defense mechanism that keeps the out-group from knowing "all the sisters' business." Mothers pass on everyday knowledge to their daughters for survival. Othermothers—aunts, grandmothers, sisters, cousins, neighbors, teachers— take on temporary or long-term child care or mentoring of younger women who are alone or whose blood mother is unable or chooses not to raise her children. These fluid boundaries reinforce the existence of the extended family through *fictive kin*. The African proverb "It takes an entire village to raise a child" is acted out in the resilience of women-centered family networks. Blood mothers and othermothers teach cultural values of resistance, survival, care, concern, personal accountability, racial pride, and empathy for the survival of all of "our children" in the church and community.[37]

Historically, black women have served as the crucible and conveyor of African American heritage and the shaper of young black minds. Since the time of slavery they have cared for all children regardless of color, ethnicity, or belief. Lacking the social and political advantages of the European American men and women, and of African American men, black women continue to remind society that things must change. Against seemingly insurmountable odds they continue to teach children (using both negative and positive methods) to be whatever they want to be, and that regardless of obstacles and disappointments they can succeed. The self-esteem and self-determination aspects of their instruction are vitally important to African Americans' ability to continue to live in spite of circumstances.[38] It is through a blend of learned relationships of faith and ethics that black mothers, grandmothers, and othermothers have instilled a social, intellectual, and cultural ethos of equal humanity in children. Black women have been the primary reservoir for purging self-hate and instilling self-assertion from slavery to the present. Ignoring the fact that black women have been caretakers of black and white children for over 380 years, a conspiracy of silence—by blacks and whites aware of shared child care responsibilities—has imposed an invisibility of values among African Americans. Racism, gender discrimination, and economic exploitation have required African Americans to create and cultivate their own values. Dominant ethics based on success and oppression rule out many African Americans.[39] However, a larger contingent strives to teach African American children how to survive and thrive in the face of societal contradictions.

In summary, African American mothers, grandmothers, and othermothers, as the primary resources for moral agency in the community, have a heritage of teaching children spiritual and community values. Through precept and example, oral tradition, formal teaching, modeling, mentoring, and love, in spite of what the world says, African American children are taught culturally specific values. These values include love of self, cultural pride, self-reliance, ethic of care, concern for others, and survival—at times by whatever means work. The Bible has been the major source of folk (oral tradition) and moral wisdom. Common sense (Mother Wit) carries one farther than book knowledge because of the presence of "educated fools" who lack heart or the ability to be culturally connected.

Black women use a variety of voices and venues to say what they believe and what they have taught their children. Black women have articulated their value systems through songs, sermons, conversations, testimonies, stories, Bible passages, prayers, stories, and writings. Black women teach their children through chastisement, modeling, example, precept, recounting family history, and one-on-one conversations.

Black children are taught guidelines for living, such as how to assert themselves as persons. "They can kill your body but not your soul" means no matter what the world does to you, you have to take a stand. My grandmother used to tell me, "We are all Aunt Haggie's children" or "God don't have no stepchildren," which implied that we are all interconnected regardless of race, gender, belief, or residence. There is no place for hatred of your brother or sister. "There is no hole deep enough to hide the truth" tells a child that the truth will always prevail. These sayings are termed "Mother Wit" in the black community and emanate from mother figures. They are examples of the community guidelines for how black children are to live and understand their place in the world.

African American spiritual values are a combination of African beliefs, Afro-Christian beliefs, and day-to-day common sense passed down from adult to child. In 1832 Maria Stewart challenged black women to stand up for themselves. In 1892 Anna Julia Cooper affirmed that the only persons who could fully articulate the beliefs, needs, and lives of black women were black women. In the twentieth century, African American women's literature provided a major source of information on the thought, beliefs, and moral wisdom of black women because it flows from the minds and lives of black women. Twenty-first century black families, black churches, and black communities can turn to black women's literary examples for strengthening their spiritual values.

3

LISTENING TO EXPERIENCE

Why Are You Actin' Like You Don't Hear Me?

Women

They were women then
My mama's generation
Husky of voice—Stout of Step
With fists as well as
Hands
How they battered down
Doors
And ironed
Starched white
Shirts
How they led
Armies
Headragged Generals
Across mined
Fields
Booby-trapped
Kitchens
To discover books
Desks
A place for us
How they knew what we
Must know
Without knowing a page
Of it
Themselves[1]

The literature of black women is about "the thoughts, words, feelings, and deeds of black women."[2] In the above poem, "Women," Alice Walker conveys, in the language of black women, the intergenerational connection of black women, their legacy of inner strength, how they transcend their cultural location, and their modeling of the need for perseverance. This chapter delineates the importance of hearing the voices of black women, the presence of womanist or African American women's literature in society in general, and the use and interpretation of literature by African American women in value transmission, lived consciousness, and spirituality. I address African American women's didactics and literature. Finally, I generate a format for the analysis of selected African American women's poetry, short stories, autobiographies, and novels to highlight a tradition of intergenerational transmission of spiritual values by grandmothers and othermothers.

There are times when I am talking with my seventeen-year-old daughter and she seems preoccupied or overtly ignores me. I immediately say, "Why are you acting like you don't hear me?" Almost simultaneously I realize that I am saying exactly what my mother, grandmother, and othermothers said to me in the same situation. My daughter's response, "I didn't hear you" or "Were you talking to me?" is like my own at the same age. Although this exchange seems harmless, it is a use of selective attention especially when one does not want to listen to or hear what another person is saying. It is an obvious power play. In essence, this tactic renders the speaker invisible or unimportant. This is also a protective device to eliminate any information that differs from one's own. My daughter learned this behavior from me, I learned it from my mother, and she learned it from my grandmother.

This same type of derisive communicative treatment is evident in academic circles where self-defined intellectuals decide whose voice is important, what is acceptable scholarship, and what language is to be used and heard as long as it parallels their own. It presides in the boardroom when one group or person reiterates what another has said and receives credit for it as if it were an original idea. It is present in churches where the one who preaches the loudest, hardest, or longest is deemed a "preacher" who everyone must hear while other "speakers" are rendered inaudible and invisible because of their gender, regardless of their abilities.

There is a socially and culturally ingrained pattern passed on through generations by European American males, African American males, and even European American females of not listening to African American women. Denigration and muffling of the voices of black women is a decisive way of dehumanizing them and "keeping them in their place." As mentioned in the previous chapters, unsubstantiated charges that black women are ignorant, sexually promiscuous, and socially deviant means they are always less than the other groups. This translates into a dominant cultural norm of denial of black women's voices, rights, power, and humanity.

In spite of this selective attending, black women have continued to speak in private and public forums. Their voices ring at family dining tables, in church services, in the classroom, and in the boardroom. Yet, there continues to be a historical ignoring or conspiratorial stifling of the existence and relevancy of the language and literature of black women.

Voices of Foremothers

In 1772, the Governor of Massachusetts convened a hearing of eighteen white men to determine the authenticity of the poetry of Phillis Wheatley. The belief was that an African, especially an African American woman, could not have written anything. The result of the "hearing" was an "Attestation" of their belief that she not only was capable of, but had actually composed, the poetry in question. Her first book, *Poems on Various Subjects, Religious and Moral*, was published with this validation by white men as the preface. This, according to Louis Henry Gates in his essay "In Her Own Write," marked the beginning of both the black American literary tradition and black women's literary tradition in the United States.[3] Although Wheatley's work was followed by Ann Plato's *Essay* in 1841 and Harriet E. Wilson's *Our Nig* in 1859, there continued to be a selective hearing of the voices of black women writers until the 1960s.

Zora Neale Hurston's 1937 *Their Eyes Were Watching God* was panned as politically naive in deference to Richard Wright's 1945 *Black Boy*. Gwendolyn Brooks's 1953 *Maud Martha* was reviewed as "homey," while Ralph Ellison's 1952 *Invisible Man* was called "the embodiment of the Negroe race." Author and literary critic Mary Helen Washington sums up the distinctions of black women's literature:

> If there is a single distinguishing feature of the literature of black women—and this accounts for their lack of recognition—it is this: their literature is about black women; it takes the trouble to record the thoughts, words, feelings, and deeds of black women, experiences that make the realities of being black in America look very different from what men have written. There are no women in this tradition hibernating in dark holes contemplating their invisibility; there are no women dismembering the bodies or crushing the skulls of either women or men; and few, if any, women in the literature of black women succeed in heroic quests without the support of other women or men in their communities.[4]

For blacks, the 1960s marked a time of turning away from the larger society and toward one another. It was a time of embracing community and getting back to basics with one another. It was also a period of pride in one's heritage. It marked the beginning of Cultural Nationalism and the Black Arts movement. Black women again audibly voiced the centuries-old tradition of self-definition and liberation. Images of black women presented by the so-called experts— white men, white women, and black men—were essentially second-hand knowledge. Black women challenged this information with their own stories of their families, needs, beliefs, and solutions to their own problems.[5] African American women pronounced their humanity in the face of objectification while others continued to pretend not to hear them, much like a thirteen-year-old groping for independence and power. Now as then, African American women persistently implore, "Why are you actin' like you don't hear me?" knowing that most of the time no one is listening or taking their literature seriously except other African American women and their children.

And by not taking their literature seriously, they are also not taking their lived experiences seriously, for what is literature but the written expression of our experiences?[6] Literature may be used to depict the historical, anticipated, real, or imagined events of a community or culture. The community in which it arises determines the acceptable oral or written literary form. The literary tradition and customs are shaped, perpetuated, taught, and affirmed by a particular community that tells and retells the story. This is what black women have done through diaries, letters, poetry, sermons, songs, short stories, novels, and speeches.[7] African American women write about the experiences of black people and the intersection of race, class, and gender. The African American female worldview defines the content, didactics (moral, philosophical, or religious themes), and cultural hermeneutic.[8]

Margaret Walker is one of the literary foremothers of 1960s writers. In her novel *Jubilee,* Walker utilizes historical narrative as she recounts the story of her maternal great-grandmother, as told by her maternal grandmother. The novel is set in nineteenth-century America. The central character, Vyry, is a slave, and her story moves from plantation life to war to Reconstruction. Told from an enslaved woman's point of view, the story presents a unique picture of slaveholders, the stereotypical *mammy* and *mulatto,* and the effect of the Emancipation Proclamation. As Union soldiers take over a plantation, the five remaining slaves are gathered in the yard to hear the commanding officer read "Mr. Lincoln's Proclamation."

> Vyry would never forget the scene of that morning on the front veranda as long as she lived. Miss Lillian stood in the door with her two children, Bob and Susan, and her arms were around their shoulders. Standing beside Vyry were Caline and May Liza, their faces working though they were trying to look solemn while the man read the paper. Vyry scarcely heard a word he said. . . . Vyry caught snatches of the long document as the man's voice droned on, "Shall be . . . forever free" and she was caught up in a reverie hearing that magic word. Could it be possible that the golden door of freedom had at last swung open?[9]

A. H. T. Levi writes that literature must shed some light on the human social structure in order to be deemed great.[10] Walker articulates the reality of slavery and its confusing aftermath. She does so through the eyes and voice of a black woman. Popular literature is always based on oral tradition.

The social and personal values of ordinary people are forged in what is heard in homes, pulpits, and social groups. Literature is a way to probe, doubt, explore, and suggest modifications of experience. David Jasper suggests that great works of art—poetry, drama, or novels—seize the imagination and transform the perceptions of the reader. The author's intentions cannot be completely interpreted, the reader must use his or her own hermeneutic or interpretation to understand the writing. This hermeneutic stems from one's worldview, experience, and connection to the community of the author's origin. As a black woman, Walker is able to identify emotions and stress experienced by black women throughout the ages, particularly in terms of finding one's place in a changing world.

Literary excellence is said to imply and require moral wisdom that shapes our lives and thoughts, and is passed on to the reader.[11] However, Western literature that is deemed classical, such as Voltaire's *Candide,* Melville's *Moby Dick,* and Dostoyevsky's *Crime and Punishment,* were all written by European males. Now the question is: How do these literary masterpieces influence or relate to the worldview of African American women? The answer is that dominant Western textual or literary tradition provides insights and moral wisdom for a primarily European male-dominated community. It lacks cultural connection or shared worldview with the self-reflective textual traditions of black women.[12]

No Longer a Stepsister

One must engage the voices of black women as valid resources for understanding the transmission of African American spiritual values by black grandmothers and othermothers. African American editor Charles Johnson's commentary on black writers is that from the first black American novel, *Clotelle, or the Colored Heroine* (1853) by William Wells Brown, black writers' hermeneutic encompassed crises of identity, the quest for liberation, development of a sense of selfhood, and the agony of social alienation in a response to European culture. He also asserts that the Harlem Renaissance marked a period of the revisioning of the lived experience of black culture. The development of the concept of "Negritude" during this period involved self-affirmation of blackness, shared experience, and the élan of African culture. Black writers sought to control and reconstruct their own images. This led to the Black Arts movement of the 1960s and 1970s, which was developed to provide a sense of blackness and racial ideologies of the African experience.[13]

The question remains: Where were women's experiences validated? Calvin Hernton agrees that African American literature was traditionally the venue of African American males, who were accepted as the sole interpreters of the black experience in America. They usually portrayed strong male heroes or protagonists and either idealized the black woman (mother) or depicted the black woman as helpless, evil, or promiscuous following the images in European American literature. This double standard persisted until the 1960s with a number of black women writers in print. Coinciding with the nascent

Black Power movement, black women were encouraged to defer their dreams for the rising power of black males.[14]

In " 'The Darkened Eye Restored': Notes Toward a Literary History of Black Women," Mary Helen Washington aptly contends that black women writers historically were treated as the "stepsisters of African American literature."[15] African American textual tradition was in the hands of males. Black women's writings were virtually suppressed until the Harlem Renaissance. They usually were dismissed by African American literary critics until "rediscovered" or "reevaluated" by feminist critics. Nineteenth-century women writers as a whole were charged with being "sentimentalists" who included little or no themes, message, or thought in their works. In the 1890s, black women intellectuals were not recognized as an official part of the "Talented Tenth" headed by W. E. B. DuBois. They were generally dismissed as nonrepresentative of African American culture. The Western textual "fathers" regularly bestowed that honor on African American males. Shirley Anne Williams writes that the proliferation of works by African American women, particularly in the 1970s, resulted from the black female portraiture, or lack of it, in black male literature. The stereotypical portrayal of black women typically meant female characters who could be beaten, raped, exploited, or had to be long-suffering for the sake of the black community. Black women characters were "strong" or abusive mothers, insignificant sex objects, or mindless women who had to have strong male leadership. Mirroring the white patriarchal picture of male characters, black male writers at times composed characters that became the conquerors of all their surroundings. Black male characters in the literature of black males often were presented as isolated, inarticulate, narcissistic, or obscure. Black women had no choice but to begin to articulate their own views of the lives of black women, black men, and ways of living in the world.[16]

Zora Neale Hurston, Harlem Renaissance author and contemporary of black poet Langston Hughes, exemplifies the deferred status of black women writers. Hurston wrote four novels, two books of black folklore, an autobiography, and fifty-five short works on black life.[17] Trained as an anthropologist with Franz Boas, Hurston was the premier black woman writer from the 1930s to the early 1950s. Due to her focus on the sexual exploitation of women, the empowerment of women, and her political writings, men heavily criticized her work. Hurston died in obscurity in 1960, but her work was unearthed in 1975 by Alice Walker. Hurston's *Their Eyes Were Watching God* is considered a classic by several womanist scholars and is required reading in a number of undergraduate literature classes across the United States. It is written in black vernacular. It details a woman's transformative journey of personal freedom from socially restrictive relationships. Hurston's protagonist is Janie Crawford. Like Hurston, Janie forges her own path and contradicts the social mores of her day. Doomed by her grandmother to loveless marriages for comfort and security Janie leaves home and finds love on her own. Returning home after she has been acquitted of killing her lover in self-defense, Janie sums up what she has learned about love.

> Ah know all dem sitters-and-talkers gointuh worry they guts into fiddle strings till dey find out whut we been talkin' 'bout. Dat's all right, Pheoby, tell 'em. Dey gointuh make 'miration 'cause mah love didn't work lak they love, if dey ever had any. Then you must tell 'em dat love ain't somethin' lak uh grindstone dat's de same thing everywhere and do de same thing tuh everything it touch. Love is lak de sea. It's uh movin' thing, but still and all, it takes its shape from de shore it meets and it's different with every shore.[18]

The novel depicts a black woman's view of a nontraditional black woman—one who takes control of her life and makes up her own mind about who and how she will be. Hurston's work was repudiated by black males as having no theme or content.[19]

Toni Cade's preeminent work, *The Black Woman,* signaled the beginning of the end of black male literary hegemony. In the anthology, Cade writes that black women continued to write and were often critiqued as shallow, superficial, emotional, or imitative.[20] Black women were demanding equality with white males, black males, and white females in every segment of society.

> The "experts" are still men, Black or White. And the images of the woman are still derived from their needs, their fantasies, their secondhand knowledge, their agreement with the other "experts." But of course there have been women who have been able to think better than they've been trained, and have produced the canon of literature fondly referred to as "feminist literature": Anais Nin, Simone de Beauvoir, Doris Lessing, Betty Friedan, etc.[21]

In response to these "experts" Cade writes that black women began to form study groups, caucuses, cooperatives, and political groups to continue their own struggle for liberation against exploitation and dehumanization.

> The question for us arises: how relevant are the truths, the experiences, the findings of white women to Black women? Are women after all simply women? I don't know that our priorities are the same, that our concerns and methods are the same, or even similar enough so that we can afford to depend on this new field of experts (white female). It is rather obvious that we are turning to each other.[22]

Black women began to write about being black women. Although they began to receive support and positive reviews from white females, they remained determined to speak for and about black women's experiences.

Black women write out of a double consciousness: being black and female. Unless there are intellectual and emotional outlets for black women's experiences, a way to share them with others, black women become (paraphrasing Dr. Prathia Hall) "perpetually pregnant." Persisting oppression due to racism, sexism, classism, ageism, collective sexual violation, intimidation, and, I would add, intellectual discrimination has been the predominant barrier to the black women's literary expression. Black scholars, preachers, scientists, doctors, professors, lawyers, and property owners are all presumed to be black males. Black women need access to all avenues of self-expression and definition in order to be liberated from societal invisibility and inaudibility.

Mary Helen Washington incisively delineates the two major approaches to the study of black women's writings.[23] Black women offer unique themes but may also overlap those themes found in the literature of black men, white women, and white men. Most frequently the subject matter is the collective and historic violation of black women or that of turning inward to create means of overcoming oppression. Black women writers may choose themes such as the intimidation of color, as in Toni Morrison's *The Bluest Eye,* which is about a young black girl who believes if she had blue eyes she would be accepted by whites. Other themes are the cyclical nature of oppression and the protagonist's collusion with or resistance to whites.

Their characters often mirror both the life and culture of black women writers and their contemporaries.[24] Editor/author Lorraine Bethel opines that black women writers choose to appear in their own works in a particular way.[25] Constantly rejected and faced with a falsification of their own lives, black women writers seek to realistically portray the socioeconomic and interpersonal situations of their characters.

Through this self-defined backdrop black women writers draw on the practice of intergenerationally passing down African American culture—music, art, oral tradition, religion or belief systems, everyday experiences, Mother Wit (common sense), and so forth—called *racial bonding*. Racial bonding along with folk culture has often been ignored or termed "backward." It is typically considered antisocial, opposed to "fitting in" with the dominant culture. Reading the canvas of individual lives and the telling and retelling of stories of the community has perpetuated racial bonding. Literature is created through this process. This bonding aids in the intellectual, psychological, physical, spiritual, and emotional development of the black community. It is a way to validate the community's existence and shared humanity.

In the African American women's groups with which I have worked there was both a thirst for and an identitification with black female characters in literature. Being able to see someone like oneself (even if she is a tragic character) represented in literature influences the self-esteem of the readers. The majority of characterizations of black women in books by black male, white male, and white female writers are negative or invisible. This pushes black women to look somewhere else to find affirmations of who they really are or will become. One of the first books I used in a Christian black women's literary group was Alice Walker's *The Color Purple*. It gave insight to the belief in an all-loving, Incarnate God that is present with black women in the face of incest, abuse, loss of loved ones, social stigma, and personal setbacks. In a letter to her sister Nettie, Celie, the protagonist, relates a conversation about God she had with her sister-friend/lover/mentor Shug Avery.

> Here's the thing, say Shug. The thing I believe. God is inside you and inside everyone else. You come into the world with God. But only them that search for it inside find it. And sometimes it just manifest itself even if you not looking, or don't know what you looking for. Trouble do it for most folks, I think. . . . It? I ast. Yeah, It. God ain't a he or a she, but a It.[26]

Discussions of the book, and the ensuing movie, fractured some relationships between black men and women for it assumes that domestic abuse is occurring within the community, that a black woman might love another black woman in a sexual way, and that God has male and female attributes. At the time of the publication of the book, the production of the movie, and the formation of African American women's support groups, these topics were not discussed openly in the black community. The book was panned as a "woman's frustrated fantasy" in yet another effort to invalidate black women's voices.

Writing in the black vernacular, African American women authors thus attempted to go beyond the Western, primarily male textual tradition to yield a rich coalescence of their own community. They sought to present a different view about their lives, in particular, and an alternative to the characterization of black women as always strong, liberated, and loud. These "Aunt Jemimas" or "Sapphires" or "Shenequas" were routinely pictured as super sex objects, domineering matriarchs, or evil illiterate shrews. Others freely described black women and decided how they "actually" were to act, look, and sound. The importance of writings by black women about black women is that they generally present more well-rounded characters or balanced depictions of the realities of being a black woman in this country.

This releasing of the weight of oppressive stereotypes and the belief that black women are permanently objects was addressed poetically by Maya Angelou in her 1978 poem "And Still I Rise." She issued a rallying cry for black women that resounds today in presentations by black women of all ages and has been used by women of other racial ethnic groups as well.[27] It depicts the survival of black women in the face of oppression and impending destruction. It evokes a faith stance that only one who has experienced overcoming can articulate with veracity. Angelou speaks of the strength gained from instruction by those who have gone before and provided space for striving to be free internally if not externally.

> You may write me down in history
> With your bitter, twisted lies,
> You may trod me in the very dirt
> But still, like dust, I rise. . . .
>
> Leaving behind nights of terror and fear
> I rise
> Into a daybreak that's wondrously clear
> I rise
> Bringing the gifts that my ancestors gave,
> I am the dream and hope of the slave.
> I rise
> I rise
> I rise[28]

Black women writers provide vocal space for other black women by identifying their current situation or status, reflecting on their past triumphs and tragedies, and bridging the possibilities for change in the status of black women in particular and the black family, church, and community in general. Believing it is necessary to understand the past in order to move forward, black women write about the conflicting relationships between men and women; alienation and antagonism of black men and women; growing up black and female; black history and, specifically, the history of black women; and the intimidation of black women by American standards of beauty (hair texture, body size or shape, and skin color).

The distinguishing characteristic of the writings of black women is that they are about women. The stories, poems, songs, sermons, and autobiographies are records of the thoughts, words, feelings, and deeds of black women.

The experience and distinctive worldview of black women lays the foundation for a black women's hermeneutic, a way of interpreting the world based on the experiences and beliefs of black women. Black women are interested in the family and community. The women in the stories relate to, confide in, and establish lifelong and often life-affirming friendships with other women— mothers, sisters, grandmothers, friends, lovers—who are vital to their growth and well-being. Intimacy with a kindred female spirit and female bonding is essential in black women's literature.[29] "By passing along cherished recipes to subsequent generations, by testifyin', by telling the story of their religious conversions, or by singing the spirituals or the blues, black women helped to revise and extend this oral tradition."[30]

In the seminal *No Crystal Stair,* Gloria Wade-Gayles also argues that black women's literature lays the foundation for the struggle against oppression and discrimination by the black woman articulating her experiences, her humanity, in her own words.[31] Black women's literature does not substitute for real life but records and reports black women's reality as a means of social, historical, anthropological, psychological, and religious witness.

Wade-Gayles delineates four features of black women's consciousness in literature: traditional characters, women aware of oppression, perpetual victims, and pioneers. Using selected works by African American women, I will illustrate Wade-Gayles's categories. In the first feature, traditional characters epitomize black womanhood as wives, mothers, and daughters. A literary example of this is Alice Walker's "Everyday Use," which contrasts the stalwart, stay-at-home mother and daughter with the daughter who goes off to see the world, becomes ashamed of her family, returns for quilts to use as wall hangings, and in her attempt to conform to the "Black Is Beautiful" cries loses the true meaning of her grandmother's quilts.

> Out came Wangero with two quilts. They had been pieced by Grandma Dee and then Big Dee and me had hung them on the quilt frames on the front porch. . . . In both of them were scraps of dresses Grandma Dee had worn fifty and more years ago. Bits and pieces of Grandpa Jarrell's paisley shirts. And one teeny faded blue piece, about the size of a penny matchbox, that was from Great Grandpa Ezra's uniform that he wore in the Civil War.[32]

Women are aware of the tridimensional oppression of sexism, racism, and classism and seek to overcome it in tandem with family and community (Wade-Gayle's second feature). This awareness of oppression is illustrated in J. California Cooper's short story "Sisters in the Rain," which follows the quest of a poor, black, twelve-year-old named Superior who wants to keep the dream of her dying mother, which is for Superior to learn how to read and to go to college. With the help of an othermother, her English teacher Miz Wild, she learned to read but did not make it to college. She lived in a time when she was to have babies, not get a degree. Superior did, however, work and make sure all of her children reached the goal she had hoped to reach herself.

> Superior was able to reach back to her great-grandmother, grandma and mama . . . to grab their dream and bring it on down to her chil-

dren. They graduated not only from school, but from college, too! Now! And they make rainbows for her! Still makin them![33]

Third, there are some characters who are unable to find the courage to sustain the struggle, who become objects of the dilemma and remain victims. Such perpetual victims appear in Alice Walker's "Her Sweet Jerome," a short story about an older black woman who falls in love with and marries a teacher ten years her junior. Much to the amusement of her friends, this once respected, wealthy woman spends inordinate amounts of money on her husband, encourages his interests, and soon becomes insanely jealous of her husband's affairs as he openly ridicules her. She decides to destroy all of his black militancy books in a final effort to secure his love. She is destroyed in the process. Alice Walker writes:

> Thirstily, in hopeless jubilation, she watched the room begin to burn. The bits of words transformed themselves into luscious figures of smoke, lazily arching toward the ceiling. . . . But the fire and the words rumbled against her together, overwhelming her with pain and enlightenment. And she hid her big wet face in her singed then sizzling arms and screamed and screamed.[34]

Fourth, there are the pioneers, those who "spit in the eyes of the Furies." This group defines themselves and names their own reality. This group insists that others must seek to understand the reality of being a black woman in America before they can reject or seek to sequester her existence. Alice Walker's "The Welcome Table" is a beautifully told story of an old black woman who dresses up to go to church and enters one of the town's white churches. After she does not respond to the minister, and one of the ushers requests that she leave, she is physically removed. The husbands of the indignant, insistent wives set her abruptly on the doorstep of the church and shut the door. The rejected old woman looks up and sees Jesus standing next to her. She begins to walk with Jesus. She tells him about her life, the number of white children she has raised, all the work she has done for whites, how they put her out of church, and how much she loved him. As the story progresses, she talks, sings, and marches down the road with Jesus. Although she is found dead later that day, in her mind she achieves ultimate victory as a child of God. Yet, others did not seem to understand her faith:

> The people in church never knew what happened to the old woman; they never mentioned her to one another or to anybody else. . . . Many of the black families along the road said they had seen the old lady high-stepping down the highway; sometimes jabbering in a low

insistent voice, sometimes singing, sometimes merely gesturing excitedly with her hands. Other times silent and smiling, looking at the sky.[35]

Contemporary black women writers are poets, novelists, academicians, critics, researchers, biographers, homileticians, musicians, intellectuals, politicians, and ideologues. They are also everyday, ordinary women who jot down their experiences, feelings, and thoughts as a legacy for their children. Since the 1970s they have begun to develop a large popular black and white, male and female, and young and mature audience.[36] Some appeal to a universal or crossover readership while others write particularly for an African American readership. Generally, African American women write for African American women, utilizing a black feminist/womanist aesthetic in form, syntax, language, sequence, and metaphor. They write in a manner with which other black women can easily identify, and use the reality of black women in the Americas.[37]

In *Black Women Writing Autobiography,* Joanne Braxton contends that black women are born into a mystic sisterhood with shared language.[38] They are able to read into a text the lives of themselves, their mothers, sisters, and grandmothers. From the first published black woman's autobiography, *Belinda, or the Cruelty of Men Whose Faces Were Like the Moon* (1787), black women have related the traditions, values of care and concern, nurturance, protection, and survival of the race. They have sought to share knowledge across generations through both the literary and oral traditions. Black women have relayed information to their children from infancy through songs, games, secret recipes, sayings, and wisdom. Grandmothers have told of the struggles of being a black woman to those gathered around them, on their laps, and during work. Female elders have learned the family history, genealogy, folk medicine, prayers, ghost stories, and rites of passage and passed them on to children or shared them with other women as a means of solidarity and community preservation. This tradition continued through the period of denial of the existence of black women writers and Western literary critics' elevation of black male literature as *the* voice of black Americans to the plethora of contemporary, published black women writers.

It's the Laying on of Hands

Anointing services, healing services, and testimonial services are a part of the worship experience in numerous black churches. A person who is "going through," experiencing some distress, or who is just in need of sensing God's presence in his or her life submits herself or himself to a "laying on of hands" by ministers, prayer warriors, or other faith-filled members of a congregation. This act is to confer spiritual blessings, to break the yoke of oppression, and to liberate one for the journey ahead.

Ntozake Shange's choreopoem *for colored girls who have considered suicide/when the rainbow is enuf* references the healing power of the laying on of hands.[39] Shange states, "I found god in myself." She states that freedom is found in the feminine side of God within her. Shange explores black male-female relationships, sexual abuse, murder, and overcoming oppression by releasing the power within. Passing on faith that provides internal strength for living in a hostile world is crucial in the nurturing process of African American grandmothers and othermothers. Life is hard and at times it is difficult to ascertain that God loves everyone. The mantra that one has a God within has served as a defense mechanism in the lives of African American peoples since the inception of slavery. Shange challenges the notion that a woman must depend on external sources, usually men, for her salvation.

Instead, like many of their heroines, contemporary black women writers reach deep inside themselves to discover who they are, to stimulate their voices long suppressed by a male-centered literary tradition, and to heal wounds caused by indifference, oppression, and discrimination.[40] These writers explore, expose, and excoriate barriers, smash icons, and define themselves while drawing on their rich heritage of storytelling and communal revelation. Many utilize womanist thought, expressions, or cultural metaphors such as the laying on of hands. Laying on of hands is a folk or cultural tradition that represents the transmission of a miraculous power that heals, restores, and transforms all it touches. Exploration of the roots of folk and cultural tradition builds vital, original, and rich emotional-spiritual lives for the writers, readers, and characters. This literary vitality is rooted in a determination to possess their own images, name themselves, and establish their place in the world. From writing only about crises in the black community, anger, and other people's view of them, contemporary black women writers have evolved to confront the past with a clear-eyed vision of the future. There is an inclination away from empty protest to informed social change. Some tackle mysticism, spirituality, and science fiction. Such variety is indicative of there being no monolithic black woman just as there is no monolithic black readership for whom she writes.

Nowhere is this more clearly articulated than in the 1978 classic *Black Macho and the Myth of the Super Woman*. Here, Michele Wallace begins an in-depth political analysis of the status of black women and their predilection for trying to be super strong, enduring all things, and denying themselves to the point of death.[41] By unearthing disenfranchisement, exploitation, oppression, and despair, black women writers, such as Shange, Walker, or Angelou, challenge not only white male hegemony but also black male sexism. By unapologetically articulating their gifts and graces women also save themselves, their families, and their communities. In later works Wallace writes that black women's literature transcends political boundaries of invisibility. However, black women are continually ignored and deemed unscholarly because they write about cultural issues. They challenge the traditional idea of what is academic by presenting what for black people is common sense, lived experience rather than academic elitism about expert information. When their voices were silenced black women spoke through sculpture, sewing, cooking, painting, performance, and music, all deemed "soft" disciplines.

Barbara Christian concurs by stating that black women's writings are viewed as low art in the same category as cooking, gardening, quilting, and storytelling. However, black women writers remember, rename, and revision the friendships, spirituality, sexuality, and mothering of African American women. Black women are moved to excavate the past and restore the words of many of the foremothers by any means necessary. They relay information in the same manner as their foremothers. Sometimes they sit in old comfortable rocking chairs and repeat stories from their lives. Other times they gently stroke the faces of children who have experienced heartbreaking racial epithets and tell them that they are somebody and God loves them.[42]

Black women portray the culture and lives of black people by showing what strengths and traditions nourished them and what are the defining actualities of their existence.[43] Novelist Itabari Njeri writes about her grandmother Ruby's black nationalistic fervor.[44] Upon visiting the eighty-nine-year-old woman in a nursing home she reflects on her vision of her grandmother compared to that of others. She had drawn strength over the years from Ruby's political activism and now must come to terms with her grandmother's frailty and "a child's naive rendering of reality."

> I never saw my grandmother in a place of her own. Perhaps she could have done more with her life despite the profound and pervasive racism that defined America most of her eighty-nine years. Some of her children seemed to think so. "Spoiled" and "lazy" were words family members often used to describe Ruby. "A con artist," too. As an adult, I have seen my grandmother play both ends against the middle, with cash as the reward. But as a child, I thought she could do no wrong.[45]

Thus, black women writers spell out the names of the obstacles that prevented or delayed their freedom. These obstacles typically include a political-social-personal interplay, for individual and community are inexorably linked.

There is a distinctive dialogue between the writers and society, and between the writers and their own psyches. Ann Petry's tragic novel *The Street* portrays a young single mother's initially hopeful, then deteriorating life in Harlem in the late 1940s.[46] In the midst of crisis Lutie Johnson remembers the teachings of her grandmother and strives for the comfort she knew as a child, wishes for her son, yet realizes comfort is out of reach in an environment of violence, oppression, and prejudice. Sensing possible harm from a building superintendent, Lutie says, "You couldn't be brought up by someone like Granny without absorbing a lot of nonsense that would spring at you out of nowhere, so to speak, and when you least expected it."[47]

Lutie infers that we are products of our upbringing. She thought her grandmother's superstitions were bothersome, yet often repeated the teachings and hummed the same songs that brought comfort to Granny. After her son is jailed and she has exhausted legal means for his freedom, she again reflects on the strength of her grandmother and yearns for her counsel and comfort.

> While she undressed, she tried to remember if she had been afraid of the dark when she was Bub's age. No, because Granny had always been there, her rocking chair part of the shadow, part of the darkness, making it known and familiar. She was always humming. It was a faint sound, part and parcel of the darkness. Going to sleep with that warm sound clinging to your ears made fear impossible. You simply drifted off to the accompaniment of a murmured "Sleepin', Sleepin', Sleepin' in the arms of the Lord." . . . No matter what time she reached the house, she knew in the back of her mind that Granny was there and it gave her a sense of security that Bub had never known.[48]

African American women writers engage oppression and provide verbalization of the needs, desires, and actualities of black women's lives. Here Petry paints a vivid picture of the frailty of human existence particularly for black, single mothers. Black women writers attempt to portray their characters with honesty and imagination, remembering that readers are both within black culture and in the broader public realm. Through inner speech or black vernacular they express shared values, perspectives, ideology, and norms. These writers present moral wisdom emanating from black women's stories through a dialect of mutuality, reciprocity, and racial identity. To begin to grasp an awareness and understanding of black women's moral wisdom one must first get rid of imposed academic invisibility and marginalization. Black women writers struggle to restructure categories of race, sex, and class that intersect differing ethical stances. Black women strive to be understood on their own terms, in their own words. Additionally, they recognize how family life, cultural expression, political organization, socioeconomic roles, and religion shape the black community. Black women are challenged to describe, document, and analyze theological and ethical ideologies they were previously subjugated to by shaping their own system of values. Black women stress the emotional and intuitive knowledge in the collective lives of African American people, and follow the rules from within the community. Through literature the ethics, theology, and social teachings of the black community are communicated as black women create their own truth, define their relationship with God, are in connection with all people, influence others, and understand themselves.[49] These teachings, often revealed in the lives of literary characters, are the lived experiences of ordinary black women.

Standing in the Gap: An Analysis of Black Women's Moral Wisdom

In "Moral Wisdom in Black Women's Literary Tradition," womanist Katie Cannon maintains that during the three-and-a-half-century "conspiracy of silence" African Americans stood against the charge that they were immoral or amoral by creating and sustaining their own inner ethical life.[50] The black community in general, and male and female elders in particular, cultivated values and virtues in their own terms. In the dominant society a moral agent was free, self-directed, and self-determined. In the black community suffering was a way of life inflicted by others. Others also determined African Americans' external freedom. As a means of survival blacks devised a set of obligations, assumptions, and duties in the African American community different from those upheld and applied by the European American community. Black women composed a black hermeneutic that included: situational ethics, different standards of beauty, multiplication of limited economic resources by any means necessary, reconstitution of disrupted family structures, reinterpretation of the white mandates against black literacy, "invisible churches" despite prohibitions of communal worship—particularly "Africanisms" in worship—and forgiveness of even those who enslaved them, because God's message was one of *agape*.[51] African Americans appropriated the Bible as the basis of their faith and ethics—"I am because we are." Self is not so much denied as incomplete without consideration of others. The assumption is that one only rises if all rise together. This is a major principle of black women's moral wisdom in reality and in literature.

Cannon observes that in black women's literary tradition the texture of black life, oral-aural tradition, and cultural values are passed from one generation to the next. Black women, particularly grandmothers or female elders, teach what is to be endured and how to survive the harsh, cruel, and inhumane vicissitudes of life. Black women writers function as symbolic conveyors and transformers of values as they chronicle black life and crack worn-out stereotypes. Their plots, characters, actions, ideas, themes, and situations interpret the nuances of black life.[52] Centuries of moral wisdom transmitted by female elders, sisters, church, and community must be reharnessed and redistributed to each succeeding generation.

Black women's literary tradition is my point of departure for an analysis of the presence of community spiritual values and for ways women conveyed them to children. Selected literature is evaluated in terms of literary elements, African American women's didactic paradigm, and a womanist moral-ethical interpretative framework.

You can't Teach What You Don't Know

That African American grandmothers and othermothers transmit values intergenerationally is shown in their pedagogy, their social location, and their relationships to the recipients of their wisdom. Over the past twelve years I have formulated an interpretive framework that I have used to gather and analyze data regarding womanist theology and ethics, African American moral wisdom, and ways in which those values are transmitted across generations. I have used a form of this grid in counseling sessions, personal interviews, and in reading African American literature.

INTERPRETIVE FRAMEWORK
  I. PEDAGOGY
    A. Teaching/Learning Paradigm
      1. Who is imparting information, wisdom, knowledge?
      2. Who is receiving information, wisdom, knowledge?
    B. Hermeneutics and Language
      1. Cultural language
        a. dialect
        b. in-group speech
        c. style
      2. Folklore
      3. Black vernacular
      4. Mother Wit
    C. Pedagogical Vehicles
      1. Attitude, action, example, narrative, biblical instruction, dialogue, lecture, interrogatory, song, sermon, literature
      2. Reinforcement—deference, dictum, positive, negative
      3. Where is teaching done? Community, home, school, neighborhood, church, car, store, and so forth

II. SOCIAL LOCATION
- A. Situation—circumstance, specific problem, event, intervention
- B. Geographical context
- C. Church Affiliation
- D. Educational Level
- E. Community Status
- F. Economic Level
- G. Age of Student and Teacher

III. RELATIONSHIPS
- A. Kinship Status
    1. Relative—blood or marriage
    2. Othermother—community, home, family, church

IV. MORAL/ETHICAL PRESUPPOSITIONS
- A. "God Don't Like Ugly."
    1. Spirituality, faith, biblical resources
        a. Awareness, identity, image and characteristics of God
    2. Black life and culture—history, memory, imagination
    3. Moral agency
        a. Behavior standards—restraint, respect, awareness of one's actions, precaution
- B. "We Are All Aunt Haggie's Children."
    1. Interconnectedness with all humanity
    2. Racial bonding, community solidarity
    3. Personhood, love of self
    4. Responsibility for self and others
    5. Reciprocity or mutuality
- C. "Trouble Don't Last Always."
    1. Survival strategies
    2. Perseverance (hope)
    3. Ethic of care, compassion
    4. Forgiveness

V. TRANSFORMATIVE POSSIBILITIES
- A. Current Situation
- B. Change Agent
    1. Who identifies the situation
    2. Who acts (grandmother, othermother, child)
- C. Type of Change Needed, Advocated, Identified
- D. What Is Advocated?
    1. Positive motivation
    2. Negative motivation
    3. Action

E. How Is Change Facilitated?

F. Did Change Take Place? Why Not?

G. Transmission of Values

    1. Other situations

    2. Other persons

    3. Community

The questions in the first three parts of the interpretative grid gather general information for critiquing each work of literature included in this study. Pedagogical vehicles will consist of example, narrative, biblical precept, one-on-one discussion, group teaching, humor, counseling, reinforcement (positive or negative), deference, or dictum. Language usage—black vernacular, dialect or in-group speech, cultural elements such as folklore, and critique of a specific social problem—will be surveyed. Physical location of teaching will include home, school, job, church, or community structures such as libraries or parks. Geographical context will be designated. Social location will encompass economic level, connection to an institutional church, grandmother or other-mother's education, and community status. Character relationship components will be the age—baby, child, adolescent, young adult, adult, or elder—and the kinship status—ancestor, blood relative (consanguineous), relative by marriage (conjugal), or fictive kin—of the grandmother and othermother and the recipient of moral wisdom.[53]

Better Mind How You Treat Your Neighbors

The fourth part is the crux of the interpretative grid. Each subsection—"God Don't Like Ugly," "We Are All Aunt Haggie's Children," and "Trouble Don't Last Always"—is culturally specific and a vital part of a womanist hermeneutic. Each will be used as a chapter topic in this analysis. The first subsection title, "God Don't Like Ugly," refers to one's understanding of who God is. The image and person of God and womanist Christology of Jesus as cosufferer is the starting point of this ethic. One is taught to revere and respect God because God knows all we say or do. We are to answer to God for all our behavior. Saying that "God don't like ugly" means "You are not acting right," "Show some restraint," "Watch what you do," or "You are about to cross the point of no return."

The second subsection title, "We Are All Aunt Haggie's Children," means that we are inexorably linked to all humanity. "Aunt Haggie" is another name for Hagar, who is seen as a recipient of the Abrahamic covenant through her son, Ishmael, and whose descendants are distinctively African. This ethic includes racial bonding, community solidarity, and personhood.

The underpinning of this ethic is responsibility for self and others and reciprocity or mutuality. In order to be in community with others one must love self. Use of this ethic means that in the vision of black women there are to be no orphans or motherless children because the grandmothers and othermothers are directed by God to become any child's "mother" regardless of age, color, race, or belief.

The dictum of the third subsection, "Trouble Don't Last Always," means that despite hardships, persecutions, oppression, or intimidation we are empowered by God to survive. With the passage of a specific difficulty one must exhibit care, compassion, and forgiveness, particularly for the one who inflicted the trouble. The belief in the relatively transitory nature of trouble is based on the biblical text "Weeping may endure for a night, but joy cometh in the morning," found in Psalm 30:5b (KJV). Everyone will encounter trouble but God is able to resolve the issue in God's time. Overcoming harsh circumstances is accomplished by having an abiding faith in God. One must also learn how to circumvent difficulties, reinterpret them, and work to change them.

By assessing the presence of moral wisdom in black women's literature I will demonstrate grandmothers' and othermothers' transmission of these specific ethical presuppositions: "God don't like ugly," "We are all Aunt Haggie's children," and "Trouble don't last always."

A Change Has Got to Come

The fifth major section for interpretation contains possibilities for individual and social transformation, identifying who is responsible for change, what change is advocated, and how the change is facilitated. Transmission of the newly learned or reinforced values to the larger community or other persons is an important part of this structure. Each of the works studied in the "God Don't Like Ugly," "We Are All Aunt Haggie's Children," and "Trouble Don't Last Always" chapters is assessed for transformative possibilities. In the process, one finds information that will prove useful in instructing contemporary children through moral wisdom and in providing programmatic insights into the transmission of spiritual values to children and adults as a means of surviving harmful social systems.

African American women have been transferring information to other black women, family, church, and community for three centuries. Through an African-based oral tradition and a rich African American written tradition since at least 1773, they have tried to articulate their beliefs and values. Usually the larger society—white men, white women, and frequently black men—have acted as if black women were voiceless, unimportant, or nonexistent. Since the 1960s, a larger number of black women writers of popular literature and scholarly publications have entered into the margins of Western textual tradition while establishing their own form and content. Since the 1970s, a small group of African American women including Toni Morrison, Gloria Naylor, J. California Cooper, Ntozake Shange, Alice Walker, Maya Angelou, Rita Dove, and Terri McMillan has permeated literary center stage and obtained national and international literary honors. Using black women's literary tradition since the 1960s as a point of departure, I will use the womanist interpretive framework as a basis for instruction in value transmission.

4.

ACTING LESSONS

God Don't Like Ugly

T he focus of the next three chapters will be the pedagogy, social location, relationships, ethical presuppositions, and transformative possibilities in African American women's transmission of values. Of particular importance are values to do with spirituality, faith, image and characteristics of God, black life and culture, and moral agency. A representative sample of gospel music, poetry, short stories, novels, and autobiographies by African American women will be analyzed using the interpretive grid described in chapter 3. The selected literature has been culled from over two hundred works written by African American women since 1960. The criteria for final selection were: the author's focus on spirituality—whether in a sacred or secular setting; language that would be inoffensive to the general reader; content about universal life lessons and, more particularly, lessons applicable to African American children or adults; varied types of grandmothers and othermothers—those with affirming and destructive instructions; and the presence of elements that could be assessed using the interpretive grid.

A foundation for a basic understanding of the theology and ethics of the black church, the role and responsibility of black women in the transmission of spiritual values intergenerationally, and the viability of black women's literature as a source for demonstrating the beliefs and practices of black women has been established. I now begin an analysis of the presence and transmission of African American spiritual values in specific works by black women using the interpretive grid, bearing in mind that spirituality in the African American context is not confined to the institutionalized church, but permeates the sacred and secular lives of the people.[1]

Three socioethical presuppositions ("God don't like ugly," "We are all Aunt Haggie's children," and "Trouble don't last always") have been gleaned from both reading of African American women's literature and research in African American and womanist ethics. Whereas each is discussed in a separate chapter they are taught simultaneously in reality and occur concurrently in African American women's literature. For the purposes of the current project each presupposition is analyzed by laying the interpretive grid over the selected literature.

The first section of this chapter highlights poetry and gospel music as vehicles for transmission of values. The second section will look at selected short stories. *Baby of the Family,* a novel by Tina McElroy Ansa, will be analyzed in the third section. Finally, autobiographical or biographical information about the lives of Gloria Wade-Gayles in *Pushed Back to Strength,* and Fannie Lou Hamer in *This Little Light of Mine,* will be evaluated in the fourth section.

God Don't Like Ugly

"God don't like ugly" is an old saying in African American families, churches, and communities that means God does not like us to behave in ways that are not

Christ-like. Adults or elders are instructed to "Train a child in the way he should go, and when he is old he will not turn from it" (Proverbs 22: 6). What we learn as children is with us throughout our lives—good, bad, or indifferent. We are called to act as if we or our parents or someone raised us to act appropriately in all circumstances. It means that we ultimately are accountable to God for every-thing we do. This saying speaks to one's individual and communal understanding of who God is and what God does in our lives. Some complete the saying with, "and He ain't too happy 'bout pretty," meaning that we are called to a higher stan-dard of behavior regardless of what society upholds as acceptable. This spiritual saying was often used by my grandmothers as a means of modifying behavior and was prefaced with some part of a biblical passage—Galatians 6:7-10 (NRSV):

> Do not be deceived; God is not mocked, for you reap whatever you sow. If you sow to your own flesh, you will reap corruption from the flesh; but if you sow to the Spirit, you will reap eternal life from the Spirit. So let us not grow weary in doing what is right, for we will reap at harvest-time, if we do not give up. So then, whenever we have an opportunity, let us work for the good of all, and especially for those of the family of faith.

We are to understand that God loves us but will penalize us for behavior that is offensive, oppressive, deceitful, or injurious to others. This is the God of the black church. This God sees, hears, and knows everything we do, say, or think. With the understanding that God makes each of us—with special talents, gifts, and graces—we are able to appreciate who we are. This means in spite of what society says about the "deficiencies" of African Americans we are able to love ourselves, respect ourselves, and value ourselves because God "don't make no junk." The black family, black church, and black community tell children and remind adults to honor their heritage—"Remember where you came from"; honor their family—"Don't shame your people"; and make contributions to the larger society—"Be a credit to your race." The denial of God's gift of life and one's familial roots is a travesty. Charges of being "uppity" or "siddity" or "tryin' to be Miss Ann" means that one is pretending to be something that he or she is not, hence one is being "ugly."

Children learn from encounters with adults and adults learn from children. The flow of learning or reinforcement of values is reciprocal. This aids in chil-dren being prepared by adults for living in the family, church, or community. It also provides adults with information about the changing world or life issues children face in their generation. A two-way communication loop may chal-lenge grandmothers or othermothers to develop new or modified values or beliefs that speak more realistically to contemporary families, churches, or communities.

Give Me a Clean Heart

Among the distinct dimensions of African American values transmitted intergenerationally, Wade Boykin and Forrest Tones list spirituality, lyricism, and movement.[2] This list emanates from Africa and continues in the family, church, and community. It means definite coded patterns or cultural methods are used for the expression of beliefs, feelings, and thoughts through art, music, sermon, testimony, prayer, humor, lectures, conversation, modeling, and literature.

For the purposes of this study a brief review of how African American women utilize lyrics of gospel music and verses of poetry will provide insight on value transmission. Lisa Pertillo Brevard, quoting Bernice Johnson Reagon's lecture " 'Wade in the Water': African American Social Music Tradition," emphasizes Reagon's claim that African American sacred song is the cornerstone of African American survival in the New World. Reagon says that the attitude of African American women in song paves the way for galvanizing the community in the process of social change. The African American spiritual, in particular, served as the primary means for the singers to claim their space in heaven and in society. The sheer power of the voice set out beliefs about the community's history, culture, and concrete reality.[3]

The gospel message of Jesus—love, joy, repentance, Holy Spirit, image of God, justice, salvation, deliverance, punishment, comfort—is the source of the lyrics in African American gospel music.[4] In the face of oppression and desolation the music generates hope and undergirds the faith of black Christians. Music focuses on immediate problems and gives means to overcome them. Black gospel music is concerned with all of life's situations.[5] The songs are used to celebrate community, detail ritual practices of worship, share the history and experience of a people, tell who God is, and relate the community's theology.

Gospel music is divided into "traditional" gospel, spanning from 1930 to 1969, and "contemporary" or "modern" gospel, from 1969 to the present. The language of gospel music is more contemporary than that of spirituals, and often either gospel music is an arrangement of a spiritual or the gospel song contains whole sections of spirituals as part of the lyrics, thus continuing the message with a change in tempo.

Throughout the period of traditional and contemporary gospel music, black women—Clara Ward, Doris Akers, Lucie Campbell, Roberta Martin, Mahalia Jackson, Sandra Crouch, Aretha Franklin, Tremaine Hawkins, Sallie Martin, Margaret Douroux, and Beatrice Brown—have been prolific writers and performers of gospel lyrics. Music of the traditional period is constantly rearranged for use in contemporary churches. Because gospel music is biblically based, lyrics are not tied to one particular time period, subject, age, gender, denomination, or racial/ethnic group. For example, Margaret Douroux wrote "Give Me a Clean Heart" in 1970. The song is about the need to change one's way of behaving in order to be of service to God. Understanding the difficulty of living in a world that negates one's existence or touts hatred rather than love, Douroux writes, "Lord, fix my heart so that I may be used by Thee.... Please give me, Lord, a clean heart, that I may follow Thee."[6]

This particular song is based on Psalm 51:10: "Create in me a clean heart, O God; and renew a right spirit within me" (KJV). It relates the power of God to transform our minds and emotions to make us amenable to God and not to the praises of humanity. Living in a competitive, "by any means necessary" world, the song teaches that "whatsoever things are pure, whatsoever things are lovely, whatsoever things are of good report; if there be any virtue, and if there be any praise, think on these things. Those things, which ye have both learned, and received, and heard, and seen in me, do: and the God of peace shall be with you" (Philippians 4:8b-9 KJV). Bible study often accompanies teaching songs to choirs in order to reinforce the biblical directive.

Given the percentage of women and children in the black church, music provides a critical opportunity to teach or share community values and beliefs. Naturally, the majority of members in black church choirs are black women. Youth and children's choirs "rehearse" and "remember" the theology, spirituality, and beliefs of their denominations primarily under the direction of women musicians and teachers. For example, in "Trees," often sung by children's choirs, Margaret Douroux expresses God's assurance of who we are and how each of us has a special part to play in God's creation.

> Trees don't want to be mountains, they just praise the Lord;
> Mountains never are valleys, they just praise the Lord;
> The Sun, the Moon and Stars are happy in their heavenly space;
> The rivers and the oceans just keep moving from place to place.
> So if I want to be a servant of that man who made the trees,
> I've got to live the life He wants me to live.
> I ain't gonna worry about the people and what they say;
> I'm gonna do what Jesus tells me each and every day.[7]

The last two lines in particular instruct the singer and listener in the importance of hearing the Word of God above the pressure of peers. The lesson is that if one seeks to do God's will and act according to God's commandments one will enjoy the abundant life Jesus promises in the Gospels to obedient believers. As legendary gospel singer Inez Andrews wrote, "The only way I know you can make it in / You've got to live right."[8]

Themes regarding conversion experiences and modification of actions related to others abound in black gospel music. Songs instruct the singer and listener in the dangers of living a life that is not pleasing to God, the opportunity for trans- formation, and at times, the difficulties and rewards of change. The lyrics of two songs published twenty-four years apart attest to the continued instruction on the need for God's presence in the regulation of human behavior. Joan Golden and Willie Morganfield penned "What Is This?" in 1961.

> What is this? I feel deep down inside. What is this? Keeps setting
> my soul on fire. Whatever it is, it won't let me hold my
> peace. . . . It makes me love all my enemies, and it
> makes me love all my friends and it won't let me be ashamed to tell
> the world I've been born again. What is this? Got me feeling so good
> now. What is this? Makes me want to run on anyhow. Whatever it is,
> it won't let me hold my peace.[9]

The Holy Spirit is an internal behavior control that enables one to express his or her faith without fear and to love without shame. In 1985, Dora Taylor com- posed "It's Not I (but Christ)," which again promotes the belief that one must be in relation with God in order to behave correctly.[10] The lyrics suggest that God is totally in charge of our emotions and ultimate transformation and salvation.

Taylor questions how she can smile when sad, continue to go forward when afraid, help others regardless of the cost, care about life, and tell the world about Jesus' love when she is uncertain of what is going to happen today and tomorrow. She says that "we can do them only with the help of Jesus" and by faith and grace.

The images and characteristics of God in gospel music are transmitted Sunday after Sunday from choir stands and in congregational singing. The advent of music videos, award shows, and national choir competitions extend the transmission of black beliefs not only to the community but cross- culturally. Music in both the black church setting and in the day-to-day life of the community is essential. In many denominations there is music connecting all parts of the service even during the end of a sermon. In the community one hears humming, singing, and often music blaring from cars or portable com- pact disc or tape players. One of my fondest memories is of my family gath- ering around the piano and singing spirituals or gospels for hours. My grandmother would hum while she worked, sat reading, or anytime the "Spirit moved her." References to gospel songs are replete in African American ser- mons as a means of uniting the community in reiteration of those special songs that kept the individual, the family, the group, the church, and the com- munity together in dire situations. Testimonies may begin with the speaker saying, "This song is my testimony" meaning "This is the song that keeps me going" or "This song most represents who I am, what I believe, and who God is for me."

Speak to Me

African American literary critic Sandi Russell contends that amidst the turmoil of the 1960s, including the one hundredth anniversary of the Emancipation Proclamation in 1963, there were cries for social change. Blacks turned to their communities and culture advocating black consciousness raising, black pride, legitimization of black values, and edification of the lives of black people. African American artists and intellectuals addressed the social, political, and spiritual needs of black people in the language of black people. African American poetry was a means of sharing the black oral tradition in self-critique and approval.[11] Poetry is the poet's direct response to aspects of personal experience through lyrics. The poet's ideas and images vividly relate the power and action of emotion and experience. Poets may symbolically contrast order and disorder, love and hate, or mind and personality. Poetry may be in the form of narratives, songs, metaphors, dramatic monologue, visions, allegories, elegy, or epic.[12]

In the African American context children are taught poetry or rhyming at an early age. Those children who are churched are given a "piece" to recite in church. The length of the "piece" increases with the speaker's age. I remember special programs where my grandmother, mother, or aunt would painstakingly rehearse works by Paul Lawrence Dunbar or Phillis Wheatley so I could stand before the entire church in my starched white dress with matching ribbons tightly placed on two long, pressed braids. Their pride came from my ability to memorize and say the words with passion, as well as how impressed others would be that their granddaughter/daughter was smart. I still remember "pieces" from my childhood and the pride that a black person *could* and *did* write something so beautiful, because all I received in school was "American literature." I find myself repeating the ritual with my daughter using Maya Angelou.

Nikki Giovanni remembers the influence of her grandmother, Louvenia Terrell, in "Legacies," a poem about the need for intergenerational contact. A grandmother calls her granddaughter in from play to teach her how to make rolls.[13] Passing down family recipes, especially from one's grandmother, is important, but the physical contact and special time to talk while walking one through the preparation of a dish is more consequential. The kitchen in a black household is like a classroom or church. Secrets of life and, at times, death are exchanged as secret ingredients are mixed together.

> But the little girl didn't want
> to learn how because she knew
> even if she couldn't say it that
> that would mean when the old one died
> she would be less
> dependent on her spirit[14]

The granddaughter avoided the lesson because she felt that if she did not know the recipe her grandmother would have to continue to make the rolls and continue to love. Children at times act as if they are unaware of information so that the adult or mentor continues to teach rather than leave them on their own. They can then hold onto the security of childhood.

> And the old woman wiped her hands on
> her apron saying "lord these children"
> and neither of them ever said what they meant
> and i guess nobody ever does[15]

Through the last two lines, Giovanni also lets us know that the grandmother realized that she needed to share information before she died but internally resisted the urge of letting go of her knowledge just as hard as the granddaughter resisted learning the secret.

The importance of observing and learning how to live or be in community with other persons regardless of circumstance is crucial to the survival of black children. Mari Evan's imagery in ". . . And the Old Women Gathered (The Gospel Singers)" depicts a group of women who have kept their faith in spite of circumstance. They band together "like supply sergeants" who dispense the necessities of life.[16] They sing out of the depth of their individual and collective experience. They sing of God's goodness in tones that drive the listeners away, not because they are lacking in harmony but because their pain is so real others seek to avoid it. The singers evidently are aware of their own behavior and the actions of God in their lives. These singers do not desert God's service but remain faithful to the journey. They passionately sing God's praises in the cognitive dissonance of shared pain. The younger listeners have yet to realize that learning from the experience of others is one of the most instructive forces in life. In spite of the listener fleeing from these othermothers, their witness influenced those who watched them even briefly. Pedagogically, a momentary encounter may be as meaningful as years of contact depending on what was imparted, who was acting, and the receptivity of the learner. In both poems the persons who are to receive information are not ready. This is vital to establishing when one teaches or transmits information. Both parties must be in a position or mind-set to communicate.

In "mrs. martha jean black" Giovanni presents an othermother who both teaches spiritual values and understands social needs.[17] Through her conversation she reminds the child of both the importance of studying the Bible and how to honor one's "father and mother that your days may be long upon the earth." She uses monetary reinforcement for learning the Bible and adds an interrogatory for parental relations.

> they call mrs. black the mother
> of the church and most sundays she says
> "gregory do you know your 'scription?"
> and i say "blessed are the meek"
> and she gives me a nickel and says
> "mind yo mama"
> and i say "yes ma'am" and go to the store
> and have candy
> i like mrs. black [18]

Giovanni uses black vernacular and features a "mother of the church." These women have a covert but understood power base in the black church. They are the spiritual centers and are expected to monitor the behavior of all members, especially children, including the pastor in many cases.

Black women's poetry is written in the language of the people and is useful in transmission of values. The social location is generally a woman speaking to a large, inclusive audience, and the scene is set often in a home, church, or community. Because of the limited information presented it is more difficult to assess transformation in poetry. However, one's particular situation and depth of engagement with the poem dictates what meaning is garnered. There are poems that have become community icons because they have been repeated by each generation, such as Langston Hughes's "Mother to Son" or "Dream Deferred," or Maya Angelou's "Still I Rise" or "Phenomenal Woman." Each speaks of the difficulty of continuing in the face of oppression, but also of the necessity of not giving up.[19] Although the repetition of the poems and meaning depends on the individual reading it, poetry is crucial to understanding the intergenerational transmission of values. Short stories and novels are generally plotted and it is easier to discern the intent of the literature. The author often delineates the purpose within the story or at least by the end of the work.

Through It All

Alice Walker says that black women seem always to be involved in a moral and/or physical struggle searching for some kind of greater freedom.[20] Their literary tradition is based on slave narratives where escape from the body (physical) and freedom for the soul (spiritual) are synonymous. Black women use their own models for attending to, creating, learning from, and realizing their own personal, spiritual, and cultural needs. Black women use everyday, ordinary experiences as a substitute for the often misrepresented, distorted, and lost archetypes in literature by black men and by whites. There is a community saying that "Ya can't teach whatcha don't know and ya can't lead where ya won't go," meaning no one can speak for me but me. The greater sin is to assume something about someone and report it as if it were true.

Short stories are one vehicle black women use to present realistic characters, events, points of view, and discourse about their lives.[21] A brief review of four short stories will demonstrate the transference of spiritual beliefs and modes of behavior from one generation to another.

"Visitations" by Brenda Bankhead illustrates the two-way communication of values between adults and children.[22] Great-aunt Ruby Fields is visiting with Dora and Janetta and does not approve of the way their mother has neglected to teach the girls how to act properly. The girls are playing in the yard catching flies in a can. Their grandmother talks with their uncle about how dirty the girls are becoming.

> "I don't know about you, John, but Mama raised the rest of us to be clean. Wilma, come see what your daughters are doing out there." . . . Ruby knew it wasn't about control really. It was about being proper. Generations of her family had been raised to be proper. This new generation was going to hell in an egg basket.[23]

Ruby did not understand that the girls were being raised with more freedom and less role definition than she had as a child. As she reflects, the grandmother is certain that the way her mother raised her led to a better adulthood than these girls are to encounter.

The generational conflict of what manner of child rearing is most effective is prevalent in today's society. Here "being proper" meant "staying in one's place." Girls did not play in the dirt when Ruby was a child. Girls were "sugar and spice and everything nice." The grandmothers believed that "playing in the dirt" as a girl would lead to a literal acting-out behavior as a woman. The girls were not destructive and were not fighting or destroying property. They were playing. Often the challenge of the generation gap is a misunderstanding of what is now acceptable for boys or girls to do.

Ruby is taught a lesson by her nieces after the death of her best friend, Bea. Ruby becomes inconsolable, stops going to church, and stays in bed most of the time. Dora and Janetta's new friend, Maria, teaches them about celebrating the Day of the Dead. The brightly dressed girls enter Ruby's bedroom, which has become her sanctuary. African Americans speak of their prayer closet as a special altar set up in the living room complete with Bible and candles—literally a closet in the house, or perhaps the car. Usually it is the bedroom where all the distractions of the world may be shut out by closing the door or getting under the covers for private time with God. The granddaughters in childlike faith and armed with information from Maria explain to their aunt the importance of mourning, life, and sharing a meal with the dead. At first Ruby resents the intrusion of the Mexican Catholic holiday on her American Catholic All Saints' Day. But after listening to the girls Ruby gets up and reluctantly enters the celebration. This demonstrates intergenerational transmission of beliefs that run child to adult, rather than adult to child.

> "Come see the altar, Aunt Ruby," Janetta pleaded. "There's candles on it for everybody, not just saints. It is like being in church, except not as sad." . . . Ruby walked to the altar. She scanned it until she came to a black-and-white snapshot. It was a picture of the young Bea. . . . A part of Ruby wanted to snatch the picture down and stuff it into her pocket. Another part of her made her reach for the bread instead.[74]

The ability of the nieces to venture past cultural and religious boundaries ultimately enriched the aunt's life and changed her behavior toward them and another faith system.

It is essential to remember that adults can also learn from children. Children often are more open to change and can interpret shifts in culture due to fewer preconceived notions.

Another othermother used field experience to teach restraint, respect, and awareness of one's actions for a group of neighborhood children. "The Lesson" by Toni Cade Bambara is about Miss Moore, who is characterized as a college educated, unmarried, go-fer, "borin' us to tears," unattractive woman who plans a lesson of the week for the children.[25] She takes them on a taxi ride to F.A.O. Schwartz. Miss Moore engages four of them in a question-and-answer period of critical thinking about expenses of life. After the children observe $1,195 sailboats, $480 prisms, and finally a $3,500 train, Miss Moore continues the lesson.

> "You know, Miss Moore, I don't think all of us together eat in a year what that sailboat costs."

> "Imagine for a minute what kind of society it is in which some people can spend on a toy what it would cost to feed a family of six or seven. What do you think?"

> "I think," say Sugar, ". . . that this is not much of a democracy if you ask me. Equal chance to pursue happiness means an equal crack at the dough, don't it?"[26]

Although the narrator is still convinced that the whole afternoon was a waste, Sugar was overjoyed that she got the point—society is unjust when there is unequal access to resources. Miss Moore's intention was accomplished by taking the children out of their normal environment and letting them try to function in another social setting. The interrogatory model allowed each student to experience the store, figure out the social and economic discrepancies they faced, and plan individually how they would engage the injustice.

There are instances where the teachings of grandmothers and othermothers give momentary relief, but the person is too overwhelmed to release or engage whatever is confronting them. There is no immediate transformation or the person shows little desire to change. Michelle Clift depicts an alcoholic actress in a drying-out ward trying to put her life back together in "Screen Memory."[27] Set in February 1963, the main character is a mixed-race woman raised by a black grandmother. At one time whites tried to take her away from her grandmother, but she ran away. Deserted by her mother, she is haunted by confused identity as she is described as "wild as the girl's mother whom the girl cannot remember and the grandmother cannot forget." Whenever she is restless or troubled she "flies to the feet of her grandmother" where she is taught lessons, listens to stories, and finds solace. As she remembers her grandmother's daily methodical polishing of an African carved piano, she begins to reach inside as instructed and relaxes. The grandmother speaks to her of passion, of the right kind. "Hastiness, carelessness, will never lead you to any real feeling, or"—she pauses—"any lasting accomplishment. You have to go deep inside yourself—to the best part."[28]

She draws strength from her memory of when she observed her grandmother's encounters with rude people, such as a white teenage grocery clerk to whom she said, "And don't you go flinging it at me like that. I've lived too long for your rudeness. I don't think the good Lord put me on this earth to teach each generation of you politeness."[29] Her grandmother always demanded and got respect from people. As she envisioned her grandmother she knew she had to find a way and reclaim the self-respect she had lost in the bottle. She was ridiculed for her parentage yet able to pass for white. She had a much easier passage through life than her grandmother but still had difficulty in maintaining social and sexual relationships. She heard her grandmother say, "We are born alone and we die alone and in the meanwhile we have to live alone." At the end of the story she has not resolved her difficulty. She decides to keep on running away until she finds that inner strength to stop her alcoholic slide. This character received "home training" yet crossed into a society with different values. She attempted to reclaim her heritage but confusion of beliefs kept her imprisoned in the bottle.

Sharing of power, intelligence, ideas, and visions by grandmothers and grandchildren is beautifully portrayed in "To Da-duh, In Memorium" by Paule Marshall.[30] A nine-year-old visits her eighty-something grandmother in the Virgin Islands and realizes the power of older women. "My mother, who was such a formidable figure in my eyes, had suddenly with a word been rendered to my status."

The grandmother was the head of a large extended family including her fourteen children in St. Andrews and St. Thomas. Everyone kowtowed to Da-duh, the anchor who monitored everyone's behavior.

> Da-duh, ashamed at their wonder, embarrassed for them, admonished them the while. "But oh Christ," she said, "why you all got to get on like you never saw people from 'Away' before? You would think New York is the only place in the world to hear wunna. That's why I don't like to go anyplace with you St. Andrews people, you know. You all ain't been colonized."[31]

She chastised adults and children who quickly became quiet. She reminded them of their shortcomings and lack of refinement because they had not assimilated British culture. She set the tone for everyone's behavior, until she met her granddaughter from New York.

The granddaughter became the stabilizing force for the grandmother who feared progress, machines, new people, and the impending changes in her settled lifestyle due to British colonization. The granddaughter loved a challenge, and learned life skills on the streets of New York. During the visit Da-duh and the granddaughter became inseparable, exploring the island daily as the grandmother pointed out the richness of her land and culture. The granddaughter countered each example with high points of her life in New York. There was a competition of age, culture, and belief but most importantly there was respect between the two. Da-duh introduced the child to everyone on the island and proudly showed her off, having her sing and dance. Their battle of wills, worked out through questions and answers, strengthened the granddaughter's resolve and resulted in the grandmother's yielding part of her power to the child.

> I came to know the signs of her surrender: the total stillness that would come over her little hard dry form, the probing gaze that like a surgeon's knife sought to cut through my skull to get at the images there, to see if I was lying; above all, her fear, a fear nameless and profound, the same one I had felt beating in the palm of her hand that day in the lorry.[32]

Often the fear of losing a part of one's self leads to a muted conflict between grandmothers and grandchildren. At the same time there is a subtle pride that the grandchild is reaching levels the grandmother was unable to attain. The granddaughter represents a loss of the grandmother's control over her life and invalidates the durability of her culture. Da-duh eventually gives up her struggle to hold onto the past, goes to bed, and soon dies. Reminiscing years later, the granddaughter becomes an artist who paints scenes from the Virgin Islands within the New York landscape. This is symbolic of the inexorable link between our heritage and our contemporary lives, ancestors and descendants, adults and children.

Through verbal confrontation the behavior and beliefs of the grandmother and granddaughter were modified. Bragging about who had the best life, who was in control, who had the most power, and who would win the battle of wills became insignificant. The time they shared and what they learned from each other were the critical factors.

Reach Out and Touch

Contemporary African American women writers reach back to the 1920s through the 1960s, the period of their mothers' lives, to determine how we value the past, what we remember, what we forget, and what we select to emphasize. In order for black women to be whole they must reconstruct their own lives from their own perspective in light of the truth of their own history.[33] The rhetoric of the 1960s stressed the necessity for the rediscovery of blackness and unity. The majority of books written for black readership included characterizations of black women—grandmothers, great grandmothers, mothers, sisters, and so forth—who sustained, taught about the self, and taught children how to dream. Themes included black women's friendship, what happens to blacks caught in the world of white values, and how black women can hold things together in difficulty.[34]

Baby of the Family by Tina McElroy Ansa is a pseudoautobiographical novel. Ansa writes stories rich in cultural linkages that allow African American women to reclaim and pass on their heritage and their history, which has been forgotten, lost, or misrepresented. She indicates that the more assimilated and integrated African Americans become the more they become ashamed of the traditional beliefs that they classify as ignorant or country. Black people need their own validity and their own voicing of beliefs.[35]

Ansa talked with older women, for example, midwives on St. Simons Island, who reminded her of these traditional folk sayings such as nose itching—someone is coming to visit; palm itching—you will receive money; or sweeping after dark—bad luck. She recalled childhood folk wisdom (Mother Wit) of her great grandmother, Nellie Lee, who told ghost stories with life morals such as "You die as you live" or "Ancestors are always with you." Ansa's great aunt, Elizabeth Lee, also told ghost stories with instruction to live upright, "You reap what you sow." Ansa states that a vital part of African American culture is spirituality, the responsibility to tell the truth, looking to ancestors for behavioral guidance, and the continuity of life and death. These lessons were passed on through stories rather than television.[36]

Ansa wrote *Baby of the Family* out of her oral tradition and life experience. She, like the lead character, Lena McPhearson, was born with a caul over her face. In black folk belief a caul or veil represents special blessings, supernatural insight, and greatness. The caul denotes psychic powers, prophetic pronouncements, and at times one to be feared by ordinary people. The covering on the face at birth, as my mother was told when my older brother was born with a caul, means the mother was deep in the spirit during the pregnancy (blessed to be chosen and touched by God, and allowed to carry a special child). It also means lifelong protection for the child, and unless the child is in touch with his or her spiritual center or guide, the child may use the powers for evil rather than good. Midwife Mother Bloom takes the caul from the delivery room to make a tea for the baby to ensure the blessing.

> That caul is a gift from God, that's what it is. This little girl has been chosen by God as a special person on this earth. She can't hardly help but to do something great in this life because God has touched her in the womb.[37]

Nurse Bloom tries to explain the spirit born in Lena to Nellie, the mother, who rejects the idea as old-fashioned. "Nurse Bloom felt as if she was trying to cram a lifetime of common sense into a few minutes." At age five Lena learned of her clairvoyance while playing in a graveyard with her brothers. Her family knew she was different and she thought she was crazy. As in many families the subject was not discussed. Afraid of her "power" due to Grandmama Lizzie's folk belief and ghost stories, and feeling ostracized by family and friends, Lena is ready to give up.

> If God made me to know, love, and serve him in this world and be happy with him in the next, why do we have to be in this world at all? Why don't we all get dressed up and go to the next world and be happy?[38]

Whenever Lena had any qualms or fears she went to her grandmother who always had a story or life lesson to share. The topic or main characters in those stories were most often supernatural.

> Like Lena he had been born in November and, according to Grandmama, whenever a person born in that month dies, another birth takes place in the family the following November. Lena liked the sound of that story. Instead of feeling responsible for Granddaddy's death, as the boys sometimes taunted her, she felt a product of his death—a seed from the lips of a dying flower.[39]

Grandmama Lizzie was deeply spiritual but did not regularly attend church. She was not a docile, quiet grandmother. She prayed, cursed, loved her family, was contentious and set in her ways, thought she was always right or knew what was best for the family, and was in many ways trying to live and understand a new society but felt out of sync.

> Grandmama was known to double back on a target if a stray thought hit her as she wandered away and everyone was sure she was finished. Lena never wanted to get caught in the crossfire of her grandmother's rage.[40]

Grandmama Lizzie was steeped in cultural folk wisdom. Taught to revere and respect elders, the family listened to whatever she said and generally accepted her word as law. When she hit her grandson, Edward, in the mouth with a cow's tongue and told him to eat some as a "cure for stuttering" Lena was disappointed but still trusted her because she at least tried to help Edward.

> "It's a cow's tongue, is what it is," her grandmother replied self-righteously. "And it's the only sure cure for stuttering. While ya'll around here with your fancy solutions to the boy's problem, his grandmama had to take matters into her own hands."[41]

The belief is that the important thing is not that one fails, but that one tries—"Nothing beats a failure but a try." As outrageous as the method was—making the boy eat a cow's tongue to make his own tongue stronger and thus stop the stuttering—Lena learned that the end, or the potential end, justifies the means. She may not have agreed or even believed her grandmother could accomplish all she said she could, but the results did not lie.

Even in a two-parent home Grandmother Lizzie was the dominant force. Lena depended on her grandmother as confidant, teacher, and one who loved her unequivocally. After her grandmother died of heart failure trying to kill an owl inside the dining room, Lena felt she had lost her best friend. Yet, her grandmother had known death was imminent—"Baby, a bird in the house is a sure sign that there's gonna be a death in the family." She had also promised Lena that she would never let anything happen to her. Lena called for her grandmother to help her find her way through life, to determine who she was, and show her once more how she was to act around people who feared she was insane. In black folk culture the "living dead" as "ministering angels" attend to those who are alive. The grandmother appeared to Lena the night of her funeral as Lena lay in Lizzie's bed again wanting to die.

> "What you are, baby, it's a gift. It's like in the Bible. It's your birthright. There's gifts that you're given in this world that you just can't throw away. If you do, its like telling somebody who love you to kiss your ass. . . . And no matter what, me and others who love you, we'll always be with you." Grandmama paused and added, "Baby, there's just some things you have to take on faith."[42]

Grandmama's life recitations did not end with physical death, but continued in her spirit. The interconnection of grandmother and granddaughter strengthened Lena's faith in herself and God's gift for her life.

Calling up the names and words of ancestors as a means of guidance in this life is rooted in African religion and black folk belief. The practice deemed old-fashioned by some people is reinstated in the black family, church, and community, especially on holidays, historical observances, Mother's Day, Father's Day, Memorial Day, birthdays, and family reunions.

Show Me the Way

The literature of African American women mirrors their life experience. Articulation of the realities of black womanhood and sharing what they have learned about how to conduct themselves are essential to the subsistence of the black woman, black family, black church, and black community. Autobiographical and biographical writings are distinct indicators of how African American women transmit values intergenerationally.

In *Pushed Back to Strength*, Gloria Wade-Gayles records her experiences from growing up in segregated Memphis, Tennessee, to work in the Southern Freedom movement to her faculty position at Spelman College in Atlanta, Georgia.[43] Wade-Gayles states that approximately 60 percent of her writing is autobiographical. Her work is an expression of "who-ness," giving meaning to the importance of validation of self and one's fertile heritage. By relating a sense of family—particularly through her mother and grandmother—she hopes to keep the black culture alive for future generations. Looking back over her life and coming to terms with the death of her mother she writes:

What I remember most vividly from my youth is my respect for women, especially my elders. To me, they were powerful beings, forces that belonged, I thought, to another world, but chose to live in this one because we needed them. As blacks, we struggled for personhood and freedom in the physical world, but that was not the only world in which we lived. Women guided us to the other world, the spiritual world, where neither race nor gender was of consequence, and there they nurtured us and made us whole. We called the women wise; they were, in fact, spiritual.[44]

This is precisely how the understanding of "God don't like ugly" was imparted in my remembrance. The idea that the "world can't do me no harm" or "this world is not my home" grew out of a deep-seated spiritual grasp of life in the midst of physical pain. I resented my grandmothers' cooking, cleaning, and caring for white families while suffering great indignities. I did not then understand how they could go day in and day out being treated like children yet stand so proudly on Sunday morning singing, "I feel like goin' on, though trials come on every hand, I feel like goin' on." It was because their realm was not here but wherever Jesus was.

Wade-Gayles says that the men in her life were the "buttresses and protectors," but the women gave her strength. Her mother, Bertha, did what she had to do to care for her two daughters, Gloria and Faye, encouraging them to continue their quest and not forget their goals. She pushed them to build for their futures with education at the center of their lives. Her Aunt Ola Mae, though socially abused, taught her how to be present in the world through "proper speech" and etiquette, and how to carry herself with dignity in all situations even in the Foote Home projects of Memphis. Her grandmother, Nola Ginger Reese, helped Gloria put her life in perspective, dulled her anger, and made her feel like she could achieve anything in her view.[45]

Her relationship with her grandmother provides the title of this work. As a teenager, Gloria says she was caught between the disdain blacks had for whites and the respect they had to afford their elders. She went to her grandmother to get an explanation of how to engage the humiliation of "Colored" water fountains, segregated theaters, and inferior schools. Her grandmother responded in the measured, all-knowing manner that black elders usually use:

"Don't tell me about white folks," she would say, barely looking up from whatever she was doing. "You don't know mean." She had deep cuts that had not been healed; we had mere scratches that barely broke the skin. . . . "They don't know it," Grandmama would respond. "They don't know it, but they're pushing you back to us, where you can get strong. Get some strength."[46]

The grandmother was not denying the granddaughter's pain but taking it to demonstrate that the pain was also instrumental in solidifying the connection between them. They each had their own pain and would be able to overcome it if they addressed it in concert. The saying "They meant it for evil, God meant it for good" was generally used to underscore this situation. The point is, yes, times are hard and we will get through them together.

Wade-Gayles writes that what she learned from the exchange is that blacks had to reaffirm their own values and define themselves while trusting in God to provide a solution. She also says that there were times her grandmother's stories calmed her down and made her feel like she was a whining child who could never become the strong person her grandmother exemplified. Other times she would become more angry and want to fight everyone she saw for the sake of her grandmother's pain as well as her own.[47] As she matured she began to understand the type of strength her grandmother possessed. Her own racial pride evolved from knowledge of her grandmother's defiance. She describes her grandmother as entrancingly resilient with the daunting retentiveness of a painful past used to maintain a healthy contemporary mindset. She taught her family not to hate whites but to love themselves.

> [They] taught me about my family's refusal to be head-dropping, side-stepping, yassiring, submissive colored folks . . . they walked outside the narrow circles of humiliation for blacks expertly drawn by whites.[48]

Miss Reese, Gloria's grandmother, was a minister's widow forced out of her home upon her husband's death by the church she had sacrificed to serve. A single mother of four, she raised her children with a strong sense of dignity, self-worth, and a belief in God. She knew implicitly biblical mandates for behavior and taught them to her children and grandchildren by precept and example. This former sharecropper from backwoods Mississippi was a prophet, a fighter, independent, vocal, and proud. "If you pushed her too hard or in the wrong direction, you would never push her again."[49]

The grandmother valued education and wanted to go to college. Because of her family responsibilities and societal prejudices she did not go. She instructed her children and grandchildren to take pride in what they knew and who they were. She told them to keep their heads up, not look down, and talk when they had something to contribute to the conversation. This was her solution for engaging people as equals, not inferiors.[50]

This behavior in African Americans is often interpreted as ignorance, sullenness, or defiance. There are cultural norms of "Don't put your business in the street" or "It is better to keep quiet and be thought a fool then to open your mouth and remove all doubt" or "Don't let your right hand know what your left hand is doing" or "They can only use the information you give them." Each is a defense mechanism used to show black children how to function in the larger society. Holding one's head up is taught by literally telling a child to raise his or her head, or manually raising the child's head. Teaching one to look another person directly in the eye when talking is also accomplished through verbal or physical reminding. This is a clear reaction to the practice of foot-shuffling, head-scratching, and directives not to look whites in the eyes, prior to the 1960s.

In spite of the harsh treatment by the African Methodist Episcopal Church, the grandmother continued to support the church and ensure that no one had to ask for financial assistance from a church. Her family had to attend church regularly. One of the vital lessons of the community is that the church is composed of people who are fallible — "sinners saved by grace." We are called to be Christ-like and love one another but sometimes even the ministers do not follow the mandate. Still, one is told, "Don't ever let anyone drive you away from your church." This does not mean allow the church membership to oppress you, but stand for what is right even if you stand alone. One must find alternative ways to live out one's Christian life, such as stopping financial contributions to the church and giving money directly to the persons who need help.

Wade-Gayles reports that through sermons, songs, Sunday school, home instruction, and community involvement with the rearing of each child she learned the "Black Commandments":

> "You must love yourself and your people."
> "You must believe that you can do anything you set your mind to."
> "You should let no circumstances remove you from the center of your
> dreams."
> "You must never forget from whence you came."
> "You must reach back to others."
> "You must serve."[51]

These so-called commandments were the foundation of African American values systems prior to the integration and assimilation crazes of the 1960s, through the 1980s "Me first" fad.

As blacks began to seek parity with whites many believed that these commandments were worthless. Observing the loss of community and spiritual values in many black homes and families, there are now efforts to reinstill or re-create them through family, church, and community mentoring programs, workshops on self-esteem, community empowerment ventures, and parenting classes.

Violence is predicated on lack of love for self and others. There is an undercurrent of self-hatred in young people active in gangs and in adults who constantly seek to modify their appearance, culture, and beliefs based on someone else's standards. In valuing self and others there is no need for competition that leads to unhealthy lifestyles, use of intoxicants, crime, or any oppressive system based on age, race, gender, or belief. Validation of one's own thoughts, faith, and physical characteristics is grounded in love of self and respect for the rights of others to be who they are as created by God.

Believing that you can do anything you set your mind to do and not allowing anyone to distract you is a challenge for black youth. If dreams are constantly deferred due to oppression or lack of opportunity, one dies. These injunctions are based on the biblical statements, "Where there is no vision the people perish" (Proverbs 29:18*a* KJV) and, "I can do all things through him who strengthens me" (Philippians 4:13 NRSV). Without constant support and reinforcement one begins to listen to the counterarguments that "you are nothing and never will be anything," and begins to act accordingly. Instead of listening to the message learned from grandmothers and othermothers—"Yes, you can"—one will continue the slide into "You never will."

Remembering where you came from is crucial amid charges that educated or middle-income or light-skinned or promoted blacks no longer remember their roots. Before moving out of the so-called black community was an option, blacks worked together for community pride. Children were told when they left home to "Remember where you came from" as a means of saying "Act like you have a home and don't do anything to bring shame on us." It also means that you can always come back home because we have all worked to make a way for you to go out into the world. One is never to be ashamed of family, church, or community. Blacks are often taught that home is the only place where they have to take you in when all others reject you. Forgetting that each advance by an individual is due to a sacrifice by scores of others is a sin. Pretending that one "pulled him or herself up by his or her own bootstraps" is a denial of culture and religion.

Reaching back for others is connected to serving others. Humanity is a collective, communal, united entity. "The body is a unit, though it is made up of many parts; and though all its parts are many, they form one body. So it is with Christ" (1 Corinthians 12:12). Informal adoption and development of extended families, behavior correction and chastisement by the entire community, and ensuring that those that follow will know how to get a job, pass a class, or raise a child are due to the belief that we are all family. African American churches teach that God has no stepchildren. Children spending weeks at another child's house is part of the interconnectedness of all persons. Being of service to others is essential to living out one's faith. Modeling Jesus' life as suffering servant, black churches teach that "we are saved to save others, blessed to bless others, and are to be a service to others."

As Wade-Gayles demonstrates in this work, blacks need to be "pushed back to strength," returned to the source, and nurtured again in family, church, and community if we are to live with dignity, restraint, respect, and spirituality in American society. The Black Commandments are not farfetched or old-fashioned, yet blacks in favor of trying to live by the values of other groups have displaced them.

Don't You Know God Is Able?

> But I say unto you which hear, Love your enemies, do good to them which hate you, Bless them that curse you, and pray for them which despitefully use you. (Luke 6:27-28 KJV)

It is difficult for many to understand why some elders say, "You got to love 'em" or "Two wrongs don't make a right" or "God will fight your battles, if you just keep still." These statements sound ridiculous in an era of stealth bombers, nuclear warheads, six-year-olds with guns, and antitheft devices. The life of Fannie Lou Hamer, however, exemplifies the biblical passage and the community saying that "God is able." Hamer bridged the incongruities of praying for those who seek to destroy and maintaining dignity while seeking to live in freedom. Her lived faith allowed her to transmit how to rise above adversity, join in the daunting struggle for freedom, and yet never lose her connection with who she was.

Hamer was an othermother during the Southern Freedom movement. She had no natural-born children but was said to have "mothered" the movement by the sheer force of her faith in God and humanity.[52] Hamer was born October 16, 1917, the youngest of twenty children in a family who worked as sharecroppers. Her early experience on the Marlowe plantation, her observations on the different standards of behavior set up for blacks and whites, her educational background, her faith development at the Strangers Home Baptist Church, and the influence of her mother contributed to her ability to sustain herself and others in the midst of the movement.

Her mother taught her that hatred made one as weak as the person hating. She also told her that if you learned to respect yourself others would eventually have to respect you. Hamer carried these values throughout her life. Her coworker, Mrs. Unita Blackwell, recalled asking Hamer if she hated whites who beat her, took her jobs, had her thrown off the plantation, and had tried to stop her every effort.

> She explained it to me that we have to love them and they are sick. That was a continuous thing—she kept that going that they were sick and America was sick and it needed a doctor and we was the hope of America.[53]

Hamer was well-versed in the Bible and stated that Christ was a revolutionary and she was called to do likewise. She believed that one should never run away from a problem. She had a low opinion of institutional churches that neglected the militant nature of Christ's ministry and being present and active with all people, particularly the grass roots.

> The most disgusting hour in the country is 11:00 A.M. Sunday morning when hypocrites from all walks of life converge on our churches for the sake of paying the ministers' way to hell and theirs too.[54]

Realizing her mission, she challenged the manner in which white Americans were treating blacks—lynching, beatings, burning, loss of employment, threats, and legalized racism. On national television she boldly asked:

> I question America, is this America, the land of the free and the home of the brave where we have to sleep with our telephones off the hooks because our lives be threatened daily because we want to live as decent human beings, in America?[55]

Bob Moses said that she had "rock hard integrity, a commitment to people she had come from and she just never left them." Known as earthy and filled with Mother Wit, she sang and cared for others, modeling how to take a stand for justice.

> "Ain't no such thing as I can hate anybody and hope to see God's face. . . . And one day, I don't know how [white people] are going to get it, but they're going to get some of it back," she said of the whites opposing civil rights workers. "They are scared to death and are more afraid now than we are."[56]

In her mind, God was about change and not about fear or anger. Persons were, however, responsible for their actions. Going against God's law, such as enslavement of others, would be the subject of retribution in God's time.

Hamer not only shared, nurtured, tutored, and encouraged others but also learned from and appreciated the black and white young people in the Student Nonviolent Coordinating Committee (SNCC) who helped her register to vote at age forty-five, with whom she traveled on Freedom Rides, and who risked their lives for the freedom of all. Hamer said that if she had not had the opportunity to work with SNCC she would not exist. For the first time in her life someone treated her as a human being. Both the black and white students in the movement respected her and listened to her. The proclamations about voting rights and freedom developed in the hearts and minds of the SNCC workers. They did not have anyone feeding them propaganda. Their deep-seated beliefs about freedom for all permeated their work. She saw the SNCC workers as the emissaries of hope for the state of Mississippi.[57]

Hamer taught love, pride, faith, and endurance through her forthright speech and her music. She became the spiritual song leader of the modern Civil Rights movement through both her theme songs, "This Little Light of Mine" and "Go Tell It on the Mountain," and her encouragement to tell everyone everywhere about injustice and the possibilities for change. When the groups were encountering danger or apprehension she began to sing. In the jails, on buses, during marches she began the songs of freedom. At the 1964 Democratic Convention, after one stinging defeat after another, she sang. Bernice Johnson Reagon, Freedom Singer and SNCC worker, said that Mrs. Hamer was a "fire warrior," constantly sharing her life story, singing, and maintaining an aura of peace and safety. Reagon describes Hamer as insistent, loving, angry, and strong. She was the type of black woman role model that Reagon needed to meet in order to continue her struggle for freedom.[58]

Through precept and example Hamer taught others how to conduct themselves in positive and negative situations. She sacrificed her own family, life, and health for her "children"—everyone she met. She died on March 14, 1977, of cancer, diabetes, heart disease, and complications from the movement lifestyle. At her funeral Stokely Carmichael, former SNCC leader, said she was the "very best of us."

> Some people who live do bad things and others are happy when they die; some live indifferent lives so no one knows when they die. But others give their blood and sweat, he said, and "these are the ones we come to honor."[59]

As demonstrated in the literature cited in this chapter, there is an expectation that we love one another, love and respect ourselves, and carry an awareness of our culture with us. Each person is to take what she has learned and pass it on to the next person regardless of age, gender, race, or belief system. The African American community has blended scriptural passages and community sayings into a web of values or Black Commandments that may serve as guidelines for our behavior. The method of passing on this information varies with each person but includes interrogatories, lectures, song, stories, poetry, recipes or cooking lessons, sewing, gardening, sermons, protests, lifestyle, shopping, and church service. Young people develop a viable value system using both negative and positive characteristics of grandmothers and othermothers, such as rage or anger. These female elders also learn from the young people, allowing each to endure and thrive in society. Transmission of values is a two-way street and allows both parties to gain information. In some cases transformation does not take place immediately but may at some point.

The interconnectedness of God's creation, "We are all Aunt Haggie's children," is discussed in the next chapter as a continuation of the "God don't like ugly" presupposition. Songs, poetry, short stories, novels, and autobiographies are examined as a means of unearthing and reestablishing African American spiritual values systems in the life of the black family, black church, and black community.

5

SPIRITUAL CONNECTIONS

We Are All Aunt Haggie's Children

We hold these truths to be self-evident, that all men are created equal, that they are endowed by their Creator with certain unalienable Rights, that among them are Life, Liberty, and the pursuit of Happiness. (Declaration of Independence, adopted by the Continental Congress, in Philadelphia, on July 4, 1776)

There is neither Jew nor Greek, slave nor free, male nor female, for you are all one in Christ Jesus. If you belong to Christ, then you are Abraham's seed, and heirs according to the promise. (Galatians 3:28-29)

A cursory reading of these passages might indicate secular and sacred assurance of equality for all persons. Black women's reality throughout history, however, is that in both arenas they are more often than not excluded. The Declaration of Independence was written at a time when "unalienable rights" meant the rights of white men to own and control all other persons.[1] The Constitution of the United States did not begin to address rights of other persons until the ratification of Article 13—abolition of slavery (December 8, 1865) and Article 15—which was intended to grant equal rights not based on race, color, or previous servitude (March 30, 1870). Individual state governments for at least another hundred years ignored this "law of the land." In essence, the mind-set of individuals in power could not be legislated. African Americans remained enslaved, lynched, and locked out of the "American Dream" of life, liberty, and happiness. Following the process of the "fathers" of the country, African Americans had to seek their own means of liberation and equality at least before the law. The issue was not that one group was better than another, but that all deserved access to the benefits of living in the "land of the free and the home of the brave."

The Bible has been used to undergird the subjugation of women and various racial/ethnic groups and keep white Protestant males, who supposedly founded the United States on Christian principles, in positions of power. Theological debates have abounded on the subservient position of Adam's "helpmate" Eve, and the mandate of "Slaves, obey your earthly masters with respect and fear, and sincerity of heart, just as you would obey Christ" (Ephesians 6:5). Faced with charges of being less human than others or being the "cursed children of Ham," African American Christians appropriated and reinterpreted biblical texts in order to live as free heirs of God's promise. The use of Galatians 3:28-29 with 1 Corinthians 12:13 ("For we were all baptized by one Spirit into one body—whether Jews or Greeks, slave or free—and we were all given the one Spirit to drink") can lead to a belief that God made us all from the same elements and no one is superior to anyone. We are all equally blessed by God.

One of the standard biblical stories used by African Americans to substantiate their right to equality is the life of Hagar found in Genesis 16. Hagar was a slave handmaiden for Sarah, who was barren. God's covenant with Abraham was that his seed would be multiplied and blessed. Sarah decided to give God some assistance and offered Hagar as Abraham's concubine. Hagar conceived Abraham's first son, Ishmael. Following a series of manipulations, confrontations, exiles, and the birth of Sarah's son Isaac, Hagar and Ishmael were forced out into the desert to die. God spoke to Hagar and promised her a portion of Abraham's inheritance and blessing through Ishmael.

African Americans have appropriated the story as the basis for their connection with all of God's children. All of us came from Abraham's seed and therefore are inexorably connected. The enslavement of black women, their rape and violation by white men, their surrogacy and mothering of white children, and the distrust or strained relationship that developed between black and white women coincides with the lives of Hagar and Sarah. "We are all Aunt Haggie's children" means that we all—black, white, red, yellow, brown—came from one source and will all receive the promise of God. No one has the right to repress or hate his or her brother or sister. We are all related. Aunt Haggie is a cultural reference to Hagar. "Aunt," "Aintie," or "Auntie" refers to othermothers in the community who may or may not be related by blood to the children or members of the community they care for or teach.[2]

The content of this chapter will be the depiction of "We are all Aunt Haggie's children" by African American women in three songs, four poems, three short stories, two novels, and one autobiography. The saying may be broken down into several areas of analysis. Every person created by God is a member, an equal member, of God's family. There are no stepchildren. The difficulty arises when one does not believe in Christian principles or believes that "God is no respecter of persons," when one is unchurched, or due to the effects of racism or brutal treatment by another person one believes there is no viable way for all persons to coexist as brothers and sisters. African American Christians usually believe that we are all related because we are children of God. We are called to love, honor, and respect one another regardless of race, creed, color, gender, denomination, age, income, neighborhood, sexual proclivity, intelligence, or residence. We are called to build and maintain community.

Racial solidarity is important as a means of securing personhood in the face of persecution. Freedom is connected to responsibility for self and others. One cannot ignore the needs of others. Living these beliefs out on a day-to-day basis is a struggle for many people. At times hatred is met with hatred, violence with violence, and prejudice with prejudice. Reciprocity or mutuality, in an African American context, does not necessarily connote equal exchange. It validates an understanding that in time of need one will be there or be supportive spiritually, financially, emotionally, intellectually, socially, or physically, if at all possible. You may hear "Ann would do the same for us" or "Girl, I know you would be here if you could but you need to keep that job." There are to be no grudges held if someone is unable to reciprocate. Regardless of the law of the land, hierarchical government, church or family structures, or onerous biblical interpretations, African American women are called to live by the ethical presupposition that "We are all Aunt Haggie's children" and we must transmit this information to our children. Black women's belief in the interconnectedness of all humanity is prevalent in their songs, poetry, prose, and autobiography.

If I can Help Somebody

> The music of the Black religious tradition operates on two levels: first, psychologically and emotionally—it locates the people's sense of heritage, their roots, where they are and where they want to go; and secondly, it mobilizes and strengthens the resolve for struggle.[3]

Civil rights activist Reverend Wyatt T. Walker writes that during the Southern Freedom movement gospel music was a vital instrument in the struggle for freedom and dignity. He says that the "psychic healthiness of self expression within the black cultural context" strengthened the resolve of the people and gave them a sense of community in song. The songs carried the oral tradition and the day-to-day experiences of blacks while validating God's presence with them. Women sang and wrote gospel music as an expression of their faith and as messages to others about community, equality, personhood, and mutuality.[4]

The opening words of my grandmother's favorite song "If I can help somebody as I pass along . . ." reverberated throughout the latter years of the Southern Freedom movement. The words are about our duty to pass on information to those who come after us. They speak of our mission to assist in raising the thought and actions of the downtrodden. We are challenged to encourage all people to live as God directs. Finally the song is about our individual responsibility to be in communion with all our sisters and brothers regardless of whom, where, why, or how they are. The song was sung, as requested, at the funeral of Dr. Martin Luther King, Jr.[6]

The lyrics of contemporary gospel music speak of a continued need for an ethic of care. In "Can You Reach My Friend?" Helen Baylor, a recovering addict, seeks God's face on behalf of a person who is feeling abandoned and possibly lost. Part of our human responsibility is to intercede on behalf of both friends and strangers. Baylor alludes to an extensive conversation with a friend who knew about God but who had not felt in full connection for some time. She sings of a request for God to provide the same security for her friend that she felt in her newfound personal spiritual relationship. She sings a prayer for her friend's conversion.[7]

Baylor includes her personal testimony on each album and encourages others to get help in overcoming their dysfunctional or addictive behavior. Her music ministry is based in affirmation of self as a gift of God and our responsibility for the well-being of one another. Witnessing or testifying is one of the pillars of Afro-Christian belief. Whenever possible one is to take the time to tell someone else about God's activity in one's life and give a hopeful word of encouragement. This is particularly true for African American women who often utilize testimony and song as alternatives to preaching.[8]

Babbie Mason and Cindy Sterling convey the theme of social transformation through collective care in their 1993 gospel song "We Can Change the World." The song speaks of care of the stranger, listening to concerns of others, moving self out of the way to try to understand the pain of someone else, and praying for the world. All this, they intone, is a simple act of faith.[9] They write that social change is possible through love of others, touch, following the tenets of Jesus Christ, offering assistance and comfort, and pursuing peace. Additionally, they intone that transformation takes place one person at a time. Realizing that we are all linked yet diverse instills the idea that one should not feel overwhelmed but aware of the possibilities for change, in small steps as well as long strides. Music functions as a connecting thread between people. At times in black worship persons are more attentive to the music than to the sermon. The life instructions, survival information, the wisdom of the ages flows out of the repetition of the lyrics and the melody, which resounds in one's head days, weeks, months, and even years after one first hears the song.

Deep Down in the Soul

African American women poets frequently communicate about interconnectedness of family, church, community, and humanity. Four selected poems reinforce this theme beginning with Margaret Goss Burroughs's "To Soulfolk." Burroughs challenges that while African Americans are relishing Afrocentric or cultural dress, hairstyles, clothing, jewelry, or foods, we must remember that this is only part of the puzzle. Our personhood is determined by our intelligence, love for others, and those who love us—that makes us whole and yields dignity. The essence of *soul* is to honor the value of all persons, regardless of who they are, where they live, how they look, or what they believe. Burroughs writes that "humanity and head and heart" are critical elements of our existence. She challenges the reader to contemplate the true meaning and depth of being *soulfolk*.[10]

Lucille Clifton continues the pride in heritage and love of one another in "listen children." It has the tone of an older woman calling a group of younger people over to let them in on the secret of life. She says that the information must be kept in that secret place we each have for our valuables. Finally, she reminds listeners that we are to tell someone else so that the legacy continues. Clifton reminds us that black children are not to be filled with self-hatred due to pigmentation. Hopelessness, fatigue, and anger are nonproductive. She challenges us to love one another regardless of the situation and circumstances of life. The most important feature of her poem is that it is the obligation of each person to pass on the value of personhood to someone else.[11]

Community and racial solidarity are reinforced through common experience and shared belief. The shame, the fatigue, the anger one might feel from time to time is overcome by the commandment to love God, self, and others. Processing the message may not be immediate. Extended observation may be necessary for the message of responsibility, mutuality, or relationships to be incorporated and passed on.

In "Family Tree," Katie Rushin states that a long line of "uppity, irate black women," who were church people, raised her.[12] Looking back at her "audacious" grandmother, Addie, who raised "umpteen" disciplined children during the Depression and purchased books and place settings for her granddaughter's future, the light slowly breaks. The grandmother gave the granddaughter more than material, transient things. Her legacy was life skills. She taught Katie to reach past the social confines of "Act like a little black girl"; "Don't speak up for yourself"; "Don't draw attention to yourself"; or "Stay in your place." Through precept and example—"being uppity"—the granddaughter learned to stand up for herself and be ready for the future. No excuses for her behavior were necessary. In the poem, she answers her critics. She has become the mirror image of her "Gramom." She was an apt student and nurtured an inner resolve to be her own person.

Elouise Lofton's "Weeksville Women" presents Mother Wit and body language as vehicles for lessons on personhood, responsibility, and solidarity.[13] The transmission of values may take place through the examples or teachings of more than one person. It may be the continuous encounter with one group like Sunday school teachers, all the women in the family, or persons in a class. For some reason someone's actions or words—for better or worse, socially acceptable or not, verbal or nonverbal—stay with you and you may not even realize that they are sharing wisdom. The women in Lofton's poem are "old Black ladies with wise written" not on paper, not in a news report, not in a movie script, not in a work of fiction, but in folds of their facial features. They willingly attempt to transmit values and life experience through eye contact or "reading" the lives of the listeners. They teach God's mysterious ways and recognize that youth are at the beginning of a lifelong learning process.

In the poem a group of women, probably domestics, ride the bus home as a younger person watches and listens. There is amazement at how they remain intact, wise, and knowing—with hints of anger simmering near the surface— "and fan and fan . . . they got so much . . . to be hot about." The women tell the observer that she will experience similar times in life. They may or may not know one another but they are all family because of their culture. Older women have an obligation to give out advice to younger people whether the young want to use it or not. "It's not so much that you fall down, it's what you do when you get up," "Listen, I been where you want to go," "Choose your battles wisely," or "Don't put your business in the street" are community adages for how to maintain one's dignity, redirect anger, and save others from pain.

Do Lord Remember Me?

African American women fulfilled a variety of occupations in order to support their families, churches, and communities. Before integration and the advent of Affirmative Action the majority of them worked as washerwomen, day workers or domestics, cooks, nursemaids, factory workers, farmhands, teachers, and nurses. Many domestics lived in maids' quarters during the week but left on their day off to care for their own families or to meet with other black women to compare the stories of "Miss Ann" or "Mr. John," discuss current events, do church work, or relax in the comfort of their own culture. It was during this period of renewal and regeneration that their humanity and sisterhood was again validated.

Karla F. C. Holloway's short story "Thursday Ladies" is her childhood reflection of what transpired as she and her sister watched a network of domestics/spiritual sisters that gathered at their home each Thursday, the maids' day off. The ritual was the only constant in their Michigan town where few blacks lived.[14] The assembly began at the death of the girls' brother as the women gave support to their mother. They were all many miles and many states away from their own children, but gathered around a sister in mourning. "Their community was well-established. They had ritualized those mornings spent in Mama's kitchen, the evenings on our porch. All of the ladies worked for white families who had come to Michigan to escape the summer heat. . . ."[15] The two girls resented the group but were also in awe of these women who were "out of place in our sophisticated preadolescent vision of the world." They did not understand why their mother would socialize with country women who did not know how to talk.

> They didn't talk like us—me, or Shirl or Mama. They sounded like
> M'dear, our grandmama back in Sedalia. They kissed (when we came

out to grab a biscuit or bacon) like those ladies in M'dear's church. Their voices were soft and their feelings were loud. And Mama smiled more on those summer Thursdays than on any other day.[16]

Each Thursday the girls would position themselves so they could listen to the conversation and make fun of the women at the same time. They had no idea that the women needed a safe haven to express themselves, feel loved, and bond. "Our house was the base for Thursday breakfast, supper, late night talk and a kind of gathering of spirit that I didn't understand then, but respected (or feared or envied) for the strength that was obviously a part of these women's meetings."[17]

Although the mother did not work she understood the pain the women were in, due to her own mother's life as a domestic. She knew that in the sight of the world and as a Christian she was equal to these women and she had to provide a sanctuary for them. These sisters became her extended family each summer. The ridicule of the children stopped one Thursday when Mamie, a woman new to the group and to the North, went to the movies but abruptly returned to use the bathroom. The woman's action overcame the girls' presumed ignorance. The mother set the record straight, making the scene an object lesson.

> "Maybe," Mama said quietly, "maybe in that little country town in Mississippi that's so funny and so foreign to you two, where Mamie works her life away in a home that will never be hers and for a family that will never love her back . . . maybe the bathrooms in the movie houses there say something that hurts her so bad she wishes she couldn't read."[18]

The girls gained a new respect for the Thursday ladies who had sacrificed more than they would ever know. Through community solidarity the women set up a healing place for one another that enabled them to go back and face the world. They were one in spirit and struggle.

A granddaughter's reflection on community support revolves around her grandmother's funeral in Ann Shockley's short story "Funeral."[19] The funeral is a critical ritual in the African American community. It is a time of gathering family, solace, sermon, and song; a time of humor and food. It is a time when the church and community family becomes enmeshed with the immediate family. As eighty-year-old Miss Eliza sat in her rocking chair, selecting scriptures from the "frayed family Bible," deciding on flowers, humming "Just a Closer Walk with Thee," coordinating her burial outfit, and deciding who would sit with Melissa—her only family—Melissa covertly drank away the pain of losing her grandmother.

Miss Eliza had planned ahead paying fifty cents per week to the Black

Brothers Burial Society. She had attended every funeral in town. " 'Goin' to ever'body's. I got no folks livin' I know of 'cept you. If I go to other peoples', they'll come to mine,' Granny used to say."[20] True to her word, all of the town came out to see Miss Eliza's last ride. Her lodge sisters sat up with her body during the wake and the women from the church monitored Melissa's well-being and made sure everything was done to Miss Eliza's specifications.

> That was what they all called her—Miss Eliza—young, old, white folks alike. She had been a fixture in the town like the Confederate soldier in front of the court house. A born and bred fixture claimed by time.[21]

Melissa came to understand that she was not alone—would never be an orphan—due to her grandmother's life of mutuality and responsibility. Miss Eliza's childhood friend Miss Reva became Melissa's othermother. Assuring Melissa that the rain on the day of the funeral meant Miss Eliza was going to heaven, the ritual of sharing community proverbs also continued through Miss Reva.

Respect and reverence for elders is an intrinsic part of African values. Whether one wanted to listen or not, a younger person was to stand and listen to the wisdom of elders. African American women who were viewed as elders in family, church, or community were virtually able to hold monologues of inspired or repetitive teachings. Called Granny, Big Momma, Mother Dear, M'dear, Grandmother, and so on, these women seemed to pack a lifetime of information, social criticism, and faith into one speech.

Terry McMillan writes about a seventy-two-year-old widow who is reflecting on her life. She had no natural-born children but adopted all her boarders. She reads the Bible to soothe her nerves and does not like the solitude of old age. Her critique of the younger generation is that they have less faith, are irresponsible, trust no one, and have limited endurance. Her peers, however, attended church faithfully, stuck together regardless of circumstance, and wanted an education but were barred from schools.

> But like I was saying before I got all off track, some of these young people don't appreciate what they got. And they don't know thangs like we used to. . . . What going to church was, being honest and faithful. Trusting each other. Leaving our front door open. We knew what it was like to starve and get cheated yearly when our crops didn't add up the way we figured. We suffered together, not separately. These youngsters don't know about suffering for any stretch of time.[22]

Contemporary social rhetoric about children having no morals, racial ethnic minorities lacking a work ethic, and a general sense of societal alienation parallels Ma'Dear's evaluation of the generational shift in values. At the same time it reflects the sense of entitlement younger people often possess mainly because many parents want a better life for their children and do not deny them anything they request.

> I ask myself, I say, Ma'Dear, what's wrong with these kids? They can read and write and do arithmetic, finish high school, go to college and get letters behind their names, but every day I hear the neighbors complain that one of they youngsters done dropped out.[23]

She is trying to share her wisdom with someone but due to advanced age and death of her close friends she sits and talks to herself. Her wisdom is lost because she has no one to pass it on to. This is the state of many elders who have little or no contact with youth. Volumes of life-saving information is lost due to elders' isolation and young people's fear of being around older people. African Americans will soon have no "memory" or "remembrance" if the trend continues.

We Are All in This Thing Together

The necessity of value transmission for family, church, or community preservation transcends social or economic level. Grandmothers and other-mothers in each group share insights on social conduct, duty, and reciprocity. As previously stated, age, residential area, distance, belief systems, church attendance, or family structure are not restrictions on who contributes to community solidarity. At times informal discussion groups, meals, parties, hospital visits, telephone calls, and "shop talk" serve as venues for communication of life-adjusting wisdom. African American women form bonds of sisterhood in order to assist one another in living in often hostile environments and precarious relationships. Those trusted sisters—othermothers—are the only persons one can turn to without explanation to understand the struggle to be considered human, of worth, of dignity, or of equal status. The identification of someone that shares your story and recognizes what you need to do before you go where they have already been is crucial to the lives of African American women.

The Women of Brewster Place by Gloria Naylor centers on seven low- to lower-middle-income African American women living in a housing project over a period of years. *Waiting to Exhale* by Terry McMillan follows the lives of four middle- to upper-income African American women living in Phoenix, Arizona. Both works are illustrative of the similarities in pedagogy and values of African American women regardless of income. The major differences are language (dialect or vernacular versus so-called standard English), occupation (unemployed or on public assistance versus entrepreneurship or corporate employment), and social location (projects versus homes and condominiums). In spite of these differences the women all face common social problems—lack of resources, divorce, underemployment, unemployment, unstable relationships, and issues of sexuality. They know that if one is down, all are down; if one rises, all must rise together. Their unity is their strength.[24]

Mattie Michaels is the main character of the Naylor work. She is a "grandmother" figure who reflects on the lives, losses, and transformations of the women living on a dead-end street, Brewster Place. Forced from her home in Rock Vale, Tennessee, after a teenage pregnancy, Mattie uses her life lessons to be the mother, counselor, and sisterfriend of six women. She also takes what she absorbed from Eva Turner—a woman who had had five husbands, seven children, and raised five grandchildren—who without question, but with compassion, took Mattie and her son Basil off the street. Over the years, Mattie, Miss Eva, Basil, and Miss Eva's granddaughter Ciel became a family unit, taking turns caring for the children. Miss Eva accepted no money because she wanted Mattie to learn to save her money and become independent. Miss Eva freely offered advice on child rearing: "Ya know, you can't keep him runnin' away from things that hurt him. Sometimes you just gotta stay there and teach him how to go through the bad and good whatever comes."[25]

Unfortunately, Mattie did not accept this advice. She became overprotective of her son and acquiesced to his every demand. He learned to take what he wanted because his mother would get him out of whatever trouble he was in at the moment. After he was tried for manslaughter and jumped bail, resulting in Mattie losing her house, she understood what Miss Eva told her when Basil was five.

Although she faithfully attended the Canaan Baptist Church, Mattie did not turn away from her friends who did not. She modeled Christian love and forgiveness. Her childhood friend, Etta Mae Johnson, was a free spirit—a prostitute who challenged everyone for her right to participate fully in life. When Etta Mae, consumed with shame, entered a risky relationship with a visiting minister Mattie waited up to console her when Etta Mae was abruptly dropped off in the middle of the night.

> Sometimes being a friend means mastering the art of timing. There is a time for silence. A time to let go and allow people to hurl themselves into their own destiny. And a time to prepare to pick up the pieces when it's all over.[26]

Mattie may have acted out the scriptural passages "To everything there is a season and a time to every purpose under the heaven" (Ecclesiastes 3:1 KJV) and "There is no difference, for all have sinned and fall short of the glory of God" (Romans 3:22*b*-23). In any event, she did not judge her friend but accepted her unconditionally. Although Etta Mae continued her lifestyle she knew who loved her, and tried to change for Mattie's sake. Grandmothers and othermothers know their sisters or children and do not need many words to convince them of a particular point. Their life experience is a "walking sermon." Lucielia (Ciel) Turner, Miss Eva's granddaughter, lived at Brewster Place as a young adult and reestablished an othermother-daughter relationship with Mattie. "It was rare that Mattie ever spoke more than two sentences to anybody about anything. She didn't have to. She chose her words with the grinding precision of a diamond cutter's drill."[27]

The blend of the austerity and body language of grandmothers and othermothers is usually sufficient for instilling the desire for behavior modification. One has the feeling that he or she has let down or disappointed the grandmother or othermother. This is different from guilt. This is a recognition of denying the sacrifices made on one's behalf and the time spent in trying to provide for a better life. The sense of one person's behavior affecting the perceptions about the entire community is prevalent in the African American context.

Mattie was the community conduct monitor. But she was not intrusive. Her demeanor set the standard for the other women. Cora Lee, the mother of seven children, knew what the other women thought about her. She was caught up in a cycle of babies, welfare, television, and lack of vision. But she liked Mattie, who softly entreated her to stop having children. Mattie was not the busybody that Sophie was. Sophie, close to Mattie's age, was always looking in windows, examining trash, proudly voicing her prejudices, and being contentious all the while quoting the Bible. Mattie was like a protector for Cora Lee. "She sincerely liked Miss Mattie because unlike the others, Mattie never found the time to do jury duty on other people's lives."[28]

Ciel also valued Mattie's discretion and fortitude. Ciel became involved in a tumultuous relationship and eventually had a daughter. During one of many heated reconciliations she left her daughter unattended and the baby was electrocuted. Ciel lost her will to live but Mattie rocked her back to health, laying on hands of life.

> And she rocked her back, back into the womb, to the nadir of her hurt and they found it—a slight silver splinter, embedded just below the surface of skin. . . . And Ciel lay down and cried. But Mattie knew the tears would end. And she would sleep. And morning would come.[29]

During times of sorrow, loss, or grief in the African American Christian community the most frequently quoted scripture is "Weeping may remain for a night, but rejoicing comes in the morning" (Psalm 30:5b). This is understood to mean that everyone will go through "the valley of the shadow of death" but God promises that the light will come, the pain will subside, and life will go on. Mattie remembered the times she wanted to give up but her othermother, Miss Eva, encouraged her not to give up. This became Mattie's dream and lesson for all of the women on Brewster Place.[30]

Terry McMillan wrote a controversial book about how four women support, love, and care for one another in an area of the country with relatively few African Americans, the Southwest. Several male critics view the book as an indictment of African American males because of McMillan's characterization of types of men whom the women are in and out of relationships with throughout the book. I selected this book because it closely mirrors my own experience as an upwardly mobile, educated African American woman who received sisterhood/othermother support and guidance from five black women. They, like me, were struggling with relationships with men, family, church, society, and self. Like the women in McMillan's book, we had to learn to depend on rather than become dependent on one another.

The main character in the book is Savannah Jackson, a thirty-five-year-old, single, resilient, career woman working in television production. Bernadine Harris is a thirty-six-year-old with two children, facing a divorce after eleven years of putting off her career for the sake of her lawyer husband's dreams. Her life is thrown into financial and emotional upheaval when her husband leaves her for a younger, white woman. Robin Stokes is in her late twenties, a secretary, responsible for her ill parents and constantly entering bad relationships. Gloria Matthews is thirty-eight-years-old, a baptized Catholic, with a teenage son, owns her own beauty salon, and seeks comfort and solace in God. Each finds time to mentor the others and work in the community through an organization called "Black Women on the Move," and all are waiting for a solid relationship. The wordplay of the title is that each of them is holding her breath until that relationship happens. How they wait, who they wait for, and what they do with the support of the others is the central theme of the book.[31]

The reason women seek out othermothers is a recurring theme in this novel. Just as in *The Women of Brewster Place,* the women seek love and support. They need to know that some sister knows what they are going through—struggles, promotions, successes, defeats, loss of love, confusion, ecstasy, poor health, child care, and loneliness. These othermothers let them act out—through cursing, tears, laughter, hostility, music, dance, prayer, or silence. They also counsel with tough love—telling one another what they need to know, not what they want to hear. Due to income, educational level, and access to resources this group's language and location is vastly different from the women in the Naylor book. However, the result is the same: they learn to love themselves and share with others. After Bernadine torched her husband's car, sold all his possessions for pennies at a yard sale, and attacked his girlfriend, she reflects on who would most likely understand her actions. Choosing who will teach or attempt to transform one's behavior is very important in sisterhood networks.

> Bernadine loved Gloria, and Robin too, but Savannah was the one person who would understand how she was feeling. She wouldn't have to apologize for it. She was one of those glass-is-half-full people.[32]

An othermother does not necessarily have to agree with the action, but accepts the perpetrator with love and accepts their right to be angry. She then finds the appropriate place and means to discuss the difficulty and direct the person to more positive actions without being demeaning. Othermother sayings such as "It's all right to be angry but what are you going to do with the anger?" or "People are seldom mad about what they say they're mad about" or "Don't let them pull you down into the gutter with them" or "You don't need to carry anyone's baggage but your own" validate one's anger and try to focus on discovering why the event took place and how to transform it into a learning experience. These sayings are used to alleviate the "Oh, poor me" syndrome or "victim" tag of "Why did I let this happen to me?" or "I can't do anything right" or "Nobody loves me." These statements become convenient tools for staying mired in the problem. The othermothers seek to empower the person to own who they are, affirm their own personhood, and be responsible for their actions.

When Robin doesn't want to hear advice she listens out of respect for the age of the other women but simply makes her own decisions. The results are usually negative. Throughout the piece she rebels against even her own better judgment and suffers for it. At the end she demonstrates little transformation and continues to chart her own course in most things.

> We fight like sisters, but I don't know what I'd do without them. When my mother was in the hospital Bernadine and Gloria were right there. And when we found out that Daddy had Alzheimer's, my mother asked me when I could pay her back the three thousand dollars because they'd be needing that money real soon. Of course I didn't know when I'd have it, so Bernadine just wrote me a check and told me to forget about it.[33]

Regardless of Robin's acceptance or rejection of the advice of the older women they support her emotionally, spiritually, and economically. They are their sister's keeper. The fact that they did not work out a payment plan for the money is support for the cultural "You'd do the same for me." Bernadine did not try to buy Robin's friendship or manipulate her life, but merely helped somebody who was in need.

A contemporary issue among African American women is how to connect with a community that sometimes is suspicious of their intentions. Do they want to give back to the community out of guilt? Do they think poor women are stupid? Are they ashamed of their sisters like the ones living on Brewster Place? Why must there always be an agenda to come together as sisters, to help one another? Thinking of the endless meetings to set agendas, Savannah decries networking:

> She hated the whole notion. It was as if black folks couldn't get together and have a good time anymore unless they were in a position to do something for each other. Whatever happened to good old-fashioned fun?[34]

These middle-income black women had taken on the corporate organization mind-set. Everything was production oriented and there was no place on the agenda for people to be in community. Historically the gathering of the people in the African American community was a time for renewed friendships, encouragement. The idea that business would be taken care of at the right time has been lost in the name of the "cost of my time." The passion and compassion of relationships has been sanitized and made emotionless.

Savannah is a community activist whose fear is that apathy would continue the decline of the community. She chairs committees in the Black Women on the Move, the black women's sisterhood in Phoenix. The organization programs include Black Family Survival Project, Sister's Nite Out, financial planning, substance abuse, maturity and aging, single parenting, mental and physical health, and youth mentoring. Each of these programs is actually replicated in cities throughout the United States.[35]

These four women exhibit strong bonds of friendship. When Bernadine finally receives a divorce settlement of close to one million dollars she immediately decides she will share it with her friends. The women supported her through the years and she feels that they deserve it as much as she does. When Gloria has a heart attack, having ignored the women's advice to lose weight, she still wakes up to a room filled with sisters who love her regardless of her size. "I think we're all responsible for her," Bernadine says, "she's our sister. Please tell us she's going to be alright."[36]

The advice is presented in many forms. One can choose to use it or ignore it. The teacher cannot force her wisdom on her student. In both novels women chose to follow or adhere to community value systems. Some experienced tragedy while others experienced transformation. The use of the values was open-ended. In transmission of values one may not use the insight for years, until a situation presents itself, a flashback brings the teaching to light, and it is translated into the current event. One may try to comply with the mandate but be distracted, misunderstand the intent, refuse to believe he or she is wrong, or lack willpower and resources. The important thing is that the one transmitting the information does not give up on the student. Savannah and Mattie did not write off anyone. They also understood that they were still in process of becoming. "We are all Aunt Haggie's children" and all make mistakes and get second chances. There is always hope that a change will come, but it cannot be relegated to a calendar, clock, or agenda item. Black women's fiction inspires and teaches about life. Black women's nonfiction is the essence of lived experience of victory over adversity.

I Can Do All Things

On January 9, 1961, Charlayne Hunter-Gault became the first African American student admitted to the University of Georgia.[37] Throughout her autobiography the journalist refers to the grandmothers and othermothers who instilled in her a sense of community, race, equality, responsibility, and mutuality that enabled her to withstand the taunts and stress of integration and helped her become the person she is today.

Her paternal grandmother, Momma Hunter, was an African Methodist Episcopal pastor's wife and was described as "saintly." She quoted scripture, especially her favorite, Psalm 23. She prayed every day at noon, and fasted and prayed each Friday. She was seen as more religious than her husband. Momma Hunter was also a teacher in her own right, and had special ideas about how children of the preacher should conduct themselves. "Never mistreat anybody," she would say, "no matter how nasty they might be to you. They might be the very ones who are feeding you. We have to live from the people, and you have to show them your gratitude."[38]

She taught Charlayne by example and discussion. Her words are often heard as, "Don't burn down your bridges," "The same people you meet on the way up you will meet on the way down," "You did not pull yourself up by your own bootstraps," "Don't cut off your nose to spite your face," or "We are standing on the shoulders of all who came before us." The moral is that someone else sacrifices for us to live, you may need that person later, and everyone in this life is important. Hunter-Gault says that she called up her grandmother's recitation of Psalm 23 when she walked through the angry white crowds at the University of Georgia as they hurled racial epithets and death threats at her. Her lessons by Sunday school teachers at St. Paul A.M.E. and St. Phillip's A.M.E. in Georgia, as well as teachings in the Catholic Church (she converted as a teenager), served as armor as she engaged social oppression.

Most of her life was spent living with her mother, maternal grandmother, and brothers. Her father was absent because he was a military chaplain and A.M.E. itinerant pastor. This grandmother had also been an A.M.E. pastor's wife but upon his death was ordered out of the parsonage. She affiliated with Bethlehem Baptist Church. She was an organizer of a burial society, club president, and speaker. She vowed not to be without or have to depend on anyone for anything. She never criticized anyone. She allowed Charlayne to help her in the kitchen and travel with her. Hunter-Gault's grandmother and mother shared friends. She learned to appreciate the company of older people and learned a tremendous amount from listening to their conversations in a time when children were to be seen but not heard. Everyone called her grandmother "Mis' Frank," though she and her daughter "didn't socialize a lot, minding their own and not other people's business, unless somebody got sick or needed help."[39]

Her grandmother was not intimidated by anyone and was full of curiosity. She set her mind to something and did it. There were times, however, when the grandmother's advice did not help Charlayne's quest for selfhood. Because of the diversity of color in the black community and the racially loaded adage "If you're white you're right, if you're yellow you're mellow, if you're brown stick around and if you're black get back," Charlayne, like many others, had to fight to prove her worth in spite of her light skin. Part of the community suicide that occurs is that the image of black skin as worthless and the image of light skin as close enough to white to be privileged pits blacks against one another for approval by whites. Charlayne was the focus of the backlash of color-struckness. She had to fight on the way to school for many reasons. Her skin color was the most frequent target. "I tried to summon the words my grandmother had taught me: 'Sticks and stones may break my bones, but words will never hurt me.' But it was small consolation."[40]

This saying meant a lot to the grandmother who no doubt heard her own mother say that one must ignore ignorance or words. The reality of communication is that words have power and at times hurt more than physical contact. Words last longer and may be resurrected when another situation rises. Charlayne had to learn to separate her own reality from the power of the word.

Othermothers played a critical role in Hunter-Gault's life. In her account of her mother sending her to the peach tree to select a switch for a spanking when she misbehaved in church, Hunter-Gault also relates the fact that the entire neighborhood, church, and school could use the same tactic without parental interference if they observed her actions in her parent's absence. "You know your mother would not like that," "Why you acting like you don't have parents," "Child I've known you since you was a baby, you like one of my own children, now come here" preceded the punishment, whether in the form of a spanking or a lecture. The entire neighborhood was responsible for each child. "In fact, if one of their parents 'caught you wrong,' it was perfectly acceptable, if not desirable, that they administer their own punishment on the spot."[41]

This reinforces the value of there being no orphans in the community. The behavior of one affected the status of everyone. In contemporary society adherence to legislation, changing judicial systems, and separation of black enclaves have decreased this model's effectiveness. The spanking of children was not viewed as child abuse but chastisement that would lead to the child being responsible for his or her own behavior. In some ways this model is being resurrected in black church youth programs. Any member of the church can dialogue with any youth member, for there is an understanding that each child belongs to the church family. No one can save black children from destruction except the black family, church, and community.

Teachers were a portentous component in Hunter-Gault's psychological, social, spiritual, and political formation. Her third grade teacher, Miss Sara Francis Thompson Hardiman, exemplified black teachers who worked with meager supplies, tutored before and after school, and attended school constantly in order for black children to receive the best education possible.

> They found out, after schools were desegregated and they had more access to information, that many of them were better qualified than the white teachers. . . . "They wanted to teach" was how Miss Sara Francis put it. "It was like a mission. They felt they had to see that their children learned."[42]

The belief that one can do the best with little is grounded in biblical stories such as taking a little meal, a little oil, or two mites, and making much out of it. The crucial words "that their children learned" implies an understood ownership of each child. The teachers were just as much mothers and fathers of the children in their care as were their natural parents. The idea that a black student is merely a statistic, quota, or problem was unheard of during this time. The current idea that a black child from a single-parent family is "at risk" and will automatically fail was absurd. Everyone had mothers and fathers and as long as one member of the community lived the child would live also. Hunter-Gault's father lived all over the world but she had her mother, grandmother, church, school, and neighborhood to help raise her.

Hunter-Gault's family was steeped in church activities. In Sunday school she memorized Bible verses, studied play lines, and "They taught us to believe in ourselves." Miss Sally Benton at St. Paul A.M.E. Church in Covington, Georgia, was depicted as stern in mannerisms and dress. She had no time to play. She worked with youth in the missionary societies, Sunday school, vacation Bible school, and conventions. She taught the youth deportment by discussions, lectures, and modeling. They traveled with her, staying in the homes of people across the South because of unequal access to public accommodations. Because of her commitment to them, they did not want to let her down.[43] Othermothers, at times, do not need to say anything. Through contact with them their expectations are understood. They know what one is capable of and will hold her or him to that standard. A look, body movement, or whispered vocalization tells the young person if the othermother is pleased or not. Even in the absence of these othermothers one remembers what they conveyed.

Mrs. Victoria Sutton was a "no-nonsense teacher from the old school, who believed in hard work, homework, and discipline." Students found her stern but she inspired confidence within them. Miss Elsie Foster Evans was protective and tried to channel her students to places where they could avoid racism.[44] Attorney Constance Baker Motely of the National Association for the Advancement of Colored People (NAACP) was a different sort of teacher. During litigation on the constitutionality of Hunter-Gault's barring from the University of Georgia, Baker Motely seemingly ignored her. Her focus was on the trial. Charlayne observed her courage, skill, and power, and wished to be closer to her. During a break in the trial they sat together in a car and as fatigue hit both of them Baker Motely gently hugged Hunter-Gault to let her know that everything would work out.[45] Othermothers are not monolithic. Something can be learned from persons with different belief systems, attitudes, sentiments, or forbearance.

Finally, during her senior year in high school and during college Hunter-Gault joined an African American sorority whose members also ministered to her during the riotous days at the University of Georgia. Pat Ryder and Gwen Walker were termed "urban sophisticates with Southern charm." Hunter-Gault wished to emulate their soft-spoken, clear-headed, self-possessed, strong, and mentally healthy demeanor. She said that her upbringing, her training in the Catholic high school, her paternal grandmother's scriptures, and the oath of members of her sorority prepared her for what she had to face in Georgia as she demanded equal treatment before the law.

> I will not shrink from undertaking what seems wise and good because hardships or obstacles confront me; but striving to preserve a calm mind with a courageous spirit, barring bitterness from my heart, I will strive all the more earnestly to reach the goal.[46]

Hunter-Gault remained intact during the extensive process of the struggle for integration due to the influence of a variety of grandmothers and othermothers. Her spirituality, personhood, racial bonding, and community support enabled her to understand that she was doing for others what the women in her life had done for her.

"We are all Aunt Haggie's children" and no law or misappropriation of scripture removes that idea from the minds of African American women. The Constitution of the United States held that a black man was three fifths of a person but did not entertain the idea that black women even existed. In the literature of African American women, however, the vitality of women's lives in terms of caring for all peoples is evident. An ethic of care and compassion for the whole Body of Christ is essential to the nature of African American women's beliefs. The universality of humanity is foundational to womanist theology and ethics. This chapter has briefly shown how these beliefs are lived out. The next chapter focuses on how African American grandmothers and othermothers transmit the ethical presupposition "Trouble don't last always," which is a continuation of "God don't like ugly" and "We are all Aunt Haggie's children." Although the presuppositions are divided for analysis in the book, they are taught concurrently in the African American context.

6

FAITH-FILLED PERSEVERANCE

Trouble Don't Last Always

The LORD is my light and my salvation; whom shall I fear? the LORD is the strength of my life; of whom shall I be afraid? . . . Wait on the LORD: be of good courage, and he shall strengthen thine heart: wait, I say, on the LORD. (Psalm 27:1,14 KJV)

We shall overcome, We shall overcome, We shall overcome someday. Oh, If in our hearts we do believe, We shall overcome someday. (Traditional)

These scriptural undergirdings for the belief that "Trouble don't last always" are frequently recited and reinforced in black churches. The understanding that one must endure with patience and not submit to the forces of trouble or evil is interpreted in the full reading of Psalm 27. God is able to redeem, reconcile, regenerate, and revive us regardless of the action of enemies, family, or friends. The lyrics of the well-known song "We Shall Overcome" were used to encourage persons in the jaws of racism and classism, especially during the Southern Freedom movement and succeeding struggles for freedom around the world. The intent of the song is that whatever one is facing will pass if one perseveres—"If we just hold out 'til tomorrow, if we just keep the faith through the night, if we just hold out 'til tomorrow, everything will be all right."

This chapter will review eleven gospel songs, seven poems, two short stories, three novels, and one autobiography as illustrations of the intergenerational transmission of the presupposition "Trouble don't last always" by African American grandmothers and othermothers. In order to hold out, to overcome, to keep the faith, to survive, one needs a strong, spiritually-based support system. The mothers, grandmothers, and othermothers of the faith provide lessons in perseverance through conversations, chastisement, action, stories, and years of trial and error. Perseverance is a learned skill and most students do not fully appreciate the lessons until they have gone through years of trial, error, and tests of faith. To learn faith-filled perseverance one must exercise an ethic of care and compassion for self and others to ensure that all may be free. One is empathetic, instructive, attentive, affirming, and encouraging as he or she assists others in learning how to take a stand, and keep standing, in spite of often harsh circumstances. Forgiveness of self and others is crucial because one must also relinquish persistent anger and mistrust in order to live a healthy, free life. The constant replaying of old tapes and revictimization will defeat the beauty of liberation. If old wounds are allowed to continue to fester, healing cannot occur. The caregiver must teach new ways of honoring the pain, yet reach forward to new opportunities for change.

The receiver of the information must comprehend that she or he is neither the first nor the last to endure troubles and trials. There are others whose witness and lives reveal how to endure and thrive within oppressive systems. Another scriptural reinforcement is "Therefore, since we are surrounded by such a great cloud of witnesses, let us throw off everything that hinders and the sin that so easily entangles, and let us run with perseverance the race marked out for us" (Hebrews 12:1). The witnesses are the ancestors, the elders, and the martyrs of the faith and the race—DuBois, Tubman, Douglas, Malcolm, King, Mama, Granddaddy, Grandmama, and Daddy—the ordinary and the famous. Constant testimony of the African American family, church, and community about the possibilities of overcoming adversity is necessary for the survival of the whole people. The community understanding that "Into each life some rain must fall" or "We may be down but we will not be down always" is a portion of the hope.

Another is the core belief that the *kerygma,* or proclamation of the life, death, resurrection, and return Parousia of Jesus, is the pattern for the majority of African Americans confronting and surmounting even death for the sake of justice for all persons. If no one tells the stories, if the people are ashamed of their situation, if the leaders remain accepting of and apathetic about any form of subjugation, or if the group constantly complains about the hopelessness of life, the ones facing new difficulties have no way to address the issues or formulate a solution. Telling a child that "Trouble don't last always" says that there is always hope for transformation of self or the situation. This does not necessarily mean the end to the trouble, but it means that God is ever-present even in the midst of the problem and will sustain you as you pass through the storm.

Nobody But Jesus

In the African American Christian worldview the person who sustains one during trials and difficulties is Jesus Christ. The testimony of how one made it through a dangerous situation, received a raise, completed some task, or heard good news is "Nobody but the Lord." This means that the respondent does not take credit for any event, any situation, or any victory—the victory came from God.

In the previous discussion of African American theology and ethics Jesus is depicted as both liberator and cosufferer. God is all-knowing (omniscient), all-powerful (omnipotent), and all-present (omnipresent). It is because of the "everywhereness" of God that African American gospel singers write and sing songs about a God who "knows all about our troubles." This God stands with one in "sunshine and rain, sickness and pain." The God of Mahalia Jackson, Rosetta Thorpe, Cassietta George, Albertina Walker, Inez Andrews, Roberta Martin, and Beatrice Brown, to name a few, traveled around the country with them and comforted them when they were turned away from hotels, had to improvise for roadside restroom facilities, and were called all kinds of names by people in power. The God of "somehow"—ultimate victory—was sung about in homes, bars, fields, concert halls, churches, on jobs, and outdoors as a witness of faith in the midst of trouble. The improvisational style and emotionalism of black gospel music affords generation upon generation the opportunity to rearrange songs and add their own particular testimony to the story of resurrection and salvation.[1]

> He's worthy, God's worthy! Almighty Creator! Alpha, Omega, Beginning and the End. Holy, holy Lord God Almighty which was and is and is to come. Blessings and glory, wisdom and power, God of my Rock, in Him will I trust! My Strong Tower and my refuge. Savior, Deliverer and soon coming King.[2]

Gospel music depicts agreed upon attributes of God as the champion of life, the hope of the oppressed, the only one deserving praise, and the only one to bring one through "many dangers, toils, and snares."

Recognition of the need for the power, presence, and purpose of God in human life is evident in work by Willie Mae Ford Smith. One of the pioneers in gospel music, Smith speaks of who God is in "He'll Fight Your Battles.[3] She says that when there are problems in her home she crosses her arms, cries, and looks at the sky. In the black church tradition, she looks to the hills to find her help, meaning that she looks to God. She says she believes that God will hear her and answer her concerns. There is a belief that God knows all about us and therefore is aware of our needs before we request God's help. Smith articulates her early religious instruction about God and God's willingness to be her refuge. She says, "I can call Him when I please and He always sends me ease." She has an assurance that regardless of the trouble, God will provide the solution. Her relationship with God is one of intimacy and trust. She speaks with God on a face-to-face, anytime, anyplace, first-name basis. She concludes the song with "He'll fight your battles if you just keep still," meaning if you trust in God and follow God's instructions rather than a poorly devised human reaction, victory is assured. This may be difficult for some scholars to fathom: in the black church one seeks God's face or prays before beginning anything—eating, job, protest, preaching, or singing.

God protects and blesses us in spite of ourselves. Belief in God's grace and mercy or unmerited love is evident throughout gospel music. God's care and compassion serve as a model for humans. Albertina Walker in "See How the Lord Has Kept Me," presents a picture of a God who heals and saves even when we do not deserve that gift.[4] This is due to God's forgiveness. Forgiveness is taught through songs about human behavior and God's love. God forgives individual misdoing and group actions. Following God's pattern we are challenged to do likewise. The scripture about forgiveness most often quoted is Jesus' response to Peter's inquiry about how often one is to forgive—"Jesus answered, 'I tell you, not seven times, but seventy-seven times'" (Matthew 18:22). We are not to keep track of forgiveness. We are simply to forgive with no strings attached. Regardless of what others do, we are called to forgive as God forgives us. We realize that even living in God's forgiveness, "I know I don't serve Him just like I should," we sometimes fall short. God affords us another opportunity to live in the fullness of his grace and mercy. Walker says that even during sickness she realized that she was healed in order to tell someone about God's goodness.

Inez Andrews writes in "Make It In" of a God who is wise in love and deep in grace, who is "so high you can't get over Him, so low you can't get under Him, so wide you can't get around Him."[5] Andrews's image of God is one of an insurmountable, unsurpassable deity who is eternally wise and present. She says that if we live right God will allow us to enter heaven after all our difficulty on earth. The lyrics imply an action or some sort of responsibility on the individual's part—"live right" in order to be delivered from troubles.

Cassietta George concurs in "To Whom Shall I Turn?"[6] The assurance of God's liberation and the uncertainty of human assistance is reinforced in her lyrics. She says that there will be obstructions along the way. Confusion and disappointment are inevitable, but yielding herself to God is the relief she requires. "He'll deliver my soul from trouble and strife" is the basis of her testimony. There is an acknowledgment that she might resist the rescue or become confused about a decision, but God is able to save her regardless. Jesus is referred to as the only source of hope and life—not family, not friends, not enemies, not community, not church—who is able to create or give life. She has evidently already experienced God's blessing and passes on her belief.

Gloria Griffin sings of gratitude and the state of life without God. She penned, "What would my life be without Him, It would be very dark and grim." She also compares God's actions and human action.

> When my friends and my foes turn against me
> And it seems I'm at the end of the road
> There's a still soft voice saying within me
> There is someone, someone greater who's carrying the load.
> When my way gets as dark as the midnight
> And my body is all racked with pain
> Christ appears with His holy light
> And by faith, faith and grace I'm whole again.[7]

Loneliness, health problems, hopelessness, and confusion are all addressed by God's presence and care. It is because of a close relationship with the Lord that Inez Andrews says that God redeems us. "Jesus is a friend who sticks closer than a brother" is repeatedly used to compare the intimacy of God with that possible between humans. Andrews says in "You Don't Know Me Like the Lord" that others may listen to the way she talks, watch the way she walks, and try to see her faults, but that no one knows her like the Lord does. God knows all our feelings and faults, and still loves us.[8]

These images are beneficial in telling children who they are to fear, who they are to respect, who has control of their lives, and who is always with them whatever they encounter. Coupled with biblical teachings the music grounds their beliefs, due particularly to the frequent repetition of the songs. We are to maintain our faith in the midst of persecution realizing that our cosufferer is taking on the pain with us.

> If it had not been for the Lord on my side, tell me where would I be?
> He kept my enemies away; He let the sun shine through the cloudy day.
> He rocked me in the cradle of His arm when He knew I had been
>   battered and scorned.[9]

Dorothy Love Coates testifies to the black church belief in the reality of Satan and the solution of threats of spiritual death. She says that we are confronted daily with adversaries, and enemies strive unceasingly to impede spiritual growth. Plots for the entrapment of Christians result in the demise of the wrongdoer. In "(I'm Holding On) I Won't Let Go of My Faith," Coates says that God impregnates us with a resolve that no one can touch. She writes, "It's wrapped in my soul and the world can't harm me."[10] This knowledge solidifies her faith in God.

These songs are about the justice of God. They call not for human retribution but for God's action in our lives. Survival or perseverance is not based solely on human skills but on God's grace. The ultimate proof of God's help for and love, forgiveness, and equality of faithful persons is the images of our welcome, our soul's dwelling in heaven.

All problems, all trouble, all strife will be over. Critics of African American religion usually view this as "pie-in-the-sky" religion. In the black church and community, however, it means that bearing one's cross on earth results in a crown in heaven, and that everyone has burdens and problems. The belief that "There's a cross for everyone and there's a cross for me" is interpreted as everyone suffers at some time. Suffering due to our choices, deterioration of society, and the need for individual repentance is an expectation of a Christian's life. This is patterned after Jesus' life, death, and resurrection. We are called to be "Christ-like" and suffer because of forces that are opposed to Christian principles. Regardless of trials one must "keep the faith, fight the good fight, walk the walk, and talk the talk." God has a reason for everything that happens in our lives. We are to carry on despite circumstances, forgive self and others, and accept the promise of ultimate reward for our striving for freedom.

These gospel-singing othermothers continue to spread their spiritual beliefs and values through music. Barred from faith expression through an ordained, preaching ministry, they chose the musicality of African American culture to tell "thus saith the Lord." They evangelized the black family, church, and community through testimonial lyrics representative of their individual and collective faith journeys. They directed children's formulation of faith by singing of their God of hope in struggle and liberation from hardship.

Keep Your Hand on the Plow—Hold on

African American women's poetry is permeated with statements of faith, hope, honor, and determination evident in the life experiences of the poets and persons they have observed, known, or learned from along the way. The seven selected poems for this section speak of afflictions imparted by others, God's intercession, and the overcoming of the difficulty by bold, loving, caring, and sacrificial actions by grandmothers and othermothers. All encourage or impart the need to maintain one's faith despite the circumstance because, "If you hold out I know deliverance surely will come." Wisdom contained in poems is not shared as often as gospel music but is accessible through school assignments, small group discussion of poetry collections, reading groups, black history seminars, and individual partiality to specific poets.

Maya Angelou is one such poet who writes about black life experiences from slavery to contemporary times. She remembers her grandmother humming and singing the gospel song "I Shall Not Be Moved" but changing the last word to "removed." Often lyrics are modified to fit the singer's particular existential dilemma. Sometimes the singer does not remember the lyrics but makes up ones that fit her life's experience. Angelou's grandmother may have felt that she had been displaced once (from Africa) and would not be moved again, hence "removed." This inspired Angelou to write the poem "Our Grandmothers" about the horrors of oppression yet the determination to ensure the survival and growth of children generations to come. Set during slavery, the poem is still instructive today due to the challenges, charges, and changes in black family life and the persistence of racism.[11]

Angelou depicts a mother fleeing enslavement, pushing her children to keep moving with each step toward freedom, reminding them that they will be killed "unless you match my heart and words saying 'I Shall Not Be

Moved.' " In spite of the name-calling and abuse this mother remains sure of her humanity. "She said, 'But my description cannot fit your tongue for I had a certain way of being in the world.' " The poem imparts the reality for many African American women today that at times there is no one to assist with or shield children and teach them about responsibility. The need for community-building to share in the responsibility and protection of all children is not new. Each person must give time to help someone else make it in the world. Angelou writes, "When you learn, teach. When you get, give." This is an ethic of care and compassion as well as mutuality. In the black community the saying "Each one teach one" means that any knowledge acquired is for the good of all, not a possession to be selfishly hoarded or lorded over others. The reality is that someone died or faced obstacles for the next one to have a small measure of freedom. The presence of God is not always evident—"When she appeared at the Temple door, no sign welcomed Black Grandmother, Enter here"—but one must keep trying. Ultimately there will be victory over subjugating powers. God's Spirit envelops the woman in the poem and allows her space to be human in spite of the circumstances.

> The Holy Spirit upon my left leads my
> feet without ceasing into the camp of the
> righteous and into the tents of the free . . .
> Centered on the world's stage,
> she sings to her loves and beloveds,
> to her foes and detractors:
> However I am perceived and deceived
> however my ignorance and conceits
> lay aside your fears that I will be undone,
> for I shall not be moved.[12]

The ancestors, grandmothers, and othermothers serve as models of how to hold on and maintain a sense of dignity. In the midst of the swirling problems of life there are prospects for victory. Clearly victory does not necessarily mean the absence of difficulty but finding a place to stand that the individual determines is for him or her, not what someone else dictates.

In another collection of poems Angelou uses self-reflection to tell how to protect one's life and honor in spite of what others do. The sixty-year-old woman's voice in the poem "When I Think About Myself" tells of how even children call her "girl." She must answer with "Yes, ma'am" just to keep her job. She finds irony in the fact that as old as she is, she has learned to bend but not break in order to survive.[13]

Many people make decisions to work in demeaning, abusive situations for the sake of earning a living. Working in these conditions does not necessarily mean one has no self-esteem or does not care about oneself. The first line of defense is the understanding that one must earn money in order for children to be cared for and live. The "too proud to bend, too poor to break" passage is the most telling information. Biblical teachings of putting on "the whole armor" of God (Ephesians 6) or the community saying of "They can kill your body but not your soul" are used as defense mechanisms as one prepares to engage an often hostile world.

As with the women in this poem, there is a belief that silence does not mean weakness and may actually prove strength because one does not give information to the enemy—"What they don't know will not hurt me." Black children who do not speak up in social situations or classes are often characterized as insolent or stupid. The reality is that they may close down as a protective device in situations that are uncomfortable or foreign. Often those who are quiet around other racial-ethnic groups are quite vocal around other African Americans. Other children are verbal and at times speak loudly and freely. They are seen as gregarious but may be the most ill at ease, nervously talking around other groups. Still others see no barriers to their self-imposed social status and seem always to be on top regardless of circumstances.

> Life?
> 'Course I'll live it.
> Let me have breath,
> Just to my death,
> And I'll live it.
> Failure?
> I'm not ashamed to tell it,
> I never learned to spell it.
> Not Failure.[14]

Angelou's "Call Letters: Mrs. V. B." presents a woman who knows who she is and will live life without outside restrictions. She speaks boldly about her life, loves, and abilities and apparently freely pursues them. This is a characterization of an othermother who challenges anyone to keep her down, tell her when to speak or how to subsist because "all things are possible."

Lucille Clifton presents another type of othermother in "Miss Rosie." This poem is about an old woman who has physically and spiritually deteriorated over the years, but through her life another woman learns to live. Observing the lives, the struggles, and the victories of other black women provides a vital sense of self for other black women. It is in living above the circumstances, sometimes the worst for wear, sometimes standing tall in the midst of a valley, that we learn to live. The reports of the misfortune of others, of the harsh lifestyles, the results of abuse of self and others, or of unrequited bitterness are usually more persuasive than reports of victories or transitory instances of good things. Evidently the bitterness and pain of Miss Rosie let the unnamed observer know that life is hard and not everyone survives intact. The observer is moved to honor the life of one who may have been overlooked by others. Because of their spiritual connectedness, the observer comes to recognize Miss Rosie's inner reserve even through her outer shell of surrender.[15]

Instilling a sense of purpose, hope, success, and impending liberation may come from the way in which grandmothers and othermothers care for children. Carol Freeman talks about her grandmother early one Christmas morning "sewing a new button on my last year rag doll" as modeling love without materialism.[16] Small kindnesses meant more than a new doll that the family obviously could not afford. Providing a sense of security and love through touch, the manner of play, preparation of favorite foods, making or altering clothing, spending time with younger persons, behavior at church and home, or hearing accounts of the grandmother's childhood is common in African American families, churches, and communities. The insularity of the community is necessary for growth of strong children. The children must be nurtured in a loving environment before they enter the larger world.

Carole C. Gregory describes "The Greater Friendship Baptist Church" where a church picnic provides calm in the midst of a storm. The sale of homemade ice cream and "fried chicken, potato salad, and fresh greens to buy new choir robes" is the counterbalance to "fathers getting fired so white men can work for their families." The vivid depiction of extended family life, such as grandmothers with switches correcting running children, is underscored by the love as the church family celebrates. In the midst of all the problems there is hope that miracles still occur and that the children will fare better than the adults.[17]

Transmitted values do not always result in positive life changes or sustained hope. Alice Walker converses with her grandmother in "Talking to My Grandmother Who Died Poor (while hearing Richard Nixon declare 'I am not a crook')."[18] Walker writes of the inequities of society based on status and heritage. She seeks her own dream and wonders what her grandmother would think about her not living up to expectations. In spite of her grandmother's paradigm on how to persevere, the granddaughter obviously believes that she does not have the strength yet to live, strive for, or exceed what her grandmother accomplished in life. The poem exhibits a sense of despair that young people often face. Some do not receive enough information on how to engage evil, confront political obstacles, or get around institutional subjugation. Others do not know how to transfer learned information to different situations. Some want material things too fast and do not consider the price paid for their access to goods and services. Some simply do not possess the stamina needed to live in American society. It may take a number of months or years for values, life lessons, or courage to surface and be utilized.

The grandmother depicted in the poem contemplates the end of her life and the missed or denied opportunities she has had and will have due to social, economic, and political barriers, which are her reality. She views the rewards for success—refreshing beverages sipped on balconies, or time to sit and relax in a cool breeze—to be pipe dreams. The harsh part of her dream is that she cannot envision success for the next generation either. While trying to understand the problem she faces, the poet tries to come to grips with possibilities for the end of her pessimism. She struggles with ascertaining who she is and how to fully become her own person while remembering the courage, care, and compassion of her grandmother. She writes of fighting the recurrence of old dreams of failure, of seeking to develop a new approach to life and valuing her grandmother's hidden strength. The poet struggles with her "lust" for material things—the new dream—and the ideal of living within her means and helping others—the old dream of her grandmother who was poor and victimized but survived on the brink of defeat. The stamina of the grandmother has overwhelmed the granddaughter.

These poems indicate the need to concentrate on the goal in spite of problems. The lessons learned may or may not be utilized by the student. The role models may not be popular, pretty, or consistent with their own beliefs but encompass the learners. The grandmother/othermothers–children/younger person dyads depicted demonstrate that persons choose when to listen and speak, when to strike out on their own, and when they need assistance from another either in reflection or at that moment. The end result of the teaching depends on the particular situation, age, and fortitude of the recipient, and the standard set by the teacher.

Learning to Stand Up Straight

The weight of marginalization and oppression, though invisible to most, can immobilize persons, stunt their psychological and spiritual growth, and impede their progress toward personhood. Some find it difficult to stand up for themselves because they are met constantly with barriers of inequality due to their race, gender, or class. At times African American children demonstrate a "bent over" social position due to stereotypes regarding their behavior and intelligence. They learn to adapt to social situations by bowing their heads, avoiding eye contact, and trying to blend into the background. They are at times viewed as less than other children simply by virtue of their heritage. Many African American female children are taught to avert their eyes and physically shrink from people just because they are female. If they do not learn to value and stand up for themselves, they will be "bent over" adults.

One of the early lessons taught to black children is to stand up straight, use good posture, look people in the eye when addressing them, hold their heads up, and be proud of who they are. Grandmothers and othermothers who have endured and survived racism and sexism teach the girls to "stand up straight," respect themselves, and speak up when they have an opinion. The resulting behavior may come off to the receiver or observer as being "uppity," "aggressive," and "out of place."

In two selected short stories life reflections again form the basis for realizing what elements are necessary to stand up for one's self and move through life as an empowered person. Annette Jones White's "Dyad/Triad" reveals a daughter's observations of conflict resolution between her mother and grandmother.[19] Reared in an extended family of grandparents and parents the daughter understood the influence and dominance of her maternal grandmother. She described her grandmother as "very strong in character" and a woman "convinced that she had most, if not all, of the answers." The grandmother "overshadowed all other personalities." In terms of what the granddaughter would wear or the family would eat, all decisions were made by the grandmother—"I thought my grandmother was the mother of us all." The position of the African American grandmother is often that of clearinghouse, information central, moral barometer, principal nurse, midwife, nutritionist, and keeper of secrets. This may have either a deleterious or a propitious effect on the family structure. Children may learn how to take leadership in decision-making situations, how to manipulate others through their imperious behavior, or a combination or range of both.

> Although my mother allowed my grandmother to be heavy-handed in my life, she was never so. She let me make choices and decisions whenever we were alone. I cherished those times even though I loved my grandmother very much. We all loved her in spite of herself.[20]

The ability to love the grandmother regardless of her positive or negative behavior was an important aspect of learning how to survive. Adjusting to the inconsistency of behaviors set a pattern for being able to maneuver in the face of unexpected obstacles. There was a need for balance and an understanding that life was not always kind. Forgiveness—release of grudges or bruised feelings—was vital to healthy existence and growth. The grandmother's motive was not destruction but self-preservation. Even while contesting the way the mother washed clothes, a challenge from the grandmother was expected and accepted.

It was my grandmother's way of holding on to her authority, of being in charge. For my mother knew as much about almost everything as my grandmother. There were no more mysteries. My grandmother realized she was losing her reputation of being all-knowing and she grasped at small things to preserve her status and her dignity.[21]

Just as most "isms"—racism, sexism, classism—are based on loss of power, the granddaughter understood that her grandmother's contentious stance was based on a perceived threat to her power. Through the grandmother's and mother's tough love and tenderhearted care the granddaughter learned how to maintain her standing in life. By sharing stories about the Ku Klux Klan, Scottsboro Boys, the Monroe, Georgia, massacre, and other lynchings, the grandmother kept the legacy of overcoming social oppression alive in the granddaughter. The mother "gave heroes and heroines to be proud of" such as Carver, DuBois, Wheatley, and Walker as reference points of how to take a stand for self and others. The grandmother passed on information to the daughter who in turn shared with the granddaughter.

In those days, Black people had few rights and lived constantly on tiptoe and in a react mode. But there was closeness, a togetherness in the community, that appears to be missing today. Perhaps, Blacks *had* to stick together then for mere survival.[22]

Racial tensions created an atmosphere of fear, yet there was courage; they created a sense of powerlessness, yet there was determination. My grandmother survived and reared her daughter to survive. My mother reared me to survive in her own fashion.[23]

Learning about the give and take of life, controlling and yielding, dominance and submission, and defeat and victory was accomplished through sharing personal and community stories of struggles to be considered human and achieve equality. In home and community affirmation of who she was, private strengthening of self-esteem, shielding from racial confrontations and assaults, and the experience of familial love, the granddaughter was enabled, when she was strong enough, to stand boldly on her own before the world.

"Survival ain't liberation," declares Kesho Yvonne Scott in her short story "Marilyn," which speaks of a need for constant striving toward change. She uses lessons learned from her aunt to transmit the importance of individual and collective liberation.[24] Scott describes the evolution of her aunt from a controlled, dominated woman to a "radical, religious, fanatic feminist." Surviving in a male dominated family, marriage, and church of the 1950s—"The women acted like life was just to be endured because you weren't gonna get no earthly reward. They acted like 'mens' was to be endured too"—gave way to a liberative, personal rebellion in the 1980s. Marilyn followed the social codes of how women were to behave—submissive, sacrificing—until her children were grown and her parents died. She then packed up her newly charted life, moved to Iowa City, Iowa, and began to study in a literature class the lives of black women.

> And that's the first time I hear about Margaret Walker, Alice Walker, Toni Cade Bambara, Toni Morrison, Gloria Naylor, Zora Neale Hurston—and I see women telling stories, using my Daddy's language and from our own point of view.[25]

Through acquiring awareness of the struggles and lives of other black women this othermother told her niece how to begin the process of liberation. Aunt Marilyn had moved through feeling overwhelmed as a wife, intimidated as a civil rights worker, depressed in the "inclusive" church, and suicidal in her relationships. When she surmised she was strong enough to remove herself from suffocating social restrictions she began, at age forty-seven, to live her own life. This character found strength and support in the stories of black women. She learned through networking with literary, spiritual othermothers how to be accepting of herself, her own story, her own dreams, and her own spirituality.

Aunt Marilyn then was able to share her story with her niece in hopes of empowering her to seek her own path. The message of Aunt Marilyn is that subsistence, day to day survival, and holding on to the status quo are not enough. One must seek personal liberation, make and take responsibility for decisions, envision a better life, work past dream-deferring obstacles, network with others in similar positions as well as those who are liberated, and develop tools to achieve and maintain freedom. Marilyn's liberation does not take place overnight, but the constancy of struggle is what is important.

If You Just Hold out

Forbearance is essential to learning that "Trouble don't last always." In a society of instant everything children must be told that success is not guaranteed and one may suffer defeats on the way to victory. Other times one's life is a series of setbacks but one must "keep on keepin' on." Still others redefine what success, survival, or liberation is for them—often the opposite of general, accepted societal definitions. Three selected novels by African American women writers relate the need for self-determination, patience, persistence, forgiveness, and care of self and others as methods for personal and communal survival.

The results of conflicting values, poor choices, societal restrictions, and self-defeating behavior are compelling in *God Bless the Child* by Kristin Hunter.[26] There are times that we become our own worst enemy and survival strategies are more detrimental than productive. The novel is about the destructive lives of a grandmother, Lourinda Huggs; a mother, Regina "Queenie" Fleming; and a daughter, Rosalie Fleming. The grandmother, a live-in domestic, wanted the American Dream for her granddaughter. Lourinda was "not really religious but she sang spirituals with an artistic air." Queenie feared her mother and abdicated mothering responsibilities whenever her mother was present. Rosalie loved her grandmother, waited for her fairy tales of the good life led by whites, and believed her mother disliked her. Regardless of what Queenie tried to tell Rosalie, Lourinda intervened and contradicted her at every turn—"You mix up everything I try to teach her." The daughter caricatured the grandmother's disrespect for the mother: "Even if she does like a taste of whiskey now and then, she's your mother. You gotta show some respect."[27]

This is one of the potential problems in extended families. When values, roles, and discipline are not clearly defined and adhered to by all members of the family, conflicts arise. The children do not gain a clear perspective of what is right or wrong or whose teachings they should follow. The mother's word was law every day but Thursday, the grandmother's day off and Rosalie's day of freedom. Conflicting interests and conflicting discipline styles often leave the child confused and ill prepared for life outside the home. The grandmother constantly touted the desirability of living like whites, and by age eighteen, Rosalie said, "I want things. I want things so bad I'd kill myself to get 'em."[28] Modified versions of this statement resound through contemporary schools and communities as some people take what they want deceitfully or violently from others. The grandmother's insistence for attaining things led Rosalie to *hustlin'*. She became a numbers runner as a mode of attaining fast cash.[29] When she began purchasing things for her grandmother and mother little was initially said about her choice of career or friends. When Rosalie's health began to fail and her mother suffered a heart attack, Queenie began to contest the lifestyle her daughter had chosen, but it was too late. News reports of children selling drugs or becoming involved with illegal activity often miss the story. Households lacking in economic resources often become blind to the extent to which a child, and even the parents, will go to supply even basic needs. This does not excuse the behavior but recognizes that at times the root cause is not simply "bad kids" but systemic economic disparity. The grandmother in this story was so possessed with attaining material things that she ignored the psychological and physical deterioration of her granddaughter. She continued to challenge Regina's concern for Rosalie.

> Now, Regina, if you can't say anything nice, just keep quiet for a
> change. Lately your mouth is always full of vinegar. If there's one
> thing I hate to see, it's a woman turning sour when they get old.[30]

Rosalie had no moral barometer to help her make decisions. She continued her slide into depravity. She learned her Granny's attitude meant, "If I don't know, it can't hurt me." She also began to understand that her grandmother had not brought her anything but "junk" her entire life and was wrapped up in her own quest for the American Dream and her "other family." "Break the law, get in trouble, kill yourself even, it's all right as long as I don't know. As long as you don't make a mess on my rugs."[31]

This is certainly not the statement of a concerned and loving grandmother. Denial of wrongdoing or contributing to the crime by acceptance of its benefits contributes to a sense of hopelessness. As Rosalie faced her failure to pull out of self-destruction through alcohol and drug use, familial greed, and purchasing a house that was literally as decayed as her moral fiber, she realized that in her drunkenness her mother loved her more than her grandmother. The entire family slowly died trying to be someone they were not. Care and compassion were rarely evident. Mother-daughter competition, a "by any means necessary" attainment value system, and a total disregard for personal or group survival or liberation permeates this novel. When there is an absence of life-affirming models and a confusion of value systems the result is devastating. The women in Rosalie's life were unable to teach her how to live or survive because they themselves did not know how. In this case, the intergenerational transmission of deviant values was obvious. There was no church backing, the presence of strong criminal elements, and only minimal positive supports—the owner of the clothing store and the man who loved Rosalie but was consumed by her.

Marita Golden's *Long Distance Life* presents a different picture of black extended family life in Washington, D.C., in the 1960s.[32] This life impression is about a grandmother, Cora Johnson, who raised her grandson, Logan Spenser, who had been deserted by her daughter, Esther Spenser, who went to find herself during the Civil Rights movement. She instructed Logan to believe in himself and to keep going in spite of gossip about his parentage—"You're what you think you are. If you don't accept a name, you can't become it." Her prayer of strength for her grandson—"Lord make him strong. And don't let him mind what nobody say"—was also one of protection.[33]

Cora contemplated the change in family structure and the acceptance of other values by black people she had seen over her life, and was disgusted by the assimilation. She reasoned that integration was more about wanting to be like whites than what was best for blacks.

"I don't know what all this sudden interest in legitimacy and illegit-imacy among colored folks is anyway," Cora said in disgust. "Negroes won't never be legitimate to white folks, don't care what we do." She laughed. "Down home, folks never worried about who your daddy was. They knew you had to have one to get here."[34]

The rejection of babies born out of wedlock was not a problem prior to acceptance of the values of larger society. The family, church, and community were responsible for each child. In answer to her grandson's anger at his par-ents' abandonment, the eighty-year-old Cora told him it was all right to be mad at God and still be loved. Logan required forgiveness in order for him to live a healthy social, psychological, spiritual, and moral life of his own. Logan had to forgive his mother for being in and out of his life, trying to become a good person, and letting him care for her when she could not care for her other son. Logan had to forgive a father who was married to another woman and could not claim Logan as his son until Logan was a teenager. At the point that his par-ents were to finally marry and another son was born, the father died. Cora taught Logan what many need to know: that anger and pain may be both painful and productive. The choice of releasing the pain and redirecting one's life is the choice of the individual.

As an adult with a career and his own family, Logan wanted to know why, in spite of all the striving and sacrifice, life does not always turn out as we want it to. It is similar to the question "Why do bad things happen to good people?" He remembered an extended conversation with his grandmother as he tried to regroup two days after her funeral. He found hope in her words even from the grave.

> You know, Logan, we always put all the blame on the Lord. Wondering why things go wrong. How come life's not perfect and just the way we want it to be. And, I've done it plenty of times myself, got mad with God 'cause He did things His way 'stead of mine. Well, I don't have no special pipeline to heaven but I *do* know that the question's not really *Why did God do this to me?* The ques-tion you got to ask is *How do I find what God give me, to get through it?*[35]

Cora let Logan know that "into each life some rain will fall" but the answer was not remaining in a "Why me?" mode, but "What can I do now?" Regardless of age each person questions God at times with a wavering faith. Cora told her grandson that everyone suffers from defeats, failures, troubles, and fear, but one must call on inner strength to get through them. She did not give him a pat "You can make it" speech but cared enough to "Speak the truth in love" so that she honored his pain and moved him toward his own answer.

> Then open up your eyes and look around you like you looking for money somebody told you was hid where you live, like you looking for love been promised and you can feel it coming to you. Look like that for the answer, Logan, and you can't help but find it.[36]

She told him that the answer to our ability to persevere and "hold out until my change has come" was already present. We need to clear away those things that blind us to our inner spirit. We attend to external things like money and other people whom we love but seldom begin with our own strengths, gifts, and graces as a remedy for our trouble or pain.

Alice Walker presents an othermother named Meridian who chooses her own beliefs to validate an existence other persons judge as peculiar.[37] At first glance she appears the weakest individual in a small extended family and community but in actuality is the strongest. As her friend Truman Held reminisces about his college meeting of Meridian Hill and her continual acceptance of him, Walker paints a picture of an extraordinary spirit who loves, cares, and forgives all around her while pressing for justice for all of them. Following her organizing work in the Student Nonviolent Coordinating Committee (SNCC) during the Civil Rights movement of the 1960s, Meridian has become catatonic, worn out but still going after issues she feels must be addressed, whether children or politics. Although other friends opted for corporate jobs, safer political ties, and families, Meridian fights her own battle with injustice—at one time walking in front of a cannon to ensure black children could see a carnival event. Her rejection by Truman Held for Lynne, a white woman, her abuse as a worker in the Freedom Schools, her distrust of the educational system, her estrangement from her family, and her belief that all humanity commands dignity leaves her often alone and viewed as maniacal. Meridian simply walks to the beat of a different drum with a vision of equality in her head. No battle is too small.

> She needed only to see a starving child or attempt to register to vote a grown person who could neither read nor write. On those occasions such was her rage that she actually felt as if the rich and racist of the world should stand in fear of her, because she—though apparently weak and penniless, a little crazy and without power—was yet of a resolute and relatively fearless character, which, sufficient in its calm acceptance of its own purpose, could bring the mightiest country to its knees.[38]

Meridian was an othermother who was willing to sacrifice her own comfort for the lives of others, particularly those in the South. She viewed the "troubles" of others as her business. She knew that someone had to take a stand and she chose to do so in her own way. Truman and Lynne turned to her as mediator for all their marital problems, including the death of their child Camara. Meridian became the problem solver, confidant, and advisor for even her enemies. An ethic of care and compassion has no boundaries. She forgave Truman's infidelity and maintained a friendship with Lynne. She set her pain aside for the good of others. This lifestyle is not for everyone, but Meridian's life presents an option for some people. She said that her value to life was to be alone and prepared to engage difficulties.

> "But that is my value," said Meridian. "Besides, all the people who are as alone as I am will one day gather at the river. We will watch the evening sun go down. And in the darkness maybe we will know the truth."[39]

Meridian reminds us that eventually all struggle will end. There is a poster from 1974 in my study that anonymously states, "The pursuit of truth will set you free—even if you never catch up with it." This was Meridian's revelation to Truman as they sat in her shack while she prepared to go on yet another crusade. Only after she leaves does Truman begin to understand what she has taught him over the years. He finally learns that there will always be trouble but one is called not to give up the fight.

These three novels use various pedagogical tools—narrative, dialogue, example, and reflection. In terms of social location Meridian Hill was a middle-class, educated woman who chose poverty, whereas Lourinda Huggs and Cora Johnson were uneducated and poor and sought to better their lives. The situations presenting themselves were all similar—How does one live a full life in the face of life-restricting obstacles? Lourinda transmitted negative values to her granddaughter while Cora and Meridian, each in her own way, transmitted positive, life-changing values to a grandson and to a friend, respectively.

In consideration of the presupposition that "Trouble don't last always," transformation comes at a different pace for each person as they become aware of the problem, assess solutions, are assisted with directives to overcome the difficulty, develop a sense of empowerment, begin acting on the problem, and envision change.

My Soul Looks Back

In the first of six autobiographical novels Maya Angelou chronicles the lives of African American women in the midst of telling the reader *I Know Why the Caged Bird Sings*.[40] Living with her paternal grandmother, Annie Henderson (Momma)—following the divorce of her parents—Marguerite Johnson

(Angelou) learned about racism, sex, determination, pride, education, forgiveness, and God's presence, power, and protection through Momma's speeches, loving care, compassion for her disabled son, and chastisement. Momma was an awesome figure in Stamps, Arkansas. She is described as a "super religious Southern grandmother with a 'church gaze' " that is a way of looking at people that leads children raised in the black church to know that they are misbehaving and that retribution is near. Momma was active in the Christian Methodist Episcopal Church as a "Mother of the Church." This is an honorific title for mature, prayerful, spirit-filled women in the black church. They are the worship conductors and set the moral tone for the congregation. Momma had deeply entrenched beliefs that she passed on to her grandchildren while cooking, washing, praying, singing, confronting, and lecturing.

> "Thou shall not be dirty" and "Thou shall not be impudent" were the two commandments of Grandmother Henderson upon which hung our total salvation. . . . But Momma convinced us that not only was cleanliness next to Godliness, dirtiness was the inventor of misery. The impudent child was detested by God and a shame to its parents and could bring destruction to its house and line.[41]

Momma used biblical mandates and social etiquette to impart how to behave at home and in the community. All adults had to be addressed as "Mister, Missus, Miss, Auntie, Cousin, Unk, Uncle, Bubbah, Sister, Brother, and a thousand other applications indicating familial relationship and the lowliness of the addressor." Children were not to "be in grown folks' business" or look an adult in the face. After a group of white children insulted Momma and men came into the store one night to lynch Marguerite's uncle, Marguerite learned for her own protection to stay away from whites and say as little as possible.

When confronted with a racial slight Momma stood her ground and began to "moan a hymn." "Maybe not to moan, but the tune was so slow and the meter so strange that she could have been moaning." Momma was showing the children how to "hold your peace, let the Lord fight your battles." She also demonstrated how she protected herself by holding in her anger in a situation where she was obviously going to eventually lose due to racism. Children must learn that in situations of powerlessness and with the absence of protection before the law the best defense is apparent inactivity. Overtly Momma was passive. Covertly she was processing everything that happened for use at a later time. One must have an alternative to violence in order to preserve the peace and save lives.

> Momma intended to teach Bailey and me to use the paths of life that she and her generation and all the Negroes gone before had found, and found to be safe ones. . . . If she had been asked and had chosen

to answer the question of whether she was cowardly or not, she would have said that she was a realist. Didn't she stand up to "them" year after year? Wasn't she the only Negro woman in Stamps referred to once as Mrs.? [42]

Marguerite learned that standing up for oneself comes in many different forms. Momma was honest, charitable, and respected by the people. She also knew when and how to fight a battle. She chose the occasion after much thought and never began anything without a plan. Methods that children may believe are outdated, old-fashioned, or infeasible at least present a starting point in the struggle for liberation. Momma was determined to share the information; it was up to Marguerite and Bailey to determine how to use it.

One of Momma's friends—Mrs. Bertha Flowers—is depicted as a "Black aristocrat, self controlled, a gentlewoman" who was the "measure of what a human being can be." She became an othermother for Marguerite and gave her "lessons in living" over tea at her home, while reading, or baking cookies.

> She said that I must always be intolerant of ignorance but understanding of illiteracy. That some people, unable to go to school, were more educated and even more intelligent than college professors. She encouraged me to listen carefully to what country people called mother wit. That in those homely sayings was couched the collective wisdom of generations.[43]

Mother Wit is life sayings that relate how to carry oneself in public, how to raise children, faith statements, how to honor your parents, reverence of God and elders, importance of family, and general value statements. For example, "There is nothing worse than an educated fool" means knowledge is wonderful but do not forget common sense. "Tell the truth and shame the devil" means honesty is the best policy and only evil people lie. "The Lord takes care of His children" means that regardless of circumstances we serve a God of "somehows." "Don't ever get so high that you forget about God" means that faith diminishes as money increases. Momma spoke out of a Mother Wit when talking to a member of the church.

> People whose history and future were threatened each day by extinction considered that it was only by divine intervention that they were able to live at all. I find it interesting that the meanest life, the poorest existence, is attributed to God's will, but as human beings become more affluent, as their living standard and style begin to ascend the material scale, God descends the scale of responsibility at a commensurate speed.[44]

Forgetting how far God has brought you is a travesty, a sin. African American preachers usually include charges of backsliding or straying away from God, occasional church attendance, and unfaithfulness in service to God once a problem is over.

Mother Wit for self-preservation begins with "Don't put your business in the street," which means finessing answers to questions, never revealing all the information, direct denial of action, protecting family at all costs, and lying if necessary in order to survive. Momma knew the hazards black children faced because they were the same ones she faced as a child. Over the years she had learned how to address the issues and was obligated to instruct her grandchildren in the strategies she had been taught.

"We have a saying among Black Americans, which describes Momma's caution. 'If you ask a Negro where he's been, he'll tell you where he's going.' "[45] She did not teach her grandchildren to be devious but showed them how to use protective devices. If someone cannot get information they cannot use it against you. One shares information at home, discusses it, formulates tactics, and then enters into society. A black child should never give a straight answer to a person in power except a parent, grandparent, or other elder in the family, church, or community or the child is considered "uppity." They have been taught not to volunteer information to power figures or to those who they feel do not have their best interests at heart.

There are catastrophic events in life when one does not believe that "Trouble don't last always." While living with her maternal Grandmother Baxter in St. Louis, Missouri, Marguerite was raped by her mother's current companion. This grandmother was a numbers runner, mother of six children, politically well connected, and also well respected in her neighborhood. She filled the home with control and secular values. Marguerite was aware of her grandmother's power and rather than tell who raped her she was silent and weeping before the man's trial. After the man was released and found murdered she did not speak for about one year because she felt responsible. Her silence was a protective device and was only ended when she returned to the security of Stamps, Momma, and Mrs. Flowers.[46]

Marguerite, as many children do, needed to return to the familiar, the caring, the loving atmosphere that affirmed her humanity. African American children forgive parents who have very different lifestyles than what are acceptable in the larger community. As long as there is the assurance they are loved, the surroundings are problematic but home.

"Trouble don't last always" is an ethical presupposition in the African American family, church, and community. This does not mean that black people continue blithely accepting adverse circumstances. It does mean, however, that there is a deep belief that God will take care of the problem if we do our part. Perseverance is necessary even in the face of racism, sexism, classism, materialism, ageism, and denominationalism (prejudice based on one's belonging to a different denomination). One must teach children in their formative years (birth to twelve) that one must never give up, even if the tunnel holds no light. Locating the core of strength within you is the beginning of liberation. One is challenged to do more than survive. One must work to make his or her place in the world better, freer, and more inclusive. There will be times of success and times of defeat, but "this too will pass." Time and patience are necessary as well as an openness to learn protective tactics and apply them when necessary. There must be ways to protect the spirit, mind, intellect, and body of persons in the struggle. Old and new ways must be paired to keep hope burning in the child. Not everyone survives. Some die trying. Some decide not to fight. Some are overwhelmed and choose other ways of salving the wounds, such as drugs, alcohol, sex, food, and so forth. Others dig deeper into their spiritual lives by becoming more involved in church or community organizations that speak to their needs and the needs of others.

Whatever the chosen technique, one is responsible for self and others and must care for others who have not yet found the hope of liberation because of the depths of their despair. Transformation takes place over a period of time, often in flashbacks to some word of encouragement or even admonition by a grandmother or othermother. The recurrence of an event may trigger a mode of operation perhaps taught during childhood. Healing takes place through repetition, revitalization, revelation, and reflection on life's lessons. Given the current societal troubles and the status of the family, church, and community there must be several methods devised to help children and young people learn how to function in today's world; how to be in relationship with others, whether or not they are the same age, race, gender, or belief system; how to endure life's pains, troubles, disappointments, and setbacks; and how to maintain a vital faith in God in the midst of the storms or tranquillity of life.

The next chapter provides suggestions for how African American women in particular, and society in general, might work together in transmitting values intergenerationally to African American children, youth, and women in order to decrease fear of others, reclaim their dignity through African American stories, songs, and sermons, and begin the process of overcoming oppression through a spiritual foundation.

7

COMMUNITY RESPONSIBILITIES

It Takes an Entire Village to Raise a Child

This chapter will explore four contemporary programs that combine the teaching of spiritual values, cultural norms, and the importance of African American history as resource tools for social transformation. The chapter's major focus will be a womanist paradigm of self-empowerment for grandmothers and othermothers in preparation for transmitting values to African American children, families, churches, and communities. Each program in some manner teaches the ethical presuppositions that "God don't like ugly," "We are all Aunt Haggie's children," and "Trouble don't last always." I will apply to the programs the same interpretive framework categories of pedagogy, social location, relationship, ethical presupposition, and possibilities for transformation that were used in the analysis of African American women's literature. Each program may be adapted to fit any cultural, racial, ethnic, gender specific, or faith group in passing on moral wisdom.

Throughout my childhood, 1951 to 1969, I heard the African proverb "It takes an entire village to raise a child" reverberating in one form or another from the lips of loved ones. Because there were few choices of public accommodations for African Americans, various ministers, friends, relatives, and even new acquaintances stayed with my grandparents during vacations or special trips. When members of my extended family experienced difficulties, space was found for an adult or child to sleep, food was stretched miraculously to feed one or two more, and clothing that never seemed to wear out was passed from household to household. Every black adult in Sedalia, Missouri, knew both sets of my grandparents and had no qualms about verbally chastising or threatening to spank my brother and I if we were found to be "actin' grown" or disobeying some community rule because, "You know your grandparents wouldn't like you doing that." Miss Susie and Mr. Carl, an older, childless, African American couple in Independence, Missouri, embodied not only the neighborhood watch but were also the surrogate parents, mentors, and the wisdom center of the neighborhood. Older children were required to tend younger children and raise them in the absence of working parents. This whole network of caregivers exemplified the black extended family at its best.

Church and school attendance, especially for women and children, was not a choice but an expectation. One attended both as a good representative of the race. The church was the social center due to limited access to public facilities and prejudice in occupational and recreational areas. The entire community cared for and freely influenced the child's psychological, social, spiritual, physical, and emotional development. The entire village—ministers, doctors, construction workers, domestics, policemen, winos, prostitutes, and even at times lucid addicts—was responsible for each child as blood and fictive kin (i.e., "play" sisters, brothers, uncles, aunts, cousins, mothers, fathers, grandmothers, and grandfathers). Each person understood his or her duty to the life of each child; each knew the litany of the importance of life and giving the children more of a chance than the adults had had. Each person grappled with this challenge and kept it to the best of his or her ability. When one faltered, refused to comply with community expectations, or was unable to fulfill a role due to personal battles—such as drugs, alcoholism, racism, poverty, unemployment, fear, immaturity, or illness—someone else, often older members of the family, church, or community stepped in and attempted to hold things together until the person recovered. The interconnectedness of the family, church, and community meant that all persons were important regardless of their status.

These features developed due to necessity. In the 1960s, 1970s, and 1980s, institutional racism limited choices blacks had as to where they could live, where they could work, and the future of their children. Constantly, people were reminded of how to act in community and in the presence of whites. There was seemingly a gradual shift in values for some members of the black community, for a plethora of reasons. The inexorable fear that whites would kill a black child has shifted over the past thirty years to an undeniable fear that black children will be killed by other black children. In the 1990s it seemed that in many cases the black family, church, and community abdicated the responsibility of raising the children in healthy environments with spiritual values that affirm life. In a race to fit into mass society some blacks have opted for removing themselves from old-fashioned ways, sayings, places, and beliefs that at one time solidified the black family, church, and community. So, Christian-based ideals of how to behave, how to be in relationship with others, and the inner empowerment that the elders sought and found in the face of blatant oppression began to slip away.

Today the village is often fragmented, the houses are divided, the churches cater to the elite, and individual political power has replaced seeking the rights of the whole. Yet there is hope. There are those women and men who seek to reclaim the children's lives in inventive and supportive ways reminiscent of the grandmothers and othermothers. And there are programs across the United States that attend to "re-membering" and "re-visioning" self-empowerment, intergenerational family care, and "returning" to an empowering spiritual base. A brief review of some of these programs is presented below.

> **"Two men in a burning house must not stop to argue."**
> Ashanti Proverb

Every day an increasing number of young black children die violently. Growing numbers of race-related hate crimes, high school dropouts, spiraling teen unemployment figures, drug and alcohol addictions, parental abuse, inept young parents, and a consuming sense of anomie or alienation deepen a sense of gloom. Though political rhetoric permeates most discussions on what we should do, many fail to face the reality that our children are still dying. Circular arguments about ineffective government and community programs are being replaced in many communities by the implementation of grassroots programs emanating from African American families, churches, and communities. The question is not whose program is best, but rather whose program meets the needs of the people.

Rites of Passage

The Rites of Passage program at Bridge Street African Wesleyan Methodist Episcopal Church in the Bedford-Stuyvesant section of Brooklyn, New York, is designed to meet the needs of African American children between the ages of nine and eighteen years old. The ethical presupposition of "God don't like ugly" entails learning how to be present in society and relate to others in an acceptable manner. "We are all Aunt Haggie's children" points to an inexorable link with all humanity. Mentoring children or youth whom one does not know or to whom one is not related is a critical element of this presupposition. I found both principles were operating in this program. Instituted in 1990 by a female youth pastor, the program mirrors African rites of initiation of male and female adolescents into adulthood. The program is about building self-esteem, pride in African heritage, conflict resolution skills, self-confidence, life skills, financial management skills, intergenerational support, academic and critical thinking, and spiritual, social, and religious values.

The Rites of Passage program for young girls is staffed by female volunteers who make one to two year commitments to be one-on-one guides and confidants. The length of the program is June to October for two years, one to two times per month, on Saturdays from 9:00 A.M. to 1:00 P.M., covering three of five curriculum areas. Resource persons, mentors, and community persons use direct teaching, lectures, and internships at businesses, identification with adult mentors, and private conversations to transmit information. The women mentor the girls and young women throughout their engagement with principles of Afrocentric thought and a five-part curriculum.

The entire group determines which area will be studied on a particular Saturday and when they should move to another study area. This is to instill group problem solving and decision making as essential to building community and responsible leadership. Mentors are accessible during the training sessions and whenever conversation, support, or redirection is necessary.

The uniqueness of the Bridge Street program is that it is a blend of Christian teachings on Christ-like behavior, responsibility, self-determination, and the love of God, neighbor, and self, and the seven principles of Nguza Saba developed by Dr. Maulana Karenga.[1] These seven principles echo those listed by Andrew Billingsley in his discussion of African values, and parallel those values intrinsic to Alice Walker's definition of *womanist* reviewed in chapter 2: love of self, respect for others, value of education, survival of an entire people (male and female), and love of God and spirit. They represent elements of the three ethical presuppositions—"God don't like ugly," "We are all Aunt Haggie's children," and "Trouble don't last always"—in the previous discussions.

The principles of **Nguza Saba** are:

Umoja (Unity) means to strive for and maintain a sense of unity in the African American family, community, nation, and race.

Kujichagulia (Self-Determination) means the ability to define ourselves, name ourselves, create and speak for ourselves.

Ujima (Collective Work and Responsibility) is to build and maintain our community together and make the problems of our sisters and brothers our own and seek to assist in solving them.

Ujamaa (Cooperative Economics) is to build and maintain our African American stores and businesses, and share the profits.

Nia (Purpose) is to make our collective vocation the building and developing of community in order to restore African Americans to their traditional greatness as members of the African Diaspora.

Kuumba (Creativity) means to do as much as African Americans can, in any way we can, in order to leave our communities more beautiful and productive than when we inherited them.

Imani (Faith) means to believe with all our hearts in African American people, our parents, our teachers, our leaders, and in the righteous and victorious nature of our struggle.

These are also called "the Seven Principles of *Kwanzaa*," an African American festival of culture, heritage, and self-empowerment celebrated December 26 through January 1 each year. This time of rededication, unity, and cultural pride has been adapted for innumerable Rites of Passage programs for African American men, women, and children.

The five curriculum areas contain elements of the ethical presuppositions specified in chapters 4–6. *Life skills management* teaches the young woman how to care for herself and others through health maintenance, hygiene, cooking, sewing, survival training, conflict resolution, and responsibility in sexuality. Community events revolve around career training, education, financial management, entrepreneurship, and celebration of African American culture.

Community involvement solidifies the traditional connection of black family, church, and community resources.

Each young woman must take part in *community service* through volunteer time in homeless shelters, soup kitchens, nursing homes, and so forth. Giving back to the community through action, money, support, visitation, and political intercession is a characteristic of African American teachings. It is often said of those who leave the community and do not look back that "It is an ungrateful child who forgets where they come from." The young women also tour prisons, court systems, and job sites of mentors as a means of information gathering, as well as exploring career possibilities.

Spirituality begins with the recognition that each person's relationship and belief in God is to be celebrated. The young woman is taught that there is no need to be ashamed of a belief in God, even when peers ridicule her. A thematic approach to contemporary situations and biblical solutions is accomplished through role-playing and Bible studies. There is an intense study of other faith systems and religions with guest speakers and question-and-answer periods. Private and public prayer and silence are also held as avenues to building a relationship with God. The girls interact with ordained and nonordained women, and discuss opportunities in living out their own ministries.

Critical thinking and decision making is accomplished through reading books, newspapers, magazines, and articles; through watching television and movies; and by observing everyday life situations. Communication skills, writing techniques, and problem solving are reviewed through analysis of media presentations.

The final area is *creative development*. Dance, drama, sports, and song are avenues for enhancing self-expression. This is a noncompetitive learning environment where each person's skills are reinforced positively.

Such Rites of Passage programs are effective in transmitting values through one-to-one interaction of adults and children. The program is time consuming but the potential results are incalculable. The honoring of culture and Christ is empowering for black youth. Too often they are told by society that they are failures and are locked into subcultures of hopelessness. The Rites of Passage programs potentially allow youth to focus on success rather than failure. Using the skills of women who have also been mentored within a church family and who are successful in the larger community opens up a world of possibilities for young women. The voices of African American othermothers transmit spiritual and cultural values not only to the young people in the program but also to their families, the church, and the community.

"When the door is closed, you must learn to slide across the crack of the sill." Yoruba Proverb

The Full Circle Intergenerational Project

The Full Circle Intergenerational Project in Denver, Colorado, was developed by Anita West Ware in 1991. It is a community-based organization that operates in an educational building of a black church. When there was no space available to house the program Ms. West Ware used her indefatigable spirit to press for a place within the womb of the black community to save children from drug and alcohol abuse. Full Circle strives to "reaffirm the learning process, sustain appropriate behavior, and provide a variety of experiences to expand the vision of our youth, parents, and elders." All three ethical presuppositions were at work in this program. The overview of the program was to teach young people how to behave in the home, school, church, and community ("God don't like ugly"), that they were interrelated to one another and the world ("We are all Aunt Haggie's children"), and how to survive or overcome the obstacles in their lives, whether a pimple or prejudice ("Trouble don't last always"). As a participant in some of the preliminary discussions on Full Circle and as an observer of its growth and development the past nine years, I know this program has exceeded its mission.

Focus areas for Full Circle are school bonding, personal development, cultural bonding, and community bonding in order to enable young people to make positive, healthy, crime-free life choices. The program is a blend of academics, physical activity, spiritual development, community outreach, and cultural reinforcement.

Youth between the ages of six and sixteen years of age are paired with trained mentors who are at least fifty years of age. One-to-one mentoring relationships provide opportunities for at-risk youth, parents, and elders to implement cultural and familial activities through fictive kinship and reinforcement of blood relationships. Mentors are solicited by the director of the program and must sign a commitment pledge, attend training sessions, and commit to one child for a period of at least seven months. These elders serve as coaches, advisors, mentors, and counselors to the assigned youth and their family. As part of the extended family, the elders are present for tutoring homework in the after school segment of the program, they attend social and cultural events with the child, and they advise on personal growth and development issues. The support offered by the elder/mentor comes from life experience and a willingness to share life lessons with youth.

The teaching is accomplished through discussion, hands-on attention, role modeling, attendance of general cultural events such as the symphony or plays, physical activities such as golf, finance seminars, and sessions on African American culture to give a sense of "somebodiness" to children who are often discounted. Parents are required to attend classes on parenting and increasing their own skills.

Like the Bridge Street Rites of Passage Program, there is an element of giving back to the community and cultural appreciation. With support of churches, communities, and families the Full Circle Intergenerational program also offers three distinct programs for selected age groups. Each program is gender specific and meets separately. "Completing the Circle" is a rite of passage for males twelve to sixteen and females ten to sixteen years of age. It is designed to assist the young people in the journey to productive adult life. It involves the mentor, community resources, and the entire family. For example, the youth write papers and design worship services honoring their elders and recognizing parents for their sacrifices and guidance. "The Learning Circle" is a cultural enrichment and summer tutorial program to expand the participants' horizons. Youth experience golf, boating, tennis, karate, cultural arts, and theater. The elders/mentors and youth participate in community-building projects such as tending a community garden.

Another program component is "Family Strengthening: Sistuh Girls—Coming Full Circle." The focus is wellness and health maintenance for girls and young women. Support groups for psychosocial development are formed with elders, youth, and resource personnel. This component addresses sexuality, self-help, and medical education for at-risk black females under the guidance of health care professionals. The resourcefulness and dedication of the director and staff, the contributions of the elders, and the willingness of the children assures that this program will continue to expand. It is evident from such programs that the model of making a way out of no way through the wisdom of the elders, and strengthening the family by preserving the children, is alive and well.

"The bell rings loudest in your own home."	Yoruba Proverb

Back to the Kitchen Table

In 1987, working as an associate minister of Christian education, raising my daughter as a single parent, and counseling families in crisis, I developed a program called "Back to the Kitchen Table" to begin to address the need for physical, spiritual, emotional, and psychological contact and care within the African American family.

The idea stemmed from my childhood memories. I remembered the time spent at the kitchen table listening to my grandmother, mother, aunts, and female neighbors talking about life experiences, giving out remedies for illnesses, sharing recipes, sewing hand-me-downs, fixing hair, chastising children, preaching the good news, crying, singing, laughing all the while planning how to survive the ravages of racism and sexism. The kitchen was their pulpit, their safe space, their network, and their classroom for moral wisdom. The eldest member guided the conversation, whether actively speaking out or through the use of assenting or rejecting body language and nonverbal cues. It was a privilege to be invited into it as an observer/girlchild. The kitchen was also the place where everyone felt that they were somebody, one's gifts and graces were appreciated, and miracles seemed to take place in a regular multiplying of food to feed large families. I had also read about similar settings in the literature of African American women. In *Mama Day* by Gloria Naylor, Miss Abigail and Mama Day ministered to their granddaughter, Bernice, in the kitchen, whether braiding her hair or mixing up her favorite dessert. They talked to her about life as they went about their work.[2]

Andrew Billingsley's social systems model of African American families depicts individual alienation at the heart of family crisis.[3] The family is also the centerpiece of the community, and society in general. The African proverb infers that taking care of home is essential for the survival of the community. If one chooses to ignore issues within one's own home—whether spiritual, financial, or interpersonal—and work exclusively for community empowerment, one overlooks the proverbial forest for the trees. This intersecting of my academic, spiritual, and social experiences birthed "Back to the Kitchen Table."

The African American families I ministered with at Shorter Community African Methodist Episcopal Church in Denver, Colorado, were middle class, single-parent and two-parent families, college educated, spiritually active people with intelligent, active, and well-behaved children. However, many families spent little time together due to school and work schedules. Parents worked to provide all those things they did not have as children, yet were often over-scheduled when it came to spending time with their children. Several requested a Christian education seminar on parenting and the church. The result was this program, which was held on Saturday mornings from 8:00 A.M. until 10:30 A.M. or until everyone went home.

The teachings of my childhood again informed the development and direction of this program. Through a review of the types of information passed on by my grandmothers and othermothers, ideas culled from discussion with other women, interviews with African American men regarding the development of their value systems, ideas taught in church and Sunday school, and mentally reviewing characters and situations in my collection of African American literature, I began to formulate cultural values and moral wisdom into the presuppositions that form the basis of this book. Conflicts between adults or parents and their children focused on the behavioral aspects of "God don't like ugly." Exclusion based on age, gender, race, belief, economics, or political astuteness spoke to the idea that "We are all Aunt Haggie's children." Finally, impending divorce, nonconformist children, threats to health, financial failure, and spiritual inquiry were engaged through the presupposition that "Trouble don't last always."

The format for the Back to the Kitchen Table program began with a preliminary survey used to ascertain areas of interest and the needs of the potential participants. The program had no budget, so all labor, speakers, and materials were donated or volunteered. The attendees recommended community resource persons. The convener selected, screened, and invited speakers in for the forty-five-minute sessions. Each session began with a covenant of persons being given equal voice in topic discussion or opinion, and a pledge of confidentiality particularly for emotionally laden topics such as sexuality. A small teaching staff contacted speakers and developed lesson plans on topics such as: "Becoming a Spirit-Filled Parent/Child," "Financial Planning and Tithing," "Appreciation of Your Child's/Parent's Music," "Preventing Suicide," "Learning to Listen to Your Child/Parent," "The Truth About Communicable Diseases," "Death and Grief," "Recognizing and Stopping Domestic Violence," and "Human Sexuality."

Part of the rationale for the program was the lack of family time during the week. The families were overscheduled with jobs, school, extracurricular activities, church obligations, and business meetings. Some rarely saw each other until Sunday. This was a purposeful meeting time to sit and talk with family members over a meal, and learn together. One projected outcome was to continue the process in individual homes. "Family" was defined as single persons, two parents, single parents, children living with grandparents, fictive kin, and any form of augmented or extended family. Each family brought one breakfast item each meeting day. Each family was assigned a day to set the tables or clean up after the meeting. The point was the families were working, praying, and studying together.

The morning began with a family prayer before we ate together at a large conference-style table. Persons shared the events of the week and one member gave a short Bible-study message. Following breakfast the group divided into age-appropriate groups with activities such as art for younger children and guest speakers for teens and adults. Participants ranged in age from infancy to approximately seventy-six years of age. The ratio of females to males was four to one. The total number of participants ranged from one hundred and fifty to fifty-four depending on the topic and the weather.

Following the small discussion groups the entire program group reconvened to report their individual learning experiences. Topics were discussed for about fifteen to twenty minutes in a large group with biblical supports and views on each topic. The morning ended with family interaction exercises that explored such values as trust, sharing, respect, loving in spite of mistakes, forgiveness, and responsibility as means of reinforcing moral wisdom. Assignments for the next week were given, including a family project to be accomplished during the week. The program ran for a little over a year and was suspended due to the convener's other responsibilities.

Northeast Denver Learning Resource Center

However, the Back to the Kitchen Table program evolved into an after-school mentoring/tutorial program called "the Northeast Denver Learning Resource Center," which opened in 1992 and closed in 1994 at the end of the granting period. This was a church-based program for at-risk neighborhood youth ages twelve to twenty-one years. The program was designed to reach middle and secondary school African American children needing to improve their academic skills, prepare for vocations, and begin the process of college readiness. The other prong of the program was to assist older students in obtaining their General Education Diploma (GED) and job skills. The necessity for a culturally sensitive tutorial program was evident from an escalating high school drop-out rate for African American children, a sense of hopelessness reported by teens, incarceration, increasing number of gang members in the community, the creation of adolescent welfare families through teen pregnancies, and potential entrance into the permanent underclass by such young people.[4]

The coordinator and a small staff obtained a federal grant to initiate the program in the fall of 1992. The program was located in a community church and was supported by five other congregations. A partnership was formed with middle and secondary schools, principals, businesses, and other social agencies in order to enhance services for the youth. The staff was composed of twenty volunteer African American adults (fourteen women and six men) and at times five adolescent peers skilled in education, psychology, sociology, medicine, religion, geology, mathematics, English, science, history, business, and technical fields. They were parents, relatives, grandparents, retirees, and friends of the youth who eventually enrolled in the program. Following preliminary training in working with and relating to at-risk youth, the mentors/counselors/tutors gave one to four nights per week from 4:00 to 7:00 P.M., Monday through Thursday, to one-to-one or small group sessions. There were also occasional Saturday morning field trips and on-the-job or in-school visits with the youth who were being mentored.

Recruitment of students was accomplished through canvassing churches, schools, and neighborhoods in northeast Denver. Students were assessed informally and by standardized evaluations by Denver public schools testing specialists. Through informal evaluation of the twenty-five to thirty youth referred by schools, parent conferences, reviews of report cards, and meetings with the center's teaching teams the coordinator determined the academic and socioemotional needs of each student. Meetings with school counselors on behavioral matters, classroom visits, and progress reports influenced individual program development. For older students, particularly those who had dropped out of school or anticipated leaving, alternative plans were discussed and implemented, such as GED preparation, counseling, vocational training, and realistic career guidance. In some cases the staff and coordinator met with juvenile authorities to monitor youth who were either gang members or gang "wannabes." Those youth who continued in the program were generally well behaved and articulated some relief that someone was finally concerned about them.

Each night academic work was accomplished one-on-one and in small groups following the syllabi of the Denver public schools and information from specific teachers. Youth were encouraged to complete assigned work and any extra credit assignments available. Students were also taught test-taking skills and self-evaluation, for example, analysis of personality assets and opportunities for self-transformation. Learning and organizational tools such as note taking, outlining, legibility, and decision making were reviewed. Group activities included team work through problem solving, creative thinking through role playing, and "competitive" team exercises in learning geography, black history, science, math, language, and social studies. Research skills were enhanced through computer literacy, library usage, critical review of news items, assessments of documentaries such as "Eyes on the Prize," reports and assessment of particular job specifications, and knowledge of various professions. Thursday night included a career component in which the group discussed and learned about interviewing, interpersonal communication, punctuality, dress, salary negotiation, and responsibility. African American business owners and professionals gave brief talks and engaged in questions and answers with the youth. Wednesday night was for social and personal skill development. Mental health professionals, ministers, social workers, psychologists, counselors, and medical personnel visited and talked about ways of self-care, identifying acceptable values for living responsibly in the world, and conflict resolution.

The final element of the program was the required parental involvement. To ensure that each youth received support at school, at the Center, and at home, parents were asked to meet with the coordinator monthly. Parents also met with Center staff to discuss needs, concerns, and progress of their children. Parents were encouraged to meet with school personnel on a regular basis, call the schools with concerns before there was a major problem, and to become members of the Parent Teacher and Student Association. Parents were also asked to become mentors for other students at the Center at least once per month or serve as a guest speaker. In those cases where the parent needed assistance, they were referred to the Adult Literacy Program, counseled in parenting, or assisted in other resource areas. They were paired with elders/foster grand-parents who were available for intermittent support.

Summary

Bridge Street Rites of Passage, Full Circle Intergenerational Project, and the Northeast Denver Learning and Resource Center are examples of the unity of black family, black church, and black community in supporting and saving children and preparing them for life. Primary values of respect, responsibility, reciprocity, reverence, and self-determination delineated in the earlier discussion of spiritual values (chapter 2) and the three ethical presuppositions "God don't like ugly," "We are all Aunt Haggie's children," and "Trouble don't last always," developed from readings of African American women's literature, are demonstrated and transmitted through male and female elders/mentors. These programs, designed to shape the lives of black youth, are just one possible option for beginning to transform society. Each program, whether culturally specific or adapted, may be replicated and expanded in any family, church, or community.

> **"Do not follow the path. Go where there is no path to begin a trail."**
> Ashanti Proverb

> Each of us has the right and the responsibility to assess the roads which lie ahead, and those over which we have traveled, and if the future road looms ominous or unpromising, and the roads back uninviting, then we need to gather our resolve and, carrying only the necessary baggage, step off that road into another direction. If the new choice is also unpalatable, without embarrassment, we must be ready to change that as well.[5]

Both the proverb and these poignant words by Maya Angelou illuminate the crux of womanist thought, lessons of my grandmothers and othermothers, the expressed and unspoken need of African American women, and my own quest for individual and communal transformation.

Sisters Working Encouraging Empowering Together (S.W.E.E.T.) is a network for sharing and expanding womanist perspectives and undergirding black women's understanding of the power to become that is within them. The model was developed as a women's ministry that I founded at Shorter Community African Methodist Episcopal Church in Denver, Colorado, in 1989.

Realizing the gaping chasm between black women in the church and community, based on false boundaries such as marital status, occupation, social club membership, church attendance, family structure, and physical appearance, I sought to bring together a group of women that would eventually be empowered to look beyond social structures and see common ground.

The basic requirement for membership was that all were welcome regardless of who or what they were. The members ranged in age from five to seventy-eight years with a diversity of educational levels, occupations, marital or family status, and faith systems. A core group of forty African American women responsible for the design and implementation of S.W.E.E.T. evolved to approximately five hundred to six hundred African American women who participated in various activities over a five-year period. The members were all black women who at some time, in some manner, felt stagnant, oppressed, limited by black men, other black women, and society in general. This sense of being bound was present in all areas of their lives: church, school, job, relationships, and businesses. They wanted to be treated as fully human and wanted to be themselves.

S.W.E.E.T. began with one rule—respect our sister's space, voice, pain, sensitivities, and ideas. There was one coordinator and no elected officers. Meetings were run on consensus. There was no admission charge and sisters donated to the treasury as they were able for any special projects. The group wanted to make sure that all women could be members. It defined itself as a spiritual, universal sisterhood with no walls, barriers, or exclusions. Each pledged to "sister" other women into wholeness. There was no need to impress one another with credentials, so everyone was referred to as "Sister," "Girlfriend," or by first names. The exception was for respected elders, othermothers, and those fifty and over, who were addressed as Mother____ or Miss____ as is the custom in the majority of black churches and communities. These othermothers were the spiritual anchors of the group. Their presence added a sense of authenticity to the belief that courageously living your own life and still loving God were possibilities. There was an understood privilege in hearing their wisdom.[6]

Teens and children met with the group unless the subject matter necessitated age-appropriate division. Their voices were also recognized as vital to the ongoing dialogue. The language was of "sisterspeak," no pretense, at home, "I love you in spite of myself," "Even if I disagree I'll honor your right to say that" speech. When disagreements arose one of the sisters facilitated the matter toward some resolution and allowed each voice to be heard.

Meetings varied in their degree of formality with annual seminars, weekly meetings, Bible studies, monthly workshops, relationship-building exercises, small group discussion, potluck dinners, informal and formal luncheons, community action projects, intergenerational mentoring groups, individual and group counseling sessions, guest speakers, speakers from within the group, panel discussions, role playing, ethnographies, health support groups, and African American women's literature study and discussion groups. Each meeting began with prayer, praise reports of successes or blessings from the week, concerns, and group-building exercises. Women were not pressured to be a member of a church but there was an understanding that the group was spiritually based. Each sister determined and articulated her own sense of spirituality, a spirituality that included the conscious awareness of God, self, and others in a total response to black life and culture.

Prayer, testimony, sharing like feelings, listening, laughter, silence, and touch were crucial elements of the sisterhood building. Sisters passed on their ideas of how to survive and thrive, and listened carefully to the othermothers in exercises such as "Who was the woman in your life who had the greatest impact on who you are today, and why?" or "Where were you ten years ago today and how have you changed?"[7] As each woman shared she also received affirmation of her situation or overcoming through similar stories repeated by another sister as well as a sort of embryonic sustenance from one another. If the situation had not been resolved, means for change were offered as possibilities, not exact solutions. The buds of extended families began as the discussions opened with "What kind of sister are you?" "Who is your sister?" or "Do you need a sister or to sister someone, and why?"

> **"She who does not know how to walk cannot climb a ladder."**
> Nigerian Proverb

Ethnographic Tools for Self-Empowerment

One of the most powerful S.W.E.E.T. small group projects (fifty women) for understanding and cultivating womanist perspectives, such as valuing self and gaining a sense of empowerment from the lives of grandmothers and othermothers, was the creation of ethnographies. The project grew out of a phrase in the first part of Walker's *womanist* definition: "Wanting to know more and in greater depth than is considered 'good' for one." The first phase of this self-empowerment program required women to discover more about themselves by knowing where they came from—the family, church, and community dynamics that gave birth to them. Each sister was asked to call, write, or visit the oldest living female member of her family and ask her about her life. She was to ask questions about spiritual, professional, familial, or personal concerns or any other information she felt she needed to know, and to record the answers.

Each woman reported back to the larger group three weeks later and answered some form of the following questions:

1. Who did you choose and why?
2. What is the historical context of her life? Date of birth? Location?
3. Brief outline of her life in ten-year increments if possible? Family members? Education? Best friend? Residences? Occupations?
4. Role of religion in her life? Spirituality? Belief in God? Religious affiliation? Religious activities?
5. Most difficult period of her life? Best part of her life?
6. Experiences of oppression? Experiences of liberation?
7. Problem-solving strategies?
8. Legacy: atypical, typical, compared to whom? Did she have a role model? Who? Why?
9. If she could change her life, what would she do? Would she want to change?
10. Was there a group of sisters, a sister, who helped her through her life?

Although initially some were hesitant to do the assignment, eventually all but three of fifty members of this small group did all or part of the project. Twenty-two did interviews in person, twenty-one did telephone interviews, and four wrote letters. Several were amazed at subjects some relatives would not talk about, such as deaths, births, family members, or religion. Others unearthed a treasure right under their noses. Those without living female relatives called fictive kin, women at least ten years older than they were. Some women received family mementos and long-awaited encouragement. Some encountered painful information about who they thought they were, or some family secret that emerged. In the group meeting their grief was respected and addressed. A number of the grandmothers and othermothers interviewed felt pleasure in a younger woman wanting to hear about them and talked at length. Others said that they were not important and had nothing to offer beyond perfunctory answers to questions.

The love/hate relationship black women have with their positions in family, church, and community was simmering beneath many discussions and reports. Some of those interviewed had opted to leave family, church, and community due to the oppressive gender roles, and their decision to seek freedom by themselves. The majority of women remained affiliated with a family that viewed them as a "strong black woman" always able to keep things going, or a church that referred to them as "the backbone" with responsibility but no power, or a community that deferred to their leadership initiative.[8] Two women had positive experiences—positions of leadership, supportive family members, opportunities to preach, inclusive language—in their church, and attributed the experience to both the mentality of the pastor and the support they received from other women. In each group, however, women had attempted and at times succeeded in creating spaces for themselves or their children that afforded them at least a modicum of dignity and self-respect. There were also reports of women who felt comfortable with their ascribed roles and taught their daughters and granddaughters that submission to men and silence was a God-given mandate. This created some lively discussions about "uppity women" (those who had decided to live as equals with men and had read about how to do so) and "unenlightened women" (older women who grew up with the submissive prototype and saw little or no reason to change).

Self-Empowerment Through the Stories and Lives of Historical African American Women

The second phase of the self-empowerment project was looking at historical African American women who exemplified the behavior or social consciousness that individual sisters desired. The focal point of this exercise was the section of Walker's *womanist* definition that speaks of a woman who "appreciates and prefers women's culture, women's emotional flexibility, and women's strength." Each member selected a biography or autobiography and agreed to form study groups with six other women and report back to the larger group answering the same type of questions used in the ethnographic study. Anna Julia Cooper, Fannie Lou Hamer, Nannie Helen Burroughs, Joanne Robinson, Maria Stewart, Daisy Bates, Jarena Lee, Amanda Berry Smith, Leontyne Kelly, Shirley Chisholm, and Barbara Jordan (fictive, spiritual grandmothers and othermothers for African American women) were a few of the women selected for study. The sisters also chose historical women not listed who they felt had a major impact on their lives or chosen professions.

Finally, the lives of the older relative-friends, the lives of the extraordinary-famous women, and the lives of the S.W.E.E.T. members were compared and contrasted in terms of social location, circumstances of life, coping mechanisms, prejudices, and goals as a source of determining how contemporary women could cultivate strategies for self and social transformation.[9] In light of what was learned about these women, the following questions fostered conversation on empowerment and intergenerational transfer of wisdom: What can be learned from the lives of African American women? What values or moral wisdom is passed down from their writings or words of encouragement? What life-changing choices did they make? What obstacles, advantages, failures, or successes did they face? How did they forge new or different paths for themselves, their family, or other women? Did they accept, reject, assimilate, or change the situation? What is your legacy for African American women and children?

Self-Empowerment Through the Lives of African American Women in Literature

The third phase involved hearing the voices of African American women in literature. Although some of the group were well read, many members were not, particularly in the literature of African American women. Self-concept, competition with other women, adverse relationships with black men, feelings of inadequacy, being shut out of the corporate world, day to day battles with racism and sexism, fear of failure for self and children, and thirst for an increased spiritual presence in their lives compelled the attention of each woman in S.W.E.E.T. at some level, and made a natural bridge of interest to literary examples of similar struggles.

Literary groups were formed around selected titles on lists provided by one of our members, Clara Villarosa, who owned an African American bookstore, and from recommendations by the membership. In a mode similar to studying the lives of black women, each group read and evaluated the books for general content, identification with characters, relationships, situations, and possibilities for change. In the study groups the *womanist* definition was used as a standard of analysis. The women decided for themselves if the protagonists exhibited *womanist* traits and if they found themselves in any characterization or a situation similar to the characters.' The work was also used as a problem-solving tool. Parallels between the circumstances, actions, and needs of the protagonist and the persons reading the text were examined. The manner in which the author resolved the situation, the characters lived out their choices, or survived in spite of the situation was also a point of conversation. The most popular books for these discussions were *Waiting To Exhale* by Terry McMillan, *The Color Purple* by Alice Walker, *Their Eyes Were Watching God* by Zora Neale Hurston, *Women of Brewster Place* by Gloria Naylor, *Song of Solomon* by Toni Morrison, and *Ugly Ways* by Tina Ansa. African American women's poetry such as *And Still I Rise* by Maya Angelou and short stories like Louise Meriweather's *Daddy Was a Numbers Runner* were reviewed at poetry and tea/coffee sessions or dinners. Examination of art, commercials, films, television programming, and plays, for example, *for colored girls who have considered suicide/when the rainbow is enuf* by Ntozake Shange, were also evaluated, in small groups or at "Sister's Night Out," and searched for meaning in contemporary life.

The engagement with African American women's literature provided an opportunity for the sisters to be mentored through written expressions and dialogue about information that intersected their lives. In many instances the chronicling of problems and transitions in black women's lives, the hopes and disappointments, opportunities and processes for transformation, and the manner in which black women survive or perish through the eyes and voices of the authors had the same impact as the personal one-on-one interview time with the elders. The intended outcome of all three processes was to open new avenues of self-love, self-determination, self-control, and an appreciation for the lives of ordinary black women as models of how one lives and teaches others how to live despite circumstances.

> **"It is impossible to break a bundle of sticks."**
>
> African Proverb

Saving Families, Transforming Communities

Another facet of womanist thought is being "committed to the survival and wholeness of an entire people, male and female." Aware of the reported disintegration of the African American family, S.W.E.E.T. members requested forums on how to save their families and transform the community. Using published articles and books such as Robert Staples's *The Black Family: Essays and Studies* or Wallace C. Smith's *The Church in the Life of the Black Family;* expertise from the membership; and invited guests such as social workers, ministers, law enforcement specialists, psychologists, and elders, seminars and forums open to the public were devised and implemented. Out of that experience intergenerational mentoring groups were set up in three areas.

The S.W.E.E.T. foster grandparents/grandchildren program, "It Takes an Entire Village" paired elders and young people who did not have living grandparents/grandchildren, those who did not know their grandparents/grandchildren, or those whose grandparents/grandchildren lived in other states. The elder (usually female and over sixty) became the advisor, confidant, tutor, and mentor while the young person (depending on age and ability) shopped, wrote letters, cleaned house, cooked, provided transportation, and offered companionship. Time commitment was two hours per week, usually on Saturdays. The program had limited success due to transportation issues but was determined to be viable when careful arrangements were made.

The S.W.E.E.T. Talent Share was a vocation/avocation mentoring program. Participants completed cards listing their occupation, education, and talents or special gifts such as gourmet cooking or stained glass art. Another card showed what they wanted to know more about in the same categories. Every two weeks persons were paired with a mentor and talents were shared. Commitment time was one hour per week. Retirees or those who had had more than one career were particularly helpful in this program. Younger women were given pointers on how to succeed in corporate structures and how to start their own businesses. New skills were acquired for leisure, of which many had little due to striving to climb tenuous corporate ladders. The result was the initiation of better time use and stress-relieving avocations.

The third intergenerational program was the "Sister/Girlfriend—I Got Your Back" mentorship. Women were asked to choose someone they did not know and find out as much information as possible in five minutes. They then introduced that person to the rest of the group. Later they committed to call that sister once per week for prayer, advice, networking, child care, tutoring, whatever the two of them needed and felt they could share. They determined their own time commitments and length of engagement. Some of the dyads failed due to personality conflicts but most led to bonds of sisterhood that had previously been fractured due to gossip and lack of knowledge about who and what the sister was. In one case, three women who had not spoken in the five or six years they had attended the same church began a friendship that has endured since the inception of the project.[10]

"You must live within your sacred truth."   Hausa Proverb

Inside the Circle, Yet Outside the Center

Each of the S.W.E.E.T. program components proved beneficial for most participants. The disheartening fact is that between meetings and activities some of the members returned to families, churches, and communities that were not supportive of their freedom or equality. As an ordained minister in a traditional black denomination I am well aware that the practice of freedom for all does not always measure up to what is preached. The portion of the *womanist* definition that has proved helpful in continuing to work with women's groups is, "possesses a revolutionary faith in a higher power." I have added, "a belief in somebody bigger than you and I." I have come to understand through conversations, interviews, listening in on testimonies, songs, sermons, and stories that both churched and unchurched black women carry a deep-seated spiritual belief in God or a being beyond themselves. For Christian women this faith in God appears senseless to many who observe the black woman's social status, her relegation to cooking, singing, and cleaning, and the violence to her psyche when she is barred from pulpits. I would term black women who have encountered these situations "recovering Christians." They strive to recover from the addictive nature of church-related oppression. It is difficult for some of them to stay away even when they know that they may come away bloodied and battered and bruised. This is where Walker's "Loves the Spirit" is helpful. Black women widen the text to find themselves as daughters of God equal with all of God's children. At the same time they hold open the text for others to locate themselves, and as the gospel song says, "keep holding on and won't let go of my faith" theology is set.

Reassessment of the role of women in churches, ministry, or private spirituality was initiated with questions such as: "Who is God and why do you believe in God?"; "Who/what does your God look like?"; "How do you name God?"; "Why do you go to church?"; "Who decides what you do at church and how?"; and "What scriptural information is available about women's roles and responsibility in religious settings?" There were no right or wrong answers, just an opportunity to air opinions, strategize about ways to make the church more inclusive of women, and help other women identify instances of discrimination and role-stereotyped ministries in churches. One of the interesting finds from the meetings was that the majority of women had never questioned what women are required to wear or do, or that the positions in the church are traditionally closed to women. Nor did they question the language, songs, and sermons that excluded women or referred to them only as tools of destruction of men.

Members who were women in ministry facilitated these discussions. Some of the women had difficulty understanding how or why a woman would seek ordination and wanted to share pain experienced in their lay ministries and strengthen their resolve to support ordained women. Bible studies or sacred texts studies led by womanist scholars or an ordained woman were crucial to nourishing the seeds of change that these discussions had planted in terms of women's roles and responsibilities in the church. Women-led studies, focusing on women in the Bible, religious female elders, and women-centered topical Bible studies yielded a more intense interpretation of faith than those settings where women felt beaten up or excluded, as they did in many regular worship services. Digging deep in the texts for stories of women and men who were in partnership with women proved empowering not only for the adult women but also for their daughters. Available resources such as *Just a Sister Away* by Renita Weems or videotapes of African American women preachers were invaluable in transmitting new paradigms of who women of faith were and could become.

One of the primary tools for transmitting values in the black church is through the sermon. The preaching ministry is one of the most revered positions in the black church and community. The preacher influences innumerable sisters and brothers of all ages in the church pulpits and community settings whether singing, praying, testifying, or preaching a major sermon. In-depth discussion or panels of women preachers resulted in questions such as: "How do you know you are called?"; "How did you decide to preach anyway?"; "What problems did you face as a woman preacher?"; "What scriptural authority do you have to preach?"; and "How do you get to stand on holy ground? You're a woman!"

Another area of worship evaluated was the lyrics for music. Small groups researched the lyricist's life, beliefs, and value system. Individual members wrote personal devotions and designed liturgies that spoke to the needs of all worshipers. Working to develop more inclusive worship services was challenging yet productive for many women, especially for those from more conservative communions. What was necessary to strengthen them to pass on life's lesson to the children, brothers, and sisters was: helping the sisters find their own sense of who they were; rediscovering the Mother Wit of how one shows reverence to God and elders; giving and getting respect; becoming more responsible for one's own decisions; and existence based in reciprocity.

The membership of S.W.E.E.T. continues to develop through mentoring of one another, for example, in a Women's Rites of Passage program and literary study groups. The program is being replicated in other cities and may expand its objectives by working with a parallel African American men's group.

> **"If we stand tall it is because we stand on the backs of those who came before us."**   Yoruba Proverb

The End of the Matter

The focus of this work has been the intergenerational transmission of African American spiritual values through grandmothers and othermothers as demonstrated in African American women's literature since 1960. Three ethical presuppositions—"God don't like ugly," "We are all Aunt Haggie's children," and "Trouble don't last always"—were developed from reading African American women's literature and a review of African American spiritual values detailed in scholarly literature on the history of the black church, black family, and black community. Each of the presuppositions has been further developed in community programs.

The Bridge Street Rites of Passage Program, the Full Circle Intergenerational Project and the Back to the Kitchen Table Program all focused on the needs of and means for black children and black families to fully develop, grow, and maintain a sense of worth and purpose in society. The S.W.E.E.T. organization began out of a decided need for African American women to obtain a sense of empowerment in the family, church, and community through the use of African American women's literature and culture. The genesis for each was grounded in an understanding of moral wisdom of the black community that is present yet overshadowed by societal reports and studies that would lead one to believe that the community has been dead or dying for years. As a result, we can affirm that through recognition of voices once silenced, use of in-house resources, mentoring by community wisdom barometers such as elders, grandmothers, othermothers, and otherfathers, and the resounding description of the realities of black life and survival from the pages of African American women's literature—songs, poetry, short stories, novels, and autobiographies—the transmission of moral wisdom intergenerationally can indeed be sustained.

Chapter 1 provided a cursory review of the composition, strengths, deficiencies, and shifts in the black family, church, and community over the past 380 years. Afrocentric interpretation of scripture, cultural hermeneutics, and particular worldviews were also pictured as vital to the intersecting sacred/secular life of African American Christians.

Principles of survival (living beyond circumstances) and the spirituality of African Americans in general, and African American women in particular, were developed in chapter 2. Womanist perspectives that grew out of African American women's literature (specifically, works by Alice Walker), history, and black theology and ethics gave voice to countless black women who endeavored to overcome multidimensional oppression in American society. The universality or equality of humanity, self-determination, or conscientization and wholeness of an entire people are hallmarks of womanist perspectives. A study of African American spiritual/cultural/social ethics was engaged through analysis of authors such as Katie Cannon, Andrew Billingsley, Wade Boykin, and Forrest Tones. Prosocial values such as spirituality, harmony, orality, love of children, reverence for a transcendent God, homage of elders, reciprocity, restraint, and respect were delineated. Pedagogical vehicles such as Mother Wit, chastisement, modeling, stories, recounting family history, biblical mandates, and one-on-one instruction were addressed.

Chapter 3 was an analysis of African American women's literature as an avenue of self-expression. The perceived leadership and authority of black men, white men, and white women in terms of who is most qualified to speak for the black people have muffled the voices of black women. Overlooked as a source of value transmission, the black woman often turned to songs, prayer, short stories, poetry, diaries, novels, and autobiographies to articulate her feelings, beliefs, desires and gifts, hopes and dreams for her children. In actuality, within the black family, church, and community it was the duty of the African American mother, grandmother, and othermother to raise black children in a Christian or at least faith-filled atmosphere. Despite social conditions, lack of sufficient economic resources, and even oppressive religious institutions black women were challenged to pass on moral wisdom to children with limited futures.

Chapters 4, 5, and 6 provided an in-depth exploration of African American women's gospel songs, poetry, short stories, novels, and autobiographies as sources for demonstration of the intergenerational transmission of African American spiritual values by grandmothers and othermothers. Using information from the preceding chapters, three ethical presuppositions were generated. The African American belief in an all-powerful, all-seeing, all-knowing, all-present, and all-loving God was connected with the belief that God sets a standard of behavior for all persons. The expectation of Christian behavior became the moral presupposition that "God don't like ugly." The womanist perspective of the universality of humanity and wholeness of a people combined with a belief that ultimately we all emanated from Adam and Eve evolved into the presupposition that "We are all Aunt Haggie's children." Regardless of our social, physical, ethnic, racial, spiritual, economic, or educational status we are all children of God. The third presupposition centers on the necessity of and constancy of hope. Notwithstanding a sense of alienation or pessimism upon hearing about the demise of the black family, the disgruntled cries about the ineffectiveness of the black church, or the inability to locate or define the contemporary black community, there is hope by believing people that "Trouble don't last always." Mother Wit reminds us that "God takes care of God's own." Persistence in the face of overwhelming odds means eventual victory spiritually if not physically.

In this chapter we have looked at four programs. The necessity of elders teaching youth, God being a primary focus in the lives of the people, and sharing messages with society is evident in all four programs. Two programs focus on youth, increasing their self-esteem and spirituality through searching those pockets of culture that seek to revitalize the gifts and grace of African Americans in order to save our children. The third is a family program used to maximize intergenerational time for social and spiritual growth and development in a middle-class community. The fourth involves African American women learning to share information across lines of age, economics, education, and belief as one method of self-empowerment and community transformation. African American folklore instructs us that "God makes three requests of his children: Do the best you can, where you are, with what you have, now." Each of the programs employs minimal resources, may be adapted to fit specific groups, and is a blend of proved ideas and methods of our foreparents, with innovative methods of implementation.

Conclusion

Grandmothers and othermothers are not the only persons passing on values to children or teaching other adults how to live through moral wisdom. However, the need to articulate the contribution of grandmothers and othermothers to the development of sacred and secular values is imperative. We are living in a society where there is an increasing number of augmented and blended families. Grandparents are caring for grandchildren for a variety of reasons and somewhere along the line credence should be given to their ability to teach those children how to survive in an often hostile and unloving world. Since our elders have been where the youth seek to go, why is it difficult to recognize the power in attending to their experience and wisdom? Somewhere along the line some of us seemed to get off track and began to overlook these resources in favor of self-help books, visits to psychiatrists, and medicating ourselves to death.

The village is partitioned, the family is fragmented, and children are perishing for "lack of knowledge." Can the village thrive? Will the people survive? The lives, words, and actions of grandmothers and othermothers, whether positive or negative in deportment, offer one possible instructive solution to this quagmire of moral malaise. The beginning of a process of change comes from using the lessons learned by the elders, translation of the situations into contemporary terms, reading about the lives of grandmothers and othermothers who found a God who "made a way out of no way," stopping to listen to someone who may have less education but significantly more Mother Wit or common sense than we will ever attain, and purposely constructing opportunities for families and churches and communities to listen to one another. Intentional hearing of all the voices around us and not closing the communication channel because one is a woman or short or blind or redheaded is not a point of comfort but a necessity if the village is to remain intact long enough for the children to learn how to live, and live above survival. The children will not hear the voices of the elders—grandmothers or othermothers—if we do not make their utterance available to them in our families, our churches, or our communities whether in song, poem, short story, novel, film, prayer, sermon, autobiography, or personal testimony. When all voices are heard, then and only then can the entire village raise the child.

APPENDIX

Remember the Children

Marian Wright Edelman, founder and president of the Children's Defense Fund, issues an annual challenge for social change as it pertains to the lives of the nation's children. In a scathing 1992 report she said that society is ethically polluted with disintegrating family and community support systems and values.[1] This deterioration crosses all races and income groups. Edelman calls the situation one of spiritual and economic paucity; she notes an absence of heroines and heroes amidst a society replete with escalating violence. Due to ethical confusion our children are seeking self-aggrandizement, are shortsighted, and lack moral or spiritual leadership. She reinforces the idea that the solution to our current situation is within our midst.

> Despite these social and cultural tidal waves, I believe there are some enduring spiritual, family, community, and national values and lessons that we need to rediscover in this last decade of this last century in this millennium. I agree with Archibald MacLeish that "there is only one thing more powerful than learning from experience and that is not learning from experience."[2]

Edelman gives seven suggestions for change as we face a new century.

1. Stop neglecting children for our own selfish and shortsighted political gain.
2. Relate to children regardless of race, gender, or class.
3. Love children.

4. Invest in children now.
5. Spend less on weapons and more on children.
6. Set clear goals for the survival and development of children.
7. Struggle to begin living less for self and more for others.[3]

I also contend that one of the most powerful solutions to contemporary societal ills is in rediscovering, remembering, and regenerating the wisdom of the grandmothers and othermothers. Many of us have developed a selective amnesia of what it is to live in community and care for all of God's creation. We have substituted the quest for transitory materialism for striving to ensure that all of God's children have a chance to live.

NOTES

Preface

1. See Margaret Walker, "Lineage," from *For My People* (New Haven: Yale University Press, 1942) reprinted in *Double Stitch: Black Women Write About Mothers and Daughters,* Patricia Bell-Scott, et al., eds. (Boston: Beacon Press, 1991), 175.

2. "Black" and "African American" will interchangeably refer to persons from the African Diaspora. "White" and "European American" will refer to persons whose heritage is based in Europe.

3. Mother Wit is a popular term in black vernacular. It means common sense, good sense not necessarily learned from books or formal education. It is the collective wisdom from the experience of generations. For additional examples and definition see *Mother Wit from the Laughing Barrel,* Alan Dundes, ed. (Jackson: University of Mississippi, 1990), introduction.

4. *Survive* means "to continue to live in spite of." *Survive* is a derivative of the Latin *survivere,* which means to outlive, to live beyond or exist, to last longer than. To survive means that one exists in spite of adversity, comes through, lasts, persists, pulls through, rides out, or outlasts.

5. See Katie G. Cannon, "Womanist Perspectival Discourse and Canon Formation," *Journal of Feminist Studies in Religion* 9:1-2 (spring-fall 1993): 29-37. Cannon says that black women writers must stay attuned to the social, cultural, and political environment of black life. African American women's literature records narrative events that are most recognizable in the lives of the black community. The literature helps the community conserve what has survived from the past and release what may shape the present and future.

6. Grandmothers and othermothers may be natural or blood relatives or those persons whom we have formed relationships with during our lives who have functioned as mothers or grandmothers through influencing our decisions, modeling behavior, or teaching beliefs. They may include sisters, cousins, aunts, teachers, or friends.

7. Luisa Teish, *Jambalaya* (San Francisco: Harper & Row, 1985), xvii, 71. Teish says that immanent spirituality is rooted in the human community, rather than individual salvation. Religion is the source of bonding, connection, or solidarity, and people getting to know one another. African American women are "kin-incarnate"; they are the mother/sister in every block. See also Lawrence Jones, "Transmitting the Faith: From Generation to Generation," *Journal of Religious Thought* 46:1 (summer-fall 1989): 32-41. Jones writes that the church has a primary role of transmission of religious language, socialization of young people, witness of the Incarnate God, modeling of how one is to behave, and sharing what one believes. Every generation needs to be nurtured in the faith of the community.

Introduction

1. Toinette Eugene, "Moral Values and Black Womanists," in *Black Theology, a Documentary History, vol. 2, 1980–1992,* James Cone and Gayaurd Wilmore, eds. (Maryknoll: Orbis, 1993), 309-20.

2. Peter Paris, *The Spirituality of African Peoples: The Search for a Common Moral Discourse* (Minneapolis: Fortress Press, 1995), 27-49, 135. Paris provides a thorough examination of spirituality—the sensitivity and attachment to religious values, behaviors, patterns, and priorities. It is the belief system about God that controls ethical choices and calms the spirit in times of stress. It is the style and content of worship and the celebration of God's presence and influence with the people. Rooted in African cultures, it is a response to and reflection of black life and culture.

1: Reaffirming Cultural Roots: You Bettah Hold Ontah Whatcha Got

1. Marian Wright Edleman, *Families in Peril: An Agenda for Social Change* (Cambridge: Harvard University Press, 1987), 7.

2. Lerone Bennett, Jr., "The 10 Biggest Myths About the Black Family," *Ebony* (August 1986): 123-33.

3. Lerone Bennett, *The Shaping of Black America: The Struggles and Triumphs of African Americans, 1619 to the 1990s* (New York: Penguin Books, 1975), 5-12. Bennett details the landing of twenty indentured blacks aboard a Dutch man-of-war who were traded for food and supplies in Jamestown, Virginia, in August 1619.

4. Marian Wright Edleman, *Families in Peril.*

5. The distinguishing characteristics of black women, their relationships with black families, and their basic beliefs will be addressed in chapter 2.

6. Barbara Omalode, *The Rising Song of African American Women* (New York: Routledge, 1994), 38, 68-78. Omalode is a former Student Nonviolent Coordinating Committee member and political writer. She writes that single black females, especially poor teenagers, have become the symbol of all that is wrong with the black family, black people, as well as any black-initiated movements for social change. She describes the black and white political and social scientist prejudicial assessment of black families, usually defining them as "broken," "illegitimate," and "incubators for

the black underclass." Failure of the black family is a group pathology whereas problems of the white family are historically related to individual failure.

7. See Jeffery Alexander, "Core Solidarity, Ethnic Outgroup, and Social Differentiation," in *Action and Its Environments* (New York: Columbia University Press, 1988), 78-96. Alexander provides a discussion of the development of primordial solidarity in group and nation formation that is vital to understanding the importance of both the solidarity and stratification of African Americans.

8. Emile Durkheim, *The Elementary Forms of the Religious Life* (New York: Free Press, 1915), 38.

9. Barbara Hargrove, *The Sociology of Religion* (Arlington Heights, Ill.: Harlan Davidson, 1979), 144-49.

10. Gayraud Wilmore, *Black Religion and Black Radicalism* (Garden City: Doubleday, 1972), 1-134, 169-85.

11. Edward Wimberly and Anne S. Wimberly, *Liberation and Human Wellness* (Nashville: Abingdon Press, 1985), 1-67.

12. Vincent Harding, *There Is a River: The Black Struggle for Freedom in America* (New York: Harcourt Brace Jovanovich, 1982), 27-44.

13. James Cone, *For My People* (Maryknoll: Orbis Books, 1984), 98-100.

14. Melva Costen, *African American Christian Worship* (Nashville: Abingdon, 1993), 83-85. See also G. Lovelace Champion, Sr., *Black Methodism: Basic Beliefs* (Nashville: The African Methodist Episcopal Church Publishing House, 1980), 77-110.

15. C. Eric Lincoln and Lawrence H. Mamiya, *The Black Church in the African American Experience* (Durham, N.C.: Duke University Press, 1990), 177.

16. Kelly Brown Douglas, *The Black Christ* (Maryknoll: Orbis, 1994), 6-84. Douglas provides a comparative study of the late-twentieth-century views of Albert Cleage, James Cone, and J. Deotis Roberts on black Christology. She also gives a historical review of the black church and the black Christ.

17. Katherine O'Sullivan See and William J. Wilson, "Race and Ethnicity," in *Handbook of Sociology*, Neal J. Smelzer, ed. (Newbury Park: Sage Publications, 1988), 225-28. Ethnic community is based on culture and affinity. One cannot escape his or her ethnicity, particularly if skin color is evidently different from the majority culture. Groups formed around sentiment and affinity are permeable because of the transitory nature of sentiment and emotion. Groups established on shared interest are limited in their ability to meet the needs of the total person. Groups formed around culture have the strongest bonds due to the commonality of behaviors, languages, values, images, meanings, and worldviews. Power and bonding in racial communities are rooted in kinship, family, blood, and legacies that transcend time and space. Allegiance to the culture-based groups depends on the meeting of individual and communal needs.

18. Emmanuel McCall, *The Black Church Experience* (Nashville: Broadmans Press, 1972), 1-29, 66-72.

19. Ibid.

20. Benjamin E. Mays and Joseph W. Nicholson, *The Negro's Church* (New York: Institute of Social and Religious Research, 1933), 30, 43-49.

21. Major Jones, *Christian Ethics for Black Theology* (Nashville: Abingdon Press, 1974), 39-63.

22. Jualyne Dodson and Cheryl Townsend Gilkes, "Something Within: Social Change and Collective Endurance in the Sacred World of Black Christian Women," in *Women and Religion in America, vol. 3, 1900–1968* (San Francisco: Harper & Row, 1986), 81-84.

23. Cain Hope Felder, *Troubling the Biblical Waters* (Maryknoll: Orbis, 1989), 5-8, 54-55. For an in-depth discussion of the principles of justice in the black church, community, and family see Felder's discussion of reciprocal, eschatological, compensatory, commutive, and charismatic distributive justice, 56-78.

24. Wallace C. Smith, *The Church in the Life of the Black Family* (Valley Forge: Judson Press, 1985), 13-42.

25. Ibid.

26. Patricia L. Hunter, "Women's Power—Women's Passion: And God Said 'That's Good' " in *A Troubling in My Soul: Womanist Perspectives on Evil and Suffering,* Emilie M. Townes, ed. (Maryknoll: Orbis, 1993), 189-98. Hunter discusses the re-imaging of God as "no longer exclusively male" as a means of reclaiming and building the self-esteem of black women.

27. Ibid.

28. Wallace C. Smith, *The Church in the Life of the Black Family,* 13-17.

29. Ibid.

30. Shirley Hartley and Ruth Wallace, "Religious Elements in Friendship: Durkheimian Theory in an Empirical Context," in *Durkheimian Sociology: Cultural Studies,* Jeffrey Alexander, ed. (Cambridge: Cambridge University Press, 1988), 93-103.

31. Patricia Hill Collins, *Black Feminist Thought* (New York: Routledge Press, 1991), 49-64.

32. Ibid.

33. Ibid.

34. Marian Wright Edelman, *Families in Peril: An Agenda for Social Change,* (Cambridge: Harvard University Press, 1987), 36, 68-74. Franklin D. Roosevelt signed the Aid to Families with Dependent Children Act in 1935.

35. Patricia Hill Collins, *Black Feminist Thought,* 58-65, 119-21.

36. Lee Rainwater and William L. Yancey, *The Moynihan Report and the Politics of Controversy* (Cambridge: Mass.: MIT Press, 1967), 27-30.

37. Ibid.

38. Ibid.

39. Bettina Aptheker, *Woman's Legacy* (Amherst: University of Massachusetts Press, 1982), 134-37.

40. bell hooks, *Ain't I a Woman?* (Boston: South End Press, 1981), 3-15, 31-66, 72-105.

41. Marian Wright Edelman, *Families in Peril,* 7-9.

42. Andrew Billingsley, *Climbing Jacob's Ladder: The Enduring Legacy of African American Families* (New York: Simon & Schuster, 1992), 28. See also E. Franklin Frazier, *The Negro Family in America* (Chicago: University of Chicago Press, 1966). Frazier's classic text on the black family traces the systems and divisions of the black family based on skin color, education, church membership, occupation, child-rearing practices, and urbanization with particular attention to 1890–1940s.

43. Ibid., 27-52, 65-80, 83-107. Billingsley defines informal adoption as the process by which children born out of wedlock are cared for by the extended family, generally the grandmother. Fictive kin is the strong basis for family union in the African American community. Appropriation means that persons live together without blood or marriage connection. Appropriated members become children, uncles, aunts, mothers, fathers, sisters, brothers, and grandparents. One does not have to share living space to be part of the family unit. Even after divorce one member may continue a close relationship with the family of the former spouse.

44. Joseph Scott and James Steward, "The Pimp-Whore Complex in Everyday Life," in *Crisis in Black Sexual Politics,* Julia and Nathan Hare, eds. (San Francisco: Black Think Tank, 1989), 57-61. Scc also Julia and Nathan Hare, "The Making of the Black Male Shortage and Its Impact on the Black Family," in *Crisis in Black Sexual Politics,* 27-30. The Hares detail the impact of shifts in economic patterns in the 1960s, most notably the increase in employment of women and the loss of jobs by black males. This, according to the Hares, resulted in an increase of absentee black fathers and single black female heads of households. They state that black women did not seek to "castrate" the black male as charged by Moynihan, but had no choice but to support their families "by any means necessary."

45. Joanne Martin and Elmer Martin, *The Helping Tradition in the Black Family and Community* (Silver Springs, Md.: National Association of Social Workers, 1985), 12-82.

46. See also Robert Staples, "The Family," in *The Black Family: Essays and Studies,* 3d ed. (Belmont, Calif.: Wadsworth Publishing, 1986), 145-48. African American sociologist Staples argues that assimilation of dominant society values has had a significant impact on the black family. The 1960s African American quest for personal freedom and job mobility led to the supplanting of traditional cultural values in the name of "fitting in." This was especially evident in changes in kinship bonds, child rearing, sharing of resources, networking, and mutual aid.

47. Elmer Martin and Joanne Martin, *The Black Extended Family* (Chicago: University of Chicago, 1978), 1-47.

48. Ibid.

49. Ibid.

50. Archie Smith, *The Relational Self: Ethics and Therapy from a Black Church Perspective* (Nashville: Abingdon Press, 1982), 15-17, 51-77, 121-22.

2: Wisdom Bearers: The Mother Wit of Sistuh Girlfriends

1. Marilyn Richardson, ed., *Maria W. Stewart, America's First Black Woman Political Writer* (Bloomington: Indiana University Press, 1987), 37-38.

2. Alice Walker, *In Search of Our Mothers' Gardens* (San Diego: Harcourt Brace Jovanovich, 1983), ix. Walker developed the term *womanist* as an interpretation of the black folk expression "You actin' womanish." The definition has been further developed over a period of twelve years to refer to the experience of black women in struggle to overcome multidimensional oppression. Womanist scholars explore the

everyday experiences of black women and how those experiences are used to effect liberation for black women, black family, black church, and black community. For the purpose of this study selected parts of the definition will be useful: "Committed to the survival and wholeness of an entire people, community, male and female; traditionally universalist, as in 'Mama why are we brown, pink, and yellow, and our cousins are white, beige, and black?'; loves herself regardless; womanist is to feminist as purple is to lavender."

3. Jualyne E. Dodson and Cheryl Townsend Gilkes, "Something Within: Social Change and Collective Endurance in the Sacred World of Black Christian Women," in *Women and Religion in America, vol. 3, 1900–1968* (San Francisco: Harper & Row, 1986), 80-127. See also Cheryl Townsend Gilkes, " 'Some Mother's Son and Some Father's Daughter': Gender and Biblical Language in Afro-Christian Tradition," in *Shaping New Visions: Gender and Values in American Culture,* Clarissa W. Atkinson, Constance H. Buchanan, and Margaret R. Miles, eds. (Ann Arbor: UMI Research Press, 1987), 73-95.

4. Henry Mitchell and Nicholas Cooper-Lewter, *Soul Theology* (San Francisco: Harper & Row, 1986), 3-6, 28-47, 47-66.

5. Ibid.

6. Archie Smith, *The Relational Self: Ethics and Therapy from a Black Church Perspective* (Nashville: Abingdon Press, 1982), 60-61, 85-87, 214-15.

7. Ibid., 25, 114-18, 125-27.

8. Ibid.

9. Cain Hope Felder, *Troubling the Biblical Waters* (Maryknoll: Orbis, 1989), 5-8, 54-55, 101.

10. James E. Evans, Jr., *We Have Been Believers* (Minneapolis: Fortress Press, 1992), 51-76.

11. Adelbert H. Jenkins, "Black Families: the Nurturing of Agency," in *Black Families in Crisis—The Middle Class,* Alice F. Coner-Edwards and Jeanne Spurlock, eds. (New York: Brunner Mazel, 1988), 115-27.

12. Ibid.

13. Wade W. Nobles, "African American Family Life—An Instrument of Culture," in *Black Families,* 2d ed., Harriette Pipes McAdoo, ed. (Newbury Park, California: Sage Publications, 1988), 49-50.

14. Margie Ferguson Peters, "Parenting in Black Families with Young Children—A Historical Perspective," in *Black Families,* Harriette Pipes McAdoo, ed., 228-41.

15. A. Wade Boykin and Forrest D. Tones, "Black Child Socialization—A Conceptual Framework," in *Black Children—Social, Educational and Parental Environments,* Harriette Pipes McAdoo and John Lewis McAdoo, eds. (Beverly Hills: Sage Publications, 1985), 33-49.

16. Andrew Billingsley, *Climbing Jacob's Ladder : The Enduring Legacy of African American Families* (New York: Simon & Schuster, 1992), 83-95, 143, 312-13, 328-33; Dwight N. Hopkins, *Shoes That Fit Our Feet: Sources of a Constructive Black Theology* (Maryknoll: Orbis, 1993), 15-19, 41-48.

17. Andrew Billingsley, *Climbing Jacob's Ladder,* 223-33.

18. Dwight N. Hopkins, *Shoes That Fit Our Feet,* 41-48.

19. Ibid.

20. Anna Julia Cooper, *A Voice from the South* (Xenia, Ohio: Aldine Publishing House, 1892; reprint, The Schomburg Library of Nineteenth-Century Black Women Writers, Louis Henry Gates, ed. (New York: Oxford, 1988), 31.

21. Paula Giddings, *When and Where I Enter: The Impact of Black Women on Race and Sex in America* (New York: William Morrow, 1984), 108-16; Louise D. Hutchinson, *Anna Julia Cooper: A Voice from the South* (Washington, D.C.: Smithsonian Institutional Press, 1982), 187-88.

22. Louise D. Hutchinson, *Anna Julia Cooper.*

23. Gloria T. Hull, Patricia Bell-Scott, and Barbara Smith, eds., *All the Women Are White, All the Blacks Are Men, But Some of Us Are Brave* (New York: Feminist Press, 1982), 75-77; Delores Williams, *Sisters in the Wilderness: The Challenge of Womanist God-Talk* (Maryknoll: Orbis, 1993), 56-79.

24. bell hooks, *Ain't I a Woman?* (Boston: South End Press, 1981), 21-53.

25. Pauli Murray, "Black Theology and Feminist Theology: A Comparative View," in *Black Theology: A Documentary History, 1966–1979,* Gayraud Wilmore and James Cone, eds. (Maryknoll: Orbis Books, 1979), 405-6.

26. Kelly Delaine Brown, "God Is as Christ Does: Toward a Womanist Theology," *Journal of Religious Thought* 46:1 (1989): 7-17; Kelly Brown Douglas, *The Black Christ* (Maryknoll: Orbis, 1994), 104-16.

27. Elsa Barkley Brown, "Womanist Consciousness: Maggie Lena Walker and the Independent Order of St. Luke," *Signs* 14 (1989): 610-33.

28. Katie G. Cannon, *Black Womanist Ethics* (Atlanta: Scholars Press, 1988), 1-10, 21-23.

29. Ibid.

30. Jacquelyn Grant, "Womanist Theology: Black Women's Experience for Doing Theology with Special Reference to Christology," *Journal of the Interdenominational Theological Center* 12 (spring 1986): 195-210; *White Women's Christ and Black Women's Jesus: Feminist Christology and Womanist Response* (Atlanta: Scholar's Press, 1989), 209-21; "Come to My Help, For I Am in Trouble," in *Reconstructing the Christ Symbol,* Margaret Stevens, ed. (Mahwah, N.J.: Paulist Press, 1993), 54-71.

31. Theresa Hoover, "Black Women and Churches: Triple Jeopardy," in Gayraud Wilmore and James Cone, *Black Theology,* 377-87.

32. Delores C. Carpenter, "Black Women in Religious Institutions: A Historical Summary from Slavery to the 1960s," *Journal of Religious Thought* 46:2 (winter-spring 1989-90): 7-27.

33. Cheryl Townsend Gilkes, "Role of Church and Community Mothers: Ambivalent American Sexism or Fragmented Familyhood?" *Journal of Feminist Studies in Religion* 2 (spring 1986): 41-59; " 'Some Mother's Son and Some Father's Daughter': Gender and Biblical Language in the Afro-Christian Worship Tradition," in *Shaping New Visions: Gender and Values in American Culture,* Clarissa W. Atkinson, Constance H. Buchanan, and Margaret R. Miles, eds. (Ann Arbor: UMI Research Press, 1987), 73-95.

34. Ibid.

35. Ibid.

36. Patricia Hill Collins, *Black Feminist Thought: Knowledge, Consciousness and the Politics of Empowerment* (New York: Routledge Press, 1991), 68-78, 96-138, 215-23.

37. Ibid.

38. Marie Peters and Cecile de Ford, "The Solo Mothers," in *The Black Family: Essays and Studies,* Robert Staples, ed. (Belmont, Calif.: Wadsworth Publishing, 1986), 166-72.

39. Katie Geneva Cannon, "Moral Wisdom in the Black Woman's Literary Tradition," in *Weaving the Vision: New Patterns in Feminist Spirituality,* Judith Plaskow and Carol Christ, eds. (San Francisco: HarperCollins, 1989), 281-92.

3: Listening to Experience: Why Are You Actin' Like You Don't Hear Me?

1. Alice Walker, "Women," in *All the Women Are White, All the Blacks Are Men, But Some of Us Are Brave,* Gloria T. Hull, Patricia Bell-Scott, and Barbara Smith, eds. (New York: Feminist Press, 1982), xiv.

2. Mary Helen Washington, ed., *Invented Lives: Narratives of Black Women, 1860-1960* (New York: Anchor Books, 1987), xxi.

3. Henry Louis Gates, Jr., "In Her Own Write," in *The Collected Works of Phillis Wheatley,* John Shields, ed. (New York: Oxford Press, 1988), vii-xxii.

4. Mary Helen Washington, ed., *Invented Lives,* xxi.

5. Toni Cade, ed., *The Black Woman: An Anthology* (New York: Mentor, 1970), 7.

6. John J. McKenzie, "The Hebrew Community and Old Testament" in "The Making of Literature," *The Interpreter's One Volume Commentary of the Bible,* ed. Charles M. Laymon (Nashville: Abingdon Press, 1971), 1072-76.

7. Molefie Kete Asante, "Locating a Text: Implications of Afrocentric Theory," in *Language and Literature in the African American Imagination,* Carol Aisha Blackshire-Belay, ed. (Westport, Conn.: Greenwood Press, 1992), 9-20. Asante suggests that one consider "Ebonics" or "in-speech" or language of African Americans in reading a text by African Americans. He states that there must be a sensitivity for sarcasm, pejorative, attitude, symbolism, and significance of the names of characters. Black women authors and womanist criticism consider issues of race, class, gender, and spirituality using coded or structured language with which African American women identify. See also John Peck and Martin Coyle, *Literary Terms and Criticism* (London: Macmillan, 1984), 1-6, 127-48. Peck and Coyle delineate guidelines for literary analysis beginning with a determination of what a work is about and how the author crafts the writing. There is a consideration of the historical context, audience, and worldview of both the reader and the author.

8. Wesley Kort, "Narrative and Theology," in *Literature and Theology,* vol. 1 (Oxford: Oxford University Press, 1987), 27-31. Narrative conveys or pursues the truth by using actual occurrences and personages to tell what can, always, and does truly happen in life. Boundaries of narratives are given instances of human life—personal existence, individual resourcefulness, and tensions between individuals and society.

African American women's narratives employ individual worldviews, relationship to an image of God, and changes in life based on interaction with others.

9. Margaret Walker, *Jubilee* (New York: Bantam, 1966), 233-34.

10. A. H. T. Levi, "The Relationship Between Literature and Theology," in *Literature and Theology,* vol. 1 (Oxford: Oxford University Press, 1987), 11-17; David Jasper, "The Limits of Formalism and the Theology of Hope: Ricoeur, Moltmann, and Dostoyevsky," in *Literature and Theology,* vol. 1, 1-9.

11. Ibid.

12. Henry Louis Gates, Jr., *The Signifying Monkey: A Theory of Afro-American Literary Criticism* (New York: Oxford University Press, 1988), xxii-xxiii.

13. Charles Johnson, *Being and Race: Black Writing Since 1970* (Bloomington: Indiana University Press, 1990), 7-26.

14. Calvin Hernton, "The Sexual Mountain and Black Women Writers," in *Wildwomen in the Whirlwind: Afra-American Culture and the Contemporary Literary Renaissance,* Joanne M. Braxton and Andree Nicola McLaughlin, eds. (New Brunswick: Rutgers University Press, 1990), 200-207.

15. Mary Helen Washington, " 'The Darkened Eye Restored': Notes Toward a Literary History of Black Women," in *Reading Black, Reading Feminist,* Henry Louis Gates, Jr., ed. (New York: Meridian, 1990), 32; Mary Helen Washington, ed., *Black Eyed Susans* (New York: Anchor Books, 1975), ix-xxi; Calvin Hernton, "The Sexual Mountain and Black Women Writers," in *Wildwomen in the Whirlwind,* 195-212.

16. Shirley Anne Williams, "Some Implications of Womanist Theory," in Henry Louis Gates, Jr., *Reading Black, Reading Feminist,* 68-75.

17. Ibid. See also Henry Louis Gates, Jr., "Afterword: Zora Neale Hurston: 'A Negro Way of Saying,' " in Zora Neale Hurston, *Their Eyes Were Watching God* (New York: HarperCollins, 1990), 185-207.

18. Zora Neale Hurston, *Their Eyes Were Watching God,* 182.

19. Ibid., 185-89.

20. Toni Cade, *The Black Woman,* 7-9.

21. Ibid.

22. Ibid.

23. Mary Helen Washington, "Teaching Black-Eyed Susans: An Approach to the Study of Black Women Writers," in *All the Women Are White, All the Blacks Are Men, But Some of Us Are Brave,* 206-17.

24. Ibid. Washington uses a psychological-historical analysis of the mirroring or social status and activism by African American women and the women portrayed in African American women's literature since the 1800s. She suggests fluid categories of analysis: (1) Nineteenth-century *suspended women,* who are subjugated and destroyed by oppression and violence; (2) 1940–50s *assimilated women,* who are also victimized, alienated, and strive to fit into mass society; (3) late 1950s–60s *emergent women,* who are influenced by the politics and freedom movements of the time, seeking their heritage and cultural connections. Washington says that there are overlapping yet distinct literary characters in African American women's literature that contemporary women identified with and whose lives may have been reinforced based on the characters about which they were reading.

25. Lorraine Bethel, "This Infinity of Conscious Pain: Zora Neale Hurston and the Black Female Literary Tradition," in *All the Women Are White, All the Blacks Are Men, But Some of Us Are Brave,* 176-86.

26. Alice Walker, *The Color Purple* (New York: Harcourt Brace Jovanovich, 1982), 166.

27. Maya Angelou, *And Still I Rise* (New York: Random House, 1978), 41-42.

28. Ibid.

29. Ibid. See also Youtha C. Hardman-Crowell, "Living in the Intersection of Womanism and Afrocentrism," in *Living the Intersection: Womanism and Afrocentrism in Theology,* Cheryl J. Sanders, ed. (Minneapolis: Fortress Press, 1995), 105-19.

30. Joanne M. Braxton, "Afra-American Culture and the Contemporary Literary Renaissance," in *Wildwomen in the Whirlwind,* xxii. Braxton outlines the importance of the literary witness of black women. Black women are privy to the spirituality of their foremothers due to the passing on of verbal lore as well as women's consciousness that would not be denied.

31. Gloria Wade-Gayles, *No Crystal Stair* (New York: Pilgrim Press, 1984), 12-19.

32. Alice Walker, "Everyday Use," in *In Love & Trouble* (San Diego: Harcourt Brace Jovanovich, 1967), 56.

33. J. California Cooper, "Sisters of the Rain," in *Some Soul to Keep* (New York: St. Martin's Press, 1987), 42.

34. Alice Walker, "Her Sweet Jerome," in *In Love & Trouble,* 34.

35. Alice Walker, "The Welcome Table," in *In Love & Trouble,* 86-87.

36. Calvin Hernton, "The Sexual Mountain and Black Women Writers," in *Wildwomen in the Whirlwind,* 204-7.

37. Ibid.

38. Joanne Braxton, *Black Women Writing Autobiography: A Tradition Within a Tradition* (Philadelphia: Temple University Press, 1989), 1-13.

39. See Ntozake Shange, *for colored girls who have considered suicide/when the rainbow is enuf* (New York: Macmillan, 1975), 48-51.

40. Joanne V. Gabbin, "A Laying on of Hands: Black Women Writers Exploring the Roots of Their Folk and Cultural Tradition," in *Wildwomen in the Whirlwind,* 246-63; See also Charles Johnson, *Being and Race,* 99-118.

41. Michele Wallace, "Variations on Negation and the Heresy of Black Feminist Creativity," in *Reading Black, Reading Feminist,* Henry Louis Gates, Jr., ed., 52-67; Barbara Christian, "The Highs and Lows of Black Feminist Criticism," in Gates, 44-49.

42. Ibid.

43. Arlyn Diamond, "Choosing Sides, Choosing Lives: Women's Autobiographies of the Civil Rights Movement," in *American Women's Autobiography: Fea(s)ts of Memory,* Margo Culley, ed. (Madison: University of Wisconsin Press, 1992), 221-31; Mae Gwendolyn Henderson, "Speaking in Tongues: Dialogues, Dialectic, and the Black Woman Writers' Literary Tradition," in Henry Louis Gates, Jr., ed., *Reading Black, Reading Feminist,* 116-42; Deborah E. McDowell, "The Changing Same: Generational Connections and Black Women Novelists," in Gates, 91-115.

44. Itabari Njeri, *Every Good-bye Ain't Gone* (New York: Vintage Books, 1991), 7, 47, 51.

45. Ibid, 51.

46. Ann Petry, *The Street* (Boston: Houghton Mifflin, 1946).

47. Ibid., 15-17.

48. Ibid., 404.

49. Ibid.

50. Katie G. Cannon, "Moral Wisdom in Black Women's Literary Tradition," in *Weaving the Visions: New Patterns in Feminist Spirituality,* Judith Plaskow and Carol Christ, eds. (San Francisco: HarperCollins, 1989), 281-91; See also Cannon, " 'Hitting a Straight Lick with a Crooked Stick': The Womanist Dilemma in the Development of a Black Liberation Ethic," in *The Annual of the Society of Christian Ethics* 16 (1988): 167-71.

51. From the time of slavery to the present "Africanisms" meant the use of drums, dance, cries, ecstatic praise, tarrying, and worship of God in nature. Although "colorism" or "colorstruckness" is evident in slavery and beyond, blacks, especially black women, understood their beauty was not validated by whites and at times black men. Women of mixed parentage because of their resemblance to whites were of higher value to slave masters than to the enslaved. Denigrated for their physical appearance, black women developed their own beauty standards defining large hips, full lips, voluptuous breasts, tightly curled (natural) hair, and distinctively African facial features as just as beautiful as those of the more slender European-like features. See Cheryl Townsend Gilkes, "The 'Loves' and 'Troubles' of African American Women's Bodies: The Womanist Challenge to Cultural Humiliation and Community Ambivalence," in *A Troubling in My Soul: Womanist Perspectives on Evil and Suffering,* Emilie Townes, ed. (Maryknoll: Orbis, 1993), 232-49.

52. Ibid.

53. The primary archetype in African American women's writings is the "ancestral" figure of the outraged mother who breaks down barriers for her children and community. She employs Christian or African spiritual strength to temper her outrage and "passes on her feminine wisdom for the good of the 'tribe' " and the survival of all black people. She embodies values of sacrifice, nurturance, and personal sacrificial courage in witness to an endangered people. See Joanne M. Braxton, "Ancestral Presence: The Outraged Mother Figure in Contemporary Afra-American Writing," in *Wildwomen in the Whirlwind,* 300-15. Also see Luisa Teish, "Ancestor Reverence," in Judith Plaskow and Carol P. Christ, *Weaving the Visions,* 87-92. "Ancestor reverence" is from African belief systems that state that ancestors make us who we are. They influence physical, hereditary, and personality traits, continue to exist and act in the world, and are called the "living dead."

4: Acting Lessons: God Don't Like Ugly

1. Ella Mitchell and Henry Mitchell, "Black Spirituality: The Values of That Ol' Time Religion," in *The Journal of the Interdenominational Theological Center* 17 (fall 1989/spring 1990): 99-105. Spirituality includes those basic beliefs about God and Creation that (a) control ethical choices and behavior; (b) support calmness of spirit in

times of stress; (c) are the style and content of worship; and (d) add typical testimony of God as Spirit as real and present with a person through personal influences with the Incarnate. God is omnipotent, omniscient, omnipresent, and the source of justice in the belief system of many black Christians. See also Celestine Cypress, ed., *Sister Thea Bowman: Shooting Star* (Winoma, Minn.: Saint Mary's Press, 1993), 38-48. Bowman refers to black spirituality as the response and reflection on black life and culture with its distinctive way of prayer, contemplating the divine, perceiving and valuing reality, and expressing of style.

2. A. Wade Boykin and Forrest D. Tones, "Black Child Socialization—A Conceptual Framework," in *Black Children—Social, Educational and Parental Environments,* Harriette Pipes McAdoo and John Lewis McAdoo, eds. (Beverly Hills: Sage Publications, 1985), 33-49.

3. Celestine Cypress, ed., *Sister Thea Bowman: Shooting Star* (Winoma: Minn.: Saint Mary's Press, 1993). Sister Thea Bowman, the late black Catholic nun, defined black music as "a living repository of the thought, feelings, and will of Black Spirituality. Its symbols, images, rhythms, and expressed values take Blacks *home*." Black music engages the whole person through conscious contact with God, self, and others, and influences one's choosing values of responsibility and is at the same time an expectation that change is possible. See also Lisa Pertillo Brevard, " 'Will the Circle Be Unbroken?': African American Women's Spirituality in Sacred Song Traditions," in *My Soul Is a Witness: African American Women's Spirituality,* Gloria Wade-Gayles, ed. (Boston: Beacon Press, 1995), 32-47. Brevard records parts of a lecture, " 'Wade in the Water': African American Social Music Tradition," by Smithsonian Institute African American curator Bernice Johnson Reagon.

4. Jon Michael Spencer, *Protest and Praise: Sacred Music of Black Religion* (Minneapolis: Fortress Press, 1990), 199-221.

5. J. Wendell Mapson, Jr., *The Ministry of Music in the Black Church* (Valley Forge: Judson Press, 1984), 15-33. See also Cheryl Townsend Gilkes, " 'Some Mother's Son and Some Father's Daughter': Gender and Biblical Language in Afro-Christian Worship Tradition," in *Shaping New Vision: Gender and Values in American Culture,* Clarissa W. Atkinson, Constance H. Buchanan, and Margaret R. Miles, eds. (Ann Arbor: University of Michigan Research Press, 1987), 73-99.

6. Margaret J. Douroux, "Give Me a Clean Heart" in *Songs of Zion* (Nashville: Abingdon Press, 1981), 182.

7. Margaret Pleasant Douroux, "Trees," in *Songs of Zion,* 191.

8. Inez Andrews, "Make It In," in *All-Star Gospel Song Book, No. 30* (Chicago: Martin and Morris Music, 1962), 32-34.

9. Joan Golden and Willie Morganfield, "What Is This?" in *All-Star Gospel Song Book, No. 30,* 7-9.

10. See Dora M. Taylor, "It's Not I (But Christ)" (Los Angeles: Birthright Music/Edwin R. Hawkins Music, 1985), 17-25.

11. Sandi Russell, *Render Me My Song: African-American Women Writers from Slavery to the Present* (New York: St. Martin's Press, 1990), 74-90.

12. John Peck and Martin Coyle, *Literary Terms and Criticism* (London: MacMillan, 1984), 11-73.

13. Nikki Giovanni, "Legacies," in *My House* (New York: William Morrow, 1972), 5.

14. Ibid.

15. Ibid.

16. See Mari Evans, ". . . And the Old Women Gathered (The Gospel Singers)," in *Black Sister: Poetry by Black American Women, 1746–1980,* Erlene Stetson, ed. (Bloomington: Indiana University Press, 1981), 146.

17. Nikki Giovanni, "mrs. martha jean black," in *Spin a Soft Black Song* (Toronto: Collins Press, 1971), 51.

18. Ibid.

19. Arnold Adoff, ed., *The Poetry of Black America* (New York: Harper & Row, 1973), 75-76; Erlene Stetson, ed., *Black Sister* (Bloomington: Indiana University Press, 1981); Maya Angelou, *And Still I Rise* (New York: Random House, 1978).

20. Alice Walker, *In Search of Our Mothers' Gardens* (New York: Harcourt Brace Jovanovich, 1983), 5-13.

21. John Peck and Martin Coyle, *Literary Terms and Criticism,* 102-26.

22. Brenda Bankhead, "Visitations," in *Sisterfire: Black Womanist Fiction and Poetry,* Charlotte Watson Sherman, ed. (New York: HarperPerennial, 1994), 276-89.

23. Ibid., 277.

24. Ibid., 289.

25. Toni Cade Bambara, "The Lesson," in *Calling the Wind: Twentieth Century African-American Short Stories,* Clarence Major, ed. (New York: HarperPerennial, 1993), 348-54.

26. Ibid., 353.

27. Michelle Clift, "Screen Memory," in *Calling the Wind,* 566-70.

28. Ibid., 568.

29. Ibid., 569.

30. Paule Marshall, "To Da-duh, In Memorium," in *Memory of Kin: Stories About Family by Black Writers,* Mary Helen Washington, ed. (New York: Anchor Books, 1991), 385-96.

31. Ibid., 388.

32. Ibid., 393.

33. Barbara Christian, "Somebody Forgot to Tell Somebody Something: African American Women's Historical Novels," in *Wildwomen in the Whirlwind: Afra-American Culture and the Contemporary Literary Renaissance,* Joanne M. Braxton and Andree N. McLaughlin, eds. (New Brunswick: Rutgers University Press, 1990), 327-33.

34. Sandi Russell, *Render Me My Song,* 91-114.

35. Shirley M. Jordan, ed., *Broken Silences: Interviews with Black and White Women Writers* (New Brunswick: Rutgers University Press, 1993), 1-27. See also Rebecca Carroll, *"I Know What the Red Clay Looks Like": The Voices and Visions of Black Women Writers* (New York: Crown, 1994), 17-26. Both works are interviews with women writers concerning their source of inspiration and the subject matter of their writings.

36. Ibid.

37. Tina McElroy Ansa, *Baby of the Family* (San Diego: Harcourt Brace Jovanovich, 1989), 16-17.

38. Ibid., 58.

39. Ibid., 103.

40. Ibid., 192.

41. Ibid., 110.

42. Ibid., 265.

43. Gloria Wade-Gayles, *Pushed Back to Strength: A Black Woman's Journey Home* (Boston: Beacon Press, 1993). See also Rebecca Carroll, *"I Know What Red Clay Looks Like,"* 102-8.

44. Gloria Wade-Gayles, *Pushed Back to Strength*, 248.

45. Ibid., 7, 8, 13, 262.

46. Ibid., 5, 7.

47. Ibid., 7.

48. Ibid., 139.

49. Ibid., 20-21.

50. Ibid., 24-25.

51. Ibid., 106.

52. Kay Mills, *This Little Light of Mine: The Life of Fannie Lou Hamer* (New York: Dutton, 1993). This is the only supportive literary work cited that is written by an Anglo female. It is, however, the most extensive work regarding Hamer's life.

53. Ibid., 17.

54. Ibid., 238.

55. Ibid., 121.

56. Ibid., 18.

57. Ibid., 41.

58. Ibid., 116.

59. Ibid., 308.

5: Spiritual Connections: We Are All Aunt Haggie's Children

1. Martin E. Marty, *Pilgrims in Their Own Land: 500 Years of Religion in America* (New York: Penguin Books, 1984), 3-72. The first colony was established by the Virginia Company on May 14, 1607. Three Protestant colonies—Virginia, New England, and New Netherland—modeled the law, religion, and customs of established churches of Europe. John Winthrop, leader of the Massachusetts Bay Colony, wrote an essay in 1630 en route to New England for the "elect and chosen people of God," the Puritans. In "A Model of Christian Charity," he stated that God intended "every man might have need of others, and from hence they might be all knit more nearly together in the body of brotherly affection." This was to be the human side of the covenant with God, but evidently this meant white Protestant males only. These pilgrims or saints believed that they were in covenant with God to establish a "city on the hill," which provided a holy commonwealth and directions for living in God's will.

2. See Delores Williams, *Sisters in the Wilderness: The Challenge of Womanist God*

Talk (Maryknoll: Orbis, 1993). See also Cheryl Sanders, "Black Women in Biblical Perspective," in *Living the Intersection: Womanism and Afrocentrism in Theology,* Cheryl Sanders, ed. (Minneapolis: Fortress Press, 1995), 121-43. In her analysis of four biblical African women Sanders discusses the importance of the Genesis 16–21 references to Hagar. African American women may identify with Hagar as a slave woman, forced sexual surrogate, and single parent exploited by another woman yet eventually empowered by God. As discussed in chapter 2, this was the lot of the majority of African women through slavery and in other ways—institutional racism, sexism inside and outside the black church, and socioeconomic pressures.

3. Wyatt Tee Walker, *"Somebody's Calling My Name": Black Sacred Music and Social Change* (Valley Forge: Judson Press, 1979), 181.

4. Ibid.

5. See Alma Bazel Androzzo, "If I Can Help Somebody" (Los Angeles: MCA Music, 1961).

6. See Martin Luther King, Jr., "The Drum Major Instinct," in *A Testament of Hope: The Essential Writings of Martin Luther King, Jr.,* James M. Washington, ed. (San Francisco: Harper & Row, 1986), 259-67. Near the end of this sermon, preached on February 4, 1968, at Ebenezer Baptist Church in Atlanta, Georgia, King responds to questions of how he would like to be remembered. He says that reports of all his social and political achievements are meaningless unless he helped somebody during his lifetime.

7. See Helen Baylor, "Can You Reach My Friend?" (Nashville: Word Music, 1990).

8. Cheryl Townsend Gilkes, " 'Some Mother's Son and Some Father's Daughter': Gender and Biblical Language in Afro-Christian Worship Tradition," in *Shaping New Visions: Gender and Values in American Culture,* Clarissa W. Atkinson, Constance H. Buchanan, and Margaret R. Miles, eds. (Ann Arbor: University of Michigan Research Press, 1987), 79-84.

9. See Babbie Mason and Cindy Sterling, "We Can Change the World" (Nashville: Word Music, 1993).

10. See Margaret Goss Burroughs, "To Soulfolk," in *Black Sister: Poetry by Black American Women, 1746–1980,* Erlene Stetson, ed. (Bloomington: Indiana University Press, 1981), 118.

11. See Lucille Clifton, "listen children," in *The Poetry of Black America: Anthology of the 20th Century,* Arnold Adoff, ed. (New York: Harper & Row, 1973), 308.

12. See Kate Rushin, "Family Tree," in *Double Stitch: Black Women Write About Mothers and Daughter,* Patricia Bell-Scott et al., eds. (Boston: Beacon Press, 1991), 176-77.

13. See Elouise Loftin, "Weeksville Women," in *The Poetry of Black America,* 515.

14. Karla F. C. Holloway, "Thursday Ladies," in *Double Stitch,* 27-31.

15. Ibid., 28.

16. Ibid.

17. Ibid., 29.

18. Ibid., 31.

19. Ann Shockley, "Funeral," in *Out of Our Lives,* Quandra Prettyman Stadler, ed. (Washington, D.C.: Howard University Press, 1975), 274-85.

20. Ibid., 281.

21. Ibid., 278.

22. Terry McMillan, "Ma'Dear," in *Breaking Ice: An Anthology of Contemporary African American Fiction,* Terry McMillan, ed. (New York: Penguin Books, 1990), 463.

23. Ibid., 462.

24. Gloria Naylor, *The Women of Brewster Place* (New York: Penguin Books, 1980); Terry McMillan, *Waiting to Exhale* (New York: Viking, 1992).

25. Gloria Naylor, *The Women of Brewster Place,* 31.

26. Ibid., 70.

27. Ibid., 91.

28. Ibid., 123.

29. Ibid., 103, 105.

30. Ibid., 188-89.

31. Terry McMillan, *Waiting to Exhale.*

32. Ibid., 92.

33. Ibid., 51.

34. Ibid., 164.

35. There is an organization called Sisters Working Encouraging Empowering Together (S.W.E.E.T.) composed of up to two hundred women in Denver, Colorado. Members are of various faith systems, personal backgrounds, educational levels, occupations, incomes, ages, and marital status. The group was formed in 1990 as a means of African American women being present with one another, mentoring one another—especially younger women, discussing problems faced by black women, education, social-political activism, and community empowerment. The mission of the group is to tear down walls that separate black women and allow each person to be who she wants to be.

36. Terry McMillan, *Waiting to Exhale,* 396.

37. Charlayne Hunter-Gault, *In My Place* (New York: Farrar, Straus & Giroux, 1992). Subsection heading is taken from Philippians 4:13: "I can do all things through Christ which strengtheneth me" (KJV).

38. Ibid., 61.

39. Ibid., 37.

40. Ibid., 36.

41. Ibid., 33.

42. Ibid., 53-54.

43. Ibid., 55-56.

44. Ibid., 107-8.

45. Ibid., 164.

46. Ibid., 200.

6: Faith-Filled Perseverance: Trouble Don't Last Always

1. *Songs of Zion* (Nashville: Abingdon Press, 1981), 172.

2. Sandra Crouch, "He's Worthy" (Los Angeles: Lexicon Music and Sanabella Music, 1983).

3. See Willie Mae Ford Smith, "He'll Fight Your Battles" in *Caravan Gospel Gems, No. 31,* Sallie Martin and Kenneth Morris, eds. (Chicago: Martin and Morris Music, 1963).

4. See Albertina Walker, "See How the Lord Has Kept Me," in *Caravan Gospel Gems, No. 31.*

5. See Inez Andrews, "Make It In," in *Caravan Gospel Gems, No. 31.*

6. See Cassietta George, "To Whom Shall I Turn," in *Caravan Gospel Gems, No. 31.*

7. Gloria Griffin, "I'm So Grateful," arr. Roberta Martin (Chicago: Roberta Martin, 1965).

8. See Inez Andrews, "You Don't Know Me Like the Lord," in *Caravan Gospel Gems, No. 31.*

9. Margaret Pleasant Douroux, "If It Had Not Been For the Lord," (Thousand Oaks, Calif.: Rev. Earl Pleasant Publishing, 1980.)

10. See Dorothy Love Coates, "(I'm Holding On) I Won't Let Go of My Faith," (Chicago: Conrad Music, 1964).

11. Maya Angelou, "Our Grandmothers," in *I Shall Not Be Moved* (New York: Random House, 1990), 33-37.

12. Ibid.

13. See Maya Angelou, "When I Think About Myself," in *Poems* (New York: Bantam, 1986), 26.

14. Maya Angelou, "Call Letters: Mrs. V. B.," in *Poems,* 165.

15. See Lucille Clifton, "Miss Rosie," in *Black Sister: Poetry by Black American Women, 1746–1980,* Erlene Stetson, ed. (Bloomington: Indiana University Press, 1981), 248.

16. Carol Freeman, "Christmas Morning I" in *The Poetry of Black America,* Arnold Adoff, ed. (New York: Harper & Row, 1973), 397.

17. See Carole C. Gregory, "The Greater Friendship Baptist Church," in *Black Sister,* 190-91.

18. Alice Walker, "Talking to My Grandmother Who Died Poor (while hearing Richard Nixon declare 'I am not a crook')," in *Her Blue Body Everything We Know: Earthling Poems 1965–1990* (San Diego: Harcourt Brace Jovanovich, 1991), 300-301.

19. Annette Jones White, "Dyad/Triad," in *Double Stitch: Black Women Write About Mothers and Daughters,* Patricia Bell-Scott et al., eds. (Boston: Beacon Press, 1991), 188-95.

20. Ibid., 189.

21. Ibid., 193.

22. Ibid., 190.

23. Ibid.

24. Kesho Yvonne Scott, " 'Marilyn': Excerpts from the Habits of Surviving, Black Women's Strategies for Life," in *Wild Women Don't Wear No Blues: Black Women Writers on Love, Men and Sex,* Marita Golden, ed. (New York: Doubleday, 1993), 15-43.

25. Ibid., 39.

26. Kristin Hunter, *God Bless the Child* (Washington, D.C.: Howard University Press, 1964).

27. Ibid., 23.

28. Ibid., 65.

29. Number running was big business before state-run lotteries or casino gambling. A numbers runner is a person who handles illegal bets on everything from sports to sunrises. People select their special numbers and place bets on the odds of that number being a winning combination. The runner handles the money and turns it over to another person. He or she is responsible for paying off the winner and keeps a percentage of the winnings.

30. Kristin Hunter, *God Bless the Child,* 213.

31. Ibid., 239.

32. Marita Golden, *Long Distance Life* (New York: Doubleday, 1989).

33. Ibid., 129.

34. Ibid., 127.

35. Ibid., 212.

36. Ibid.

37. Alice Walker, *Meridian* (New York: Harcourt Brace Jovanovich, 1976).

38. Ibid., 206.

39. Ibid., 227.

40. Maya Angelou, *I Know Why the Caged Bird Sings* (New York: Bantam, 1969).

41. Ibid., 21, 22.

42. Ibid., 39.

43. Ibid., 83.

44. Ibid., 101.

45. Ibid., 164.

46. Ibid., 74-77.

7: Community Responsibilities: It Takes an Entire Village to Raise a Child

1. Unisei Eugene Perkins, *Afrocentric Self-Inventory and Discovery Workbook* (Chicago: Third World Press, 1992), 5.

2. Gloria Naylor, *Mama Day* (New York: Ticknor & Fields, 1988).

3. Andrew Billingsley, *Climbing Jacob's Ladder* (New York: Simon & Schuster, 1992), 68. Billingsley cites the end of the 1980s as a time of intense discussion about the crisis of the African American family. He lists twenty-two areas of concern including marital conflict, domestic abuse, homelessness, school failure, health problems, and homicide among other issues.

4. See Alice Walker, *Meridian* (New York: Harcourt Brace Jovanovich, 1976). Meridian,

the main character, risks her life and sacrifices her own comfort and happiness to "other-mother" her community, to stand up for the rights of others regardless of their race.

5. Maya Angelou, *Wouldn't Take Nothing for My Journey Now* (New York: Random House, 1993), 24.

6. Maya Angelou, *I Know Why the Caged Bird Sings* (New York: Bantam, 1969). The imperative to respect elders is depicted as Angelou describes her grandmother, Annie Henderson.

7. See Gloria Naylor, *The Women of Brewster Place* (New York: Penguin Books, 1980). Naylor's characters, a group of women living in a housing project, learn to rely on one another for survival. Their source of wisdom is Miss Mattie Michaels, the community monitor, who uses her life experience as a vehicle for inductive moral wisdom teaching.

8. See Charlayne Hunter-Gault, *In My Place* (New York: Farrar, Straus & Giroux, 1992). Hunter-Gault's autobiography is replete with depictions of women who knew their history and passed it on to their children, students, and community. The influence of women in Gaults's life was crucial to her strength and empowerment in integrating the University of Georgia.

9. See Gloria Wade-Gayles, *Pushed Back to Strength* (Boston: Beacon Press, 1993). Wade-Gayles reflects on the life of her grandmother following the death of her mother. It is a powerful testimony about the "ordinary" women who have the most lasting impression on our lives.

10. See Terry McMillan, *Waiting to Exhale* (New York: Viking, 1992). McMillan's four protagonists—Bernadine, Savannah, Robin, and Gloria—seemingly have nothing in common in terms of education, lifestyle, faith, or age yet form a bond of friendship that surpasses societal expectations.

Appendix

1. Marian Wright Edelman, *The Measure of Our Success* (Boston: Beacon Press, 1992), 81-94. The Children's Defense Fund is a child advocacy agency which evolved from the Mississippi Freedom summer project of 1964 and the Headstart Programs of 1965. Edelman is a civil rights attorney.

2. Ibid., 17.

3. Ibid., 93-94.

BIBLIOGRAPHY

LITERATURE

Ansa, Tina McElroy. *Baby of the Family*. New York: Harcourt Brace Jovanovich, 1989.

Golden, Marita. *Long Distance Life*. New York: Doubleday, 1989.

Hunter, Kristen. *God Bless the Child*. Washington, D.C.: Howard University Press, 1984.

Hurston, Zora Neale. *Their Eyes Were Watching God*. New York: HarperCollins, 1990.

McMillan, Terry. *Waiting to Exhale*. New York: Viking Press, 1992.

Naylor, Gloria. *The Women of Brewster Place*. New York: Penguin Books, 1982.

_____. *Mama Day*. New York: Ticknor & Fields, 1988.

Njeri, Itabari. *Every Goodbye Ain't Gone*. New York: Vintage Books, 1991.

Petry, Ann. *The Street*. Boston: Houghton Mifflin, 1946.

Walker, Alice. *Meridian*. New York: Washington Square Press, 1976.

_____. *The Color Purple*. New York: Pocket Books, 1982.

Walker, Margaret. *Jubilee*. Boston: Houghton Mifflin, 1966.

SHORT STORY COLLECTIONS

Bell-Scott, Patricia, Beverly Guy-Sheftall, Jacqueline Jones Royster, and the Sage Women's Publications Group, eds. *Double Stitch: Black Women Write About Mothers and Daughters*. Boston: Beacon Press, 1991.

Cade, Toni. *The Black Woman*. New York: Mentor Books, 1970.

Cooper, J. California. *Some Soul to Keep*. New York: St. Martin's Press, 1987.

Golden, Marita, ed. *Wild Women Don't Wear No Blues: Black Women Writers on Love, Men and Sex*. New York: Doubleday, 1993.

McMillan, Terry, ed. *Breaking Ice: An Anthology of Contemporary African American Fiction*. New York: Penguin Books, 1990.

Major, Clarence, ed. *Calling the Wind: Twentieth Century African American Short Stories*. New York: HarperCollins, 1993.

Sherman, Charlotte W., ed. *Sisterfire: Black Womanist Fiction and Poetry.* New York: HarperPerennial, 1994.

Stradler, Quandra Prettyman, ed. *Out of Our Lives: A Selection of Contemporary Black Fiction.* Washington, D.C.: Howard University Press, 1981.

Walker, Alice. *In Love & Trouble.* San Diego: Harcourt Brace Jovanovich, 1967.

Washington, Mary Helen, ed. *Black-Eyed Susans.* Garden City, N.Y.: Anchor Press, 1975.

_____. *Invented Lives: Narratives of Black Women, 1860–1960.* Garden City: Anchor Press, 1987.

_____. *Memory of Kin: Stories About Family by Black Writers.* New York: Anchor Books, 1991.

Poetry

Adoff, Arnold, ed. *The Poetry of Black America.* New York: Harper & Row, 1973.

Angelou, Maya. *And Still I Rise.* New York: Random House, 1978.

_____. *Poems.* New York: Bantam, 1989.

_____. *I Shall Not Be Moved.* New York: Random House, 1990.

Giovanni, Nikki. *Spin a Soft Black Song.* New York: Farrar, Straus & Giroux, 1971.

_____. *My House.* New York: William Morrow, 1972.

Shange, Ntozake. *for colored girls who have considered suicide/when the rainbow is enuf.* New York: Macmillan, 1975.

Stetson, Erlene, ed. *Black Sisters: Poetry by Black American Women, 1746–1980.* Bloomington: Indiana University Press, 1981.

Walker, Alice. *Her Blue Body Everything We Know: Earthling Poems, 1965–1990.* San Diego: Harcourt Brace Jovanovich, 1991.

Autobiography–Biography–Narratives

Angelou, Maya. *I Know Why the Caged Bird Sings.* New York: Bantam Books, 1970.

_____. *Wouldn't Take Nothing for My Journey Now.* New York: Random House, 1993.

Cooper, Anna Julia. *A Voice from the South by a Colored Woman from the South.* Xenia, Ohio: Aldine Publishers, 1892.

Edelman, Marian Wright. *The Measure of Our Success.* Boston: Beacon Press, 1992.

Hunter-Gault, Charlayne. *In My Place.* New York: Farrar, Straus & Giroux, 1992.

Mills, Kay. *This Little Light of Mine: The Life of Fannie Lou Hamer.* New York: Dutton, 1993.

Richardson, Marilyn. *Maria W. Stewart: America's First Black Woman Political Writer.* Bloomington: Indiana University Press, 1987.

Gospel Music Sources

Edwin Hawkins Choral Collection. Los Angeles: Edwin R. Hawkins Music, 1985.

Martin, Sallie, and Kenneth Morris. *All-Star Gospel Song Book, No. 30.* Chicago: Martin and Morris Music, 1962.

_____. *Caravan Gospel Gems, No. 31*. Chicago: Martin and Morris Music, 1963.
Songs of Zion. Nashville: Abingdon Press, 1981.

Literary criticism

Braxton, Joanne. *Black Women Writing Autobiography: A Tradition Within A Tradition*. Philadelphia: Temple University Press, 1989.

Braxton, Joanne, and Andree McLaughlin. *Wildwomen in the Whirlwind: Afra-American Culture and Contemporary Literary Renaissance*. New Brunswick: Rutgers University Press, 1990.

Carroll, Rebecca. *"I Know What the Red Clay Looks Like": The Voices and Visions of Black Women Writers*. New York: Crown, 1994.

Christian, Barbara. *Black Women Novelists: The Development of Tradition, 1982–1976*. Westport, Conn.: Greenwood Press. 1961.

Culley, Margo, ed. *American Women's Autobiography: Fea(s)ts of Memory*. Madison: University of Wisconsin Press, 1992.

Gates, Henry Louis, ed. *The Signifying Monkey: A Theory of Afro American Literary Criticism*. New York: Oxford University Press, 1988.

_____. *Reading Black, Reading Feminist: A Critical Anthology*. New York: Meridian, 1990.

Hull, Barbara T., Patricia Scott, and Barbara Smith, eds. *All the Women Are White, All the Blacks Are Men, But Some of Us Are Brave*. New York: Feminist Press, 1987.

Johnson, Charles. *Being and Race: Black Writing Since 1970*. Bloomington: Indiana University Press, 1990.

Jordan, Shirley, ed. *Broken Silences: Interviews with Black and White Women Writers*. New Brunswick: Rutgers University Press, 1993.

Peck, Martin, and Martin Coyle. *Literary Terms and Criticism*. London: MacMillan, 1984.

Russell, Sandi. *Render Me a Song: African American Women Writers From Slavery to the Present*. New York: St. Martin's Press, 1990.

Wade-Gayles, Gloria. *No Crystal Stair: Visions of Race and Sex in Black Women's Fiction*. New York: Pilgrim Press, 1970.

Supportive Scholarly Works

Aptheker, Bettina. *Woman's Legacy*. Amherst: University of Massachusetts Press, 1982.

Bennett, Lerone. *The Shaping of Black America: The Struggles and Triumphs of African Americans, 1619 to the 1990s*. New York: Penguin, 1995.

Billingsley, Andrew. *Climbing Jacob's Ladder: The Enduring Legacy of African American Families*. New York: Simon & Schuster, 1992.

Brown Douglas, Kelly. *The Black Christ*. Maryknoll: Orbis, 1994.

Cannon, Katie G. *Black Womanist Ethics*. Atlanta: Scholars Press, 1988.

Champion, George Lovelace. *Black Methodism: Basic Beliefs*. Nashville: The African Methodist Episcopal Church Publishing House, 1980.

Collins, Patricia Hill. *Black Feminist Thought*. New York: Routledge, 1991.

Cone, James. *For My People*. Maryknoll: Orbis, 1984.

Cone, James, and Gayraud Wilmore, eds. *Black Theology: A Documentary History, 1980–1992*. Maryknoll: Orbis, 1993.

Conner-Edwards, Alice, and Jeanne Spurlock, eds. *Black Families in Crisis—The Middle Class*. New York: Brunner Mazel, 1988.

Costen, Melva. *African American Christian Worship*. Nashville: Abingdon Press, 1993.

Cypress, Celestine. *Sister Thea Bowman: Shooting Star*. Winona, Minn.: Saint Mary's Press, 1993.

Dundes, Alan, ed. *Mother Wit: From the Laughing Barrel*. Jackson: University of Mississippi Press, 1990.

Durkheim, Emile. *The Elementary Forms of the Religious Life*. New York: Free Press, 1915.

Evans, James H. *We Have Been Believers*. Minneapolis: Fortress Press, 1992.

Felder, Cain Hope. *Troubling the Biblical Waters*. Maryknoll: Orbis, 1989.

Giddings, Paula. *When and Where I Enter: An Agenda for Social Change*. Cambridge, Mass.: Harvard University Press, 1987.

Grant, Jacqueline. *White Women's Christ and Black Women's Jesus: Feminist Christology and Womanist Response*. Atlanta: Scholars Press, 1989.

Harding, Vincent. *There Is A River: The Black Struggle for Freedom in America*. New York: Harcourt Brace Jovanovich, 1982.

Hare, Nathan, and Julia Hare, eds. *The Crisis in Black Sexual Politics*. San Francisco: Black Think Tank, 1984.

Hargrove, Barbara. *The Sociology of Religion*. Arlington Heights, Ill.: Harlan Davidson, 1979.

hooks, bell. *Ain't I a Woman? Black Women and Feminism*. Boston: South End Press, 1981.

Hopkins, Dwight. *Shoes That Fit Our Feet*. Maryknoll: Orbis, 1993.

Jones, Major. *Christian Ethics for Black Theology*. Nashville: Abingdon Press, 1974.

Leslau, Charlotte, and Wolf Leslau. *African Proverbs*. White Plains, N.Y.: Peter Pauper Press, 1962.

Lincoln, C. Eric, and Lawrence Mamiya. *The Black Church in the African American Experience*. Durham, N.C.: Duke University Press, 1990.

McAdoo, Harriette Pipes, ed. *Black Families*. 2d ed. Newbury Park, Calif.: Sage Publications, 1986.

McAdoo, Harriette Pipes, and John Lewis McAdoo, eds. *Black Children: Social, Educational, and Parental Environments*. Beverly Hills: Sage Publications, 1985.

McCall, Emmanuel. *The Black Church Experience*. Nashville: Broadmans Press, 1972.

Mapson, Wendell. *The Ministry of Music in the Black Church*. Valley Forge: Judson Press, 1984.

Martin, Elmer, and Joanne Martin, eds. *The Black Extended Family*. Chicago: University of Chicago Press, 1976.

_____. *The Helping Tradition in the Black Family and Community*. Silver Springs, Md.: National Association of Social Workers, 1985.

Marty, Martin, *Pilgrims in Their Own Land*. New York: Penguin Books, 1984.

Mays, Benjamin, and Joseph Nicholson. *The Negro's Church*. New York: Institute of Social and Religious Resources, 1933.

Mitchell, Henry, and Nicholas Cooper-Lewter. *Soul Theology*. San Francisco: Harper & Row, 1986.

Omalade, Barbara. *The Rising Song of African American Women*. New York: Routledge Press, 1994.

Paris, Peter. *Social Teachings of the Black Church*. Philadelphia: Fortress Press, 1985.

_____. *The Spirituality of African Peoples: The Search for a Common Moral Discourse*. Minneapolis: Fortress Press, 1995.

Perkins, Useni E. *Afrocentric Self-Inventory and Discovery Workbook*. Chicago: Black World Press, 1992.

Plaskow, Judith, and Carol P. Christ. *Weaving the Visions: New Patterns in Feminist Spirituality*. New York: HarperCollins, 1989.

Rainwater, Lee, and William Yancy. *The Moynihan Report and the Politics of Controversy*. Boston: MIT Press, 1967.

Sanders, Cheryl, ed. *Living the Intersection: Womanism and Afrocentrism in Theology*. Minneapolis: Fortress Press, 1995.

Smith, Archie. *The Relational Self: Ethics and Therapy from a Black Church Perspective*. Nashville: Abingdon Press, 1982.

Smith, Wallace C. *The Church in the Life of the Black Family*. Valley Forge: Judson Press, 1985.

Spencer, Jon Michael. *Protest and Praise: Sacred Music of Black Religion*. Minneapolis: Fortress Press, 1990.

Staples, Robert. *The Black Family: Essays and Studies*. Belmont, Calif.: Black Think Tank, 1989.

Teish, Luisa. *Jambalya*. San Francisco: Harper & Row, 1985.

Townes, Emilie. *A Troubling in My Soul: Womanist Perspectives on Evil and Suffering*. Maryknoll: Orbis, 1993.

Vanzant, Iyanla. *Acts of Faith: Daily Meditations for People of Color*. New York: Simon & Schuster, 1993.

Wade-Gayles, Gloria. *My Soul Is a Witness: African American Women's Spirituality*. Boston: Beacon Press, 1995.

Walker, Alice. *In Search of Our Mother's Gardens*. San Diego: Harcourt Brace Jovanovich, 1983.

Walker, Wyatt Tee. *"Somebody's Calling My Name": Black Sacred Music and Social Change*. Valley Forge: Judson Press, 1979.

Washington, James. *A Testament of Hope*. San Francisco: Harper & Row, 1986.

Williams, Delores. *Sisters in the Wilderness: The Challenge of Womanist God-Talk*. Maryknoll: Orbis, 1993.

Wimberly, Edward, and Anne S. Wimberly. *Liberation and Human Wellness*. Nashville: Abingdon Press, 1985.

Articles

Alexander, Jeffery. "Core Solidarity, Ethnic Outgroup, and Social Differentiation." In *Action and Its Environment*. New York: Columbia University Press, 1988.

Asante, Molefie Kete. "Locating the Test: Implications of Afrocentric Theory." In *Language and Literature in the African American Imagination*, edited by Carol Aisha Blackshire-Belay, 9-20. Westport, Conn.: Greenwood Press, 1992.

Bennett, Lerone. "The Ten Biggest Myths About the Black Family." *Ebony* (August 1986): 123-33.

Cannon, Katie G. " 'Hitting a Straight Lick with a Crooked Stick': The Womanist Dilemma in the Development of a Black Liberation Ethic." *The Annual of the Society of Christian Ethics* (1988): 165-77.

_____. "Womanist Perspectival Discourse and Cannon Formation." *Journal of Feminist Studies in Religion* 9 (spring-fall 1993): 29-37.

Carpenter, Delores. "Black Women in Religious Institutions: A Historical Summary from Slavery to the 1960s." *Journal of Religious Thought* 46 (winter-spring 1989-90): 7-27.

Dodson, Jualyne, and Cheryl Townsend Gilkes. "Something Within: Social Change and Collective Endurance in the Sacred World of Black Christian Women." In *Women and Religion in America, Vol. 3, 1960–1968*, 80-130. San Francisco: Harper & Row, 1981.

Eugene, Toinette. "Moral Values and Black Womanists." *Journal of Religious Thought* 44 (winter-spring 1988): 23-34.

Gates, Henry Louis. "In Her Own Write." In *The Collected Works of Phillis Wheatley*, edited by Jon Shields, vii-xxii. New York: Oxford Press, 1988.

Gilkes, Cheryl Townsend. "The Role of Church and Community Mothers." *Journal of Feminist Studies in Religion* 2 (spring 1986): 41-59.

_____. " 'Some Mother's Son and Some Father's Daughter': Gender and Biblical Language in Afro-Christian Worship Tradition." In *Shaping New Vision: Gender and Values in American Culture*, edited by Clarissa Atkinson, Constance Buchannan, and Margaret Miles, 73-99. Ann Arbor: UMI Research Press, 1982.

Grant, Jacqueline. "Come to My Help, For I Am in Trouble" in *Reconstructing the Christ Symbol*, edited by Margaret Stevens, 54-71. Mahwah, N.J.: Paulist Press, 1993.

Hartley, Shirley, and Ruth Wallace. "Religious Elements in Friendship: Durkheimian Theory in an Empirical Context." In *Durkheimian Sociology: Cultural Studies*, edited by Jeffery Alexander, 93-103. Cambridge: Cambridge University Press, 1988.

Jasper, David. "The Limits of Formalism and Theology of Hope: Ricoeur, Moltmann, and Dostoyevsky." In *Literature and Theology*, vol. 1, 1-9. Oxford: Oxford University Press, 1987.

Jones, Lawrence. "Transmitting the Faith: From Generation to Generation." *Journal of Religious Thought* 46 (summer-fall 1989): 32-41.

Kort, Wesley. "Narrative and Theology." In *Literature and Theology*, vol. 1, 27-31. Oxford: Oxford University Press, 1987.

Levi, A. H. T. "The Relationship Between Literature and Theology." *Literature and Theology,* Vol. 1, 11-17. Oxford: Oxford University Press, 1987.

McKenzie, John J. "The Hebrew Community and the Old Testament." In *The Interpreter's One Volume Commentary of the Bible,* edited by Charles M. Laymon, 1072-76. Nashville: Abingdon Press, 1971.

Mitchell, Ella, and Henry Mitchell. "Black Spirituality: The Values of That Ol' Time Religion." *Journal of the Interdenominational Theological Center* 17 (fall 1989-spring 1990): 98-109.

See, Katherine O'Sullivan, and William J. Wilson. "Race and Ethnicity." *Handbook of Sociology,* edited by Neal J. Smeltz, 225-28. Oak Park: Sage Publications, 1988.

INDEX